6 'N The Morning:

West Coast Hip-Hop Music 1987-1992

& the Transformation of Mainstream

Culture

by Daudi Abe

Cover layout and design done by Cory Shaw for Buildestroy.com

Photo's courtesy of Scottie Spencer – from his upcoming book "How The West Was #1" Except Warren G, Snoop & Dolomite courtesy of Publisher Paul Stewart

Copyright © 2013 Over The Edge Publishing

ISBN 10: 1483990664

ISBN 13: 9781483990668

Printed in the United States of America

Acknowledgements

Love and thanks to: Dana and Leila, Mom and Dad, Peter, Danielle, Elijah, Demetri, Carol, Vince, Dre, D. Parker, Hux, Ally-Al, George, Scott Weed-dawg, Musa, Linda, Wyking, 206 Zulu, Kun Luv, Kuc, Okello, Omara, LaCoby, Uncle Frank, the Bass family and Park Printing, Sid, 3rd, Geneva Gay, the College of Education at the University of Washington, Marilyn, Greg B., Paul, Melanie, Al Griz, Dr. Livingston, Dr. Killpatrick, the Humanities and Social Science division at Seattle Central Community College, Kim Pollock, the Social Science division at Bellevue College, Zion Prep, Johnny, John John and Jerami in Chicago, Zeb, Topspin, Sam C., the Hype Show and KSCU and the entire Abe and White families.

My sincere appreciation to Ice-T, Greg Mack, Davey D, Jerry Heller, Sassy C of JJ Fad, and Young MC for the willingness to share stories and insights from this incredible time.

RIP Grandmas Irene and Ruth, Atim, Sally, China, Zakiya, J-Dub and Noni.

Profound thank you to Michael Logan and his editing skill.

Finally, massive respect and love to Mr. Paul Stewart for believing in this book.

Table of Contents

6 'N The Morning: West Coast Hip-Hop Music 1987-1992
& the Transformation of Mainstream Culture

Intro

Throughout the brief history of hip-hop the general public has discounted the culture changes hip-hop has brought to society at large. To a large degree mainstream media has told hip-hop's story to through the lens of record sales, music videos and revenue streams. However, this approach ignores the massive shift in mainstream culture that was sparked by the rise of hip-hop. In fact, West Coast hip-hop from 1987-1992 represents not only the most important time in hip-hop history, but is one of the most historic and influential cultural and artistic movements of the 20th century.

Ice Cube = Malcolm X? Young MC = Martin Luther King Jr.? Tension generated by the hardcore/militant stance versus a less threatening inclusive philosophy has provoked a contentious, ongoing debate in the African-American struggle for respect, recognition and equality in America. While the two opposing positions appeared socially intractable, young people from a variety of racial, ethnic, and socioeconomic backgrounds found the extremes, and the diversity of hip-hop messages and sounds that fell in between them, irresistible. The perfect storm of rhythms, rhymes, parties, gangs, drugs, poverty, violence, civil unrest, films and music videos that represented West Coast hip-hop in the late 1980s and early 1990s reduced social divisions within American society by providing a common point of cultural interest for millions of young people.

West Coast rap music between 1987 and 1992 revolutionized the mainstream culture. Perhaps more than any other era, it helped diminish artificial social barriers such as race and class which had defined United States history to that point. It also allowed the hip-hop generation to gradually adjust mainstream cultural norms and expectations that helped set the stage for the election of the first Black President less than twenty years later.

"Black culture has always been positioned between the poles of fear and entertainment in its relationship to the White mainstream."

-Dr. Todd Boyd from *Young, Black, Rich and Famous*

Throughout United States history there have been consistent examples of entertainment (mainstream-friendly) vs. fear (mainstream-threatening) dynamics, especially in relation to African-American driven changes in mainstream culture. Harriet Tubman non-violently guided scores of pre-Civil War slaves to freedom along the Underground Railroad in the mid-1800s. Conversely, an example of someone at the other end of the spectrum was Nat Turner, who led a slave rebellion in Virginia, known as the Southampton Insurrection, which killed some 60 White people in 1831.

In the early 1900s, Booker T. Washington represented a mainstream-friendly approach, though he was seen by some African-Americans as too accommodating to Whites with his 'go slow' approach to gaining full participation in an integrated society. His stance was philosophically opposed by 'radical' Black Nationalists like Marcus Garvey, who urged people of African descent to return to Africa while demanding that European colonial powers leave it.

During the Civil Rights era, Dr. Martin Luther King Jr. led non-violent protests and delivered his famous "I Have A Dream" speech in front of the Lincoln Memorial during the 1963

March on Washington. King was a palatable mainstream alternative to the militant stance of Malcolm X. Because he viewed the tone of the march as a watered down, sanitized commentary on racial harmony in the United States, Malcolm X ridiculed the event by calling it the "Farce on Washington." In addition, Malcolm was a member of the Nation of Islam which the mainstream viewed as radical and militant. Malcolm's image is memorialized in one of the most enduring photographs of the 60s, a portrait of him looking out of a window while holding an automatic rifle.

As the hip-hop movement began to break out of New York in the mid-1980s, a new frontier emerged as a force within this quickly expanding culture. The West Coast was the first area outside of New York to establish itself as a consistent hip-hop incubator with national impact. However, like the Black cultural movements that preceded it, West Coast hip-hop produced figures who existed simultaneously at extreme ends of, and also between the poles of fear and entertainment in the eyes of the mainstream. On the 'friendly' side stood artists like MC Hammer and Young MC; they actively courted the mainstream with their music and public image, going out of their way to be non-threatening. Meanwhile, others such as Ice-T, NWA, and Ice Cube, struck fear into the hearts of many within the general population because of their fierce politics, tales of street violence, profane delivery, and misogynistic themes. But there was one key difference between this movement and those of the past. Where slavery and the struggle for civil rights were based upon conflict and survival, the hip-hop movement was based inside the entertainment media. This meant two things: First, it was naturally more attractive to the mainstream and able to attract people because artistic expression is generally seen as something less threatening than a movement based within a life or death scenario, which was certainly the case for slaves and civil rights workers. Second, it allowed people to participate in the culture on their own terms. For example, if things got too intense, one could simply press stop on the tape player and return later.

Cable television was vital to the ascendency of hip-hop culture within the mainstream. While radio had always been the traditional means of delivering music to the masses, shows that debuted on cable networks, such as MTV's "Yo! MTV Raps" (1988) and BET's "Rap City" (1989), changed the dynamic in three important ways. First, prior to cable local radio stations were generally constricted to a regional listening audience.

Broadcast signals that reached more than fifty miles were rare on a good day. Cable made it possible to deliver music to consumers simultaneously all over the country.

The second major impact came from the rise of the music video. Music videos brought in a visual element of storytelling and choreography that expressed and exposed portions of hip-hop culture in new and exciting ways. While images of self-proclaimed 'bad' Black males broadcast on television were not necessarily new, the fact that they were being delivered to eager White teenage viewers in Nebraska, for example, was. The rise of a new pervasive media form, combined with major motion pictures, such as *New Jack City* and *Boyz N the Hood*, opened up alternative narrative vehicles for some of the most popular rap music of the era and expanded hip-hop's influence on mainstream culture.

The third and final change was the success of West Coast style; it helped debunk the conventional wisdom that rap had to be from the northeastern United States in order to be considered legitimate. Although there were isolated instances of rap bubbling up from other places in the late 1980s, Two Live Crew from Miami, Florida, and the Ghetto Boys from Houston,

Texas, are two examples, but for the most part many hip-hop listeners around the country thought anything not from New York was considered small-time or illegitimate. The influential rise of the West Coast cemented the localization of hip-hop while expanding a diverse sound of styles and opinions, demonstrating that rap music was real and authentic no matter where it originated.

Foreword

The second half of the 1980s marked the start of an era in which West Coast hip-hop engaged and influenced the U.S. mainstream on multiple levels. Elizabeth Grant, in her article, "Gangsta Rap, the War on Drugs, and the Location of African-American Identity in Los Angeles, 1988-1992," argued, "by 1990, Los Angeles had become the indisputable capital of the hip-hop nation, a geographic dislocation accompanied by a shift in rap's basic tonal and narrative style." This era lies smack in the middle of what hip-hop scholars have labeled the 'golden age' of rap music, roughly the mid 1980s to the mid 1990s. West Coast sensibilities were flavored by the sociopolitical climate of the time which was dominated by crack, gang violence, law enforcement, disproportionate drug sentencing guidelines, and the Rodney King video, trial, verdict, and uprisings. Within this context, the period between Ice-T's song "6 'N The Morning" and Dr. Dre's album *The Chronic* produced a body of work that created the critical artistic foundation for hip-hop's cultural infiltration and eventual takeover of the mainstream.

West Coast hip-hop media had something for everyone as it covered an entire spectrum of style and content. Young MC and MC Hammer went out of their way to be non-threatening and generally avoided topics such as race, class, and gender. Tone-Loc and Digital Underground, while still avoiding tough social issues for the most part, pushed the envelope with a suggestive PG-13 sexuality. Too $hort, NWA, and Ice-T radically mixed social-political commentary, misogyny, and explicit lyrics. All of these styles were happening over some of the illest beats ever devised as hip-hop evolved out of the early breakbeat culture of East Coast production.

From music to movies like *Boyz N The Hood*, *Colors* and *New Jack City*, the West Coast from 1987-1992 was unsurpassed in pushing hip-hop everywhere into a dominant force, not just in mainstream America, but in the global culture as well. This book will discuss the key elements of that time and place within the context of acceptance by millions of young people from diverse backgrounds.

NOTE: This text is not meant to be a complete and comprehensive history of all West Coast hip-hop music released during that time. It simply highlights and discusses a few key events and artistic contributions that accelerated the marriage between hip-hop and the mainstream.

It was my pleasure to exist in the middle of this time as a college student and host of a college radio hip-hop show in the Bay Area from 1988-1992. Hip-hop's tone during this period was a critical and intellectual challenge to the status quo while simultaneously examining the effects of the African Diaspora and connections between African-Americans and Africa. In the midst of a largely African-American creative explosion there were ominous signs such as the FBI's letter to NWA, which underscored the United States government's concern with the 'subversive qualities of hip-hop.' Given the historically shortened life span of intelligent, articulate young Black males who agitated for social justice in this country, it was no surprise those in power actively tried to divert or destroy hip-hop's sociopolitical consciousness. I think it is important to note that there are many who would argue: Mission Accomplished.

Even with all of that, or maybe in part because of it, the

creative energy in and around the music during these years was irresistible and powerful. Strictly on a head-bobbing level, it was non-stop heat. The West Coast sound was a new production style that embraced yet re-conceived the sounds of older African-American artists like George Clinton, Bootsy Collins, and Parliament Funkadelic. New sounds inspired new styles of MCing, and the content was as varied as the flows themselves. From the hardest of the hard to the safest of the mainstream, the West Coast was your one stop shop for hip-hop from 1987-1992...

--Dr. Abe

First Person Account: ICE-T

Prior to "6 'N The Morning," the hip-hop scene was really a 'techno' scene in LA. Now, they didn't call it techno, but it was spearheaded by probably the biggest name out there at the time, Egyptian Lover, and Egypt was the DJ for Uncle Jamm's Army. Roger Clayton was basically, to me, the godfather of that whole West Coast music scene. He was the main promoter, and with another guy named Gibb threw the biggest parties in Los Angeles, which was [the] Uncle Jamm's [scene]. They actually would play at the LA Sports Arena and pack it just for a dance, and no one could actually mess with them. There were other groups and party promoters, but Uncle Jamm's Army was the biggest thing. It was a phenomenon, and as I mentioned, the DJs were Egyptian Lover along with Bobcat [who would later go on to DJ for LL Cool J]. That was really the first semi-hip-hop scene in Los Angeles, and it was all based around people under 21. So the kids couldn't go to the clubs, but they could go to Uncle Jamm's. One of the first groups to break out of the Uncle Jamm's/Egyptian Lover scene was the LA Dream Team, then there was Russ Parr on the radio at KDAY, who was also Bobby Jimmy from Bobby Jimmy and the Critters. This was around 1984-85, when LA was right in the middle of the gang scene, a lot of Fila was being worn, you had the players and the hustlers and the gangsters and all that, but they all showed up at Uncle Jamm's Army.

Now I was the first person that Roger ever let rap at one of his shows. I was the only 'rap' rapper, like I used to say they did aerobic music cause they would use a lot of heavy breathing on their records, but I was the first person to really put a rap together. So they used to let me get in front of Uncle Jamm's Army crowds and rap, and I was wack but at the same time I was rappin in front of big audiences. At that time, LA was just starting to get into hip-hop, which had kind of started to break from New York and New Yorkers were break dancing and LA was popping and locking, and that whole scene was starting to move toward the west. There was a time, of course in the west where if you rapped somebody was gonna say, "Oh you tryin' to do that New York shit," but you just kept rapping.

While that whole Uncle Jamm's scene was happening, [Dr.] Dre and them were in Compton, and they had a club called Dudoes and out of that they created the World Class Wrecking Cru, which was also kind of aerobic, more breathing and also very techno based. Then they did a group called CIA [which stood for Cru In Action and included Ice Cube] which was a little bit more but it wasn't hardcore, it was kinda like [the World Class Wreckin Cru song] "Cabbage Patch." Also Greg Mack was on the radio at KDAY, and he used to throw these parties at the Casa Camino Royale and the Olympic Auditorium, and by that time they started to bring New York rappers to LA.

In 1982 I had returned from military service having heard "Rapper's Delight," and tried to rap using the instrumental, but I was no rapper. I was just saying rhymes I'd made up because truthfully I had started rapping when I was in high school but I didn't know what it was. I used to make up gang raps, rhymes that didn't have a music base. For example:

> Goin thru the city in the middle of the night
> Niggas on my left niggas on my right
> Yellin C-C-C-rip every nigga I see
> If you bad enough come fuck wit me

I seen another nigga I said Crip again
He said "fuck a Crip nigga this is Brim"
So we pulled out the Roscoe, Roscoe said "Crack!"
I looked again nigga was shootin back
So we fell to the ground aimed for his head
One more shot the nigga was dead
So we walked over to him took his gun
Spit in his face and began to run
So if you see another nigga layin dead in the street
In a puddle of blood from his head to his feet
Hope it's time all you busters get hip
Fuck a Brim nigga this is west side rollin 60 Crip

I was sayin this in 1976 but I didn't even know about rap, I made up these rhymes to entertain my friends! You have to entertain the people you're with, so if I'm hanging around with thugs they wanna hear this shit. Here go another one:

Fall into a party on a Saturday night
I left the pad down and out for a fight
Had on a waistline leather and my Levis cuffed
Under the coat I knew I was buffed
Cause I was drivin an iron getting ready for that set
And I was packin a punch a nigga never forget

The ring in my ear was hangin halfway to the floor

And I was so tight I walked sideways out the door

My hooptie was lifted front side and rear

Glass was all tinted wasn't none of it clear

Cragered down with a cold ass pearl

Deepest diamond tuck in the goddam world

I had quadraphonic headphones with a tone you could fix

Under the seat I had a 30 odd six

On the way to the party I was scrapin and hoppin

Cause I knew by the end of the night there was gonna be some poppin

When I got to the set I just let it lay on the ground

And a Buddhist came to check it out from Chinatown

When I fell in the party there was niggas for days

I was lookin crazy in some hellafied ways

As I walked in the corner I just listened as they talked

First James Brown record I jumped up and Crip walked

Now I was walkin so hard couldn't no one compete

I'm bout to turn out the party with my goddam feet

But then some nigga went and got outta line

His nose my fist had no trouble to find

After drivin an iron so hard all that day

I drive his grill in one hell of a way

But his partners fell out and so did mine

And the squabbin went on for quite a long time

Then all of sudden I heard some poppin

I knew not too soon this fight would be stoppin

I seen 22s 38s and a 45

I knew not too much would be left alive

Niggas broke out in a goddam rage

I even think I seen a sawed off gauge

But brotha I was sent from hell not heaven

I broke out with a chrome plated .357

The name of the game is simply survival

At the end of the night ten was dead on arrival

And me and my partners we was gone like the wind

The police blamed it on the Crips or the Brims

But some niggas knew in the corner of the dark

Them crazy niggas reside in Triangle Park

They go by the name of Burnett, Zell and Trey

And they belong to the association called the E.P.A.

And that was another clique we had called the Eliminators Pimpin Association! I made that up when I was like in the 11th grade! This was 11th grade shit talkin about Levis cuffed and Cragers, and I still have that shit memorized today!

Now when I started to rap in 1982, I did "The Coldest Rap," which was done over a track that was owned by Jimmy Jam and Terry Lewis. I was in a beauty parlor called Good Fred's in the hood and I was sayin these other rhymes to some girls and this guy walks up and asks, "Do you wanna make some money?" and I said, "What?" and he said "Do you wanna do that over some music?" I was hustling at the time, I was like, "I don't got no time for this!" and I was worried about fame, I used to have a phobia of cameras and all kinds of shit. But he was like, "Let's go!" So he took me to a studio, he had a record with Jimmy Jam and Terry Lewis playin with some girls singin and I rapped over it. I just said every rap I knew off of my head that day in the studio and if you listen to "The Coldest Rap" that's the one where I'm sayin:

> *The pimp, the player the woman layer*
> *I got so many clothes in my wardrobe each day*
> *When I put some in I gotta throw some away*

I was talkin all this pimp shit, so when that record came out I got a call from these cats that had a club in McArthur Park called Radio, later to be Radiotron from the movie *Breakin*. These cats were a White guy named Alex Juordinov and another guy named K-K and they were some Russian hip-hoppers by way of New York. So they had this underground club and they had been playin my record there and asked me to come and perform. This was my first performance as an artist with a record out. So I went to the club and it was all White kids, like new wave kids, and when "The Coldest Rap" came on they knew every word to that record because it had been playin in that club for months. So I roll into the club and the White kids is listenin to the record, so I kinda dug this club and I started to come back every weekend.

In fact, you know who was an early hip-hopper? Madonna! Madonna was there, Adam Ant, Malcolm McLaren, all these people used to show up at this club and I used to let people get on the stage, actually Madonna performed on that stage, and I kinda became like the stage manager. I practiced my raps there and the DJ, who was actually a guy that used to carry the equipment in, the owner of the club nicknamed him "The Glove" cause he was wearin gloves carryin the equipment in, and me and him made the song "Reckless" together.

So what happened was I'm in this club and these people walk in and go "Hey, we're gonna make a movie [*Breakin*], you'll be the rapper and these guys will be the breakers." That's how [Boogaloo] Shrimp and all them got on, cause they was at the club. They just kind of picked the people out of the club. But what they did low, Hollywood stepped in, the club was called Radio, they didn't wanna pay Alex and K-K anything so they bought the club and changed the name to Radiotron. Rat muthafuckas! So the movie *Breakin* came out and by that time I had done "The Coldest Rap" and "Reckless" [which appeared on the *Breakin* soundtrack]. Meanwhile I had worked with this guy named David Storrs, who was a White cat that lived in Hollywood and had all the equipment. He was cool, and he was already workin with Kid Frost, so I went and recorded a couple of songs with him, "Killas" and "Body Rock." So at that point I decided I might be able to make a little paper with this and hooked up with the Unknown DJ, Andre Manuel, who had a little label called Techno-Hop with King Tee and Compton's Most Wanted. He was like, "I'm about to jump this label off and I want you to be the first artist." So I was like, "Well fuck it, let's do a record."

Now at that time LL [Cool J] was talkin big shit. LL had come out and said he's the best rapper in the world, he used to come to LA and tell muthafuckas, "I'ma show you how to do this, y'all are garbage." So I was like, "Ok, if I'm gonna be the shit out here, I have to attack this dude. Whether I think I can get LL or not, it don't matter. I gotta go at him or basically he's punkin us." So I came at him and did a record called "You Don't Quit," which sampled some Bugs Bunny music because that was when Doug E. Fresh and them was usin [the theme music from the cartoon series] "Inspector Gadget" [in their song "The Show"]. That was the trend, so we said "Fuck it, we gonna do that." So then when I did that record, my homies, this was when "6 'N The Morning" came about, my homies was like, "Cuzz, you so worried about LL Cool J and talkin shit, you losin all the pimp shit!"

Goin back to those rhymes I recited earlier from Crenshaw, that's what my boys knew me for, so they was like, "Why you rappin about that? Nigga you missin the target, talk about us! You used to rap this, now you rappin like that. Yeah this is good, you cuttin this nigga's head off, but come on Ice, what's happenin?" Cause we was rollin muthafuckin candy apple [Cadillac] Broughams with bumper kits and pimp buckles and perms, we was on some whole other shit, so to them hip-hop was kinda corny. They was like, "Nigga we players, man, what are you, a punk? Rap? Hip-hop? Breakdancing? What are you doin nigga?"

So I was in this club in Santa Monica when "P.S.K." by Schoolly D came on, and when that shit came on that shit was so dust, to me I considered "P.S.K." what I called a 'dust' record cause dust was out and people was smokin sherm. When the beat came on I was like, "Oh this shit makes you feel high, and you ain't high." And Schoolly's delivery was so high, I mean who raps like that? So I was like "This shit is dope! This shit is really, really dope!" At the same time I was influenced by the Beastie Boys, who had a record out called "Hold It Now, Hit It." So what I did was take a beat kinda like "Hold It Now, Hit It" and then kinda took the 'dust' delivery of Schoolly D. But then the whole trick was to rhyme about LA.

At that time they was raidin us, the [LAPD's] battering ram was rollin, Toddy-T was singin about the battering ram, and anybody who's ever dealt with the cops knows when they come. I mean I've been in the spot when the flash bangs came through the window, EARLY, niggas was sleep, in socks, and all that shit when it be like, boom, and they screamin, and it's like "What in the fuck? Couldn't y'all have waited till later?" And I used to come home from the clubs like Carolina West early in the morning and see the [LAPD Drug] Task Force out at like 3 and 4 am getting ready for the raids. So I was like, "Well we all know that's when these muthafuckas is comin."

Meanwhile I had done another record called "Doggin The Wax," which was supposed to be "You Don't Quit" part two. Very violent, very aggressive, more about how tough an MC I was. But then my boy Randy Mack had an 808 drum machine and we made the beat and said, "Just fuck around on this record." So really "6 'N The Morning" was a b-side, which was basically just fucking around, like how simple and how stupid a story can you tell. I've always been a story teller so I just started rhyming some shit and made sure I said all my friend's names because, you see, my friends wanted me to rap about them. That's what you do; as a rapper you're kinda like a cheerleader for a neighborhood. That's what a lot of people will ask, "Why do you always say the name of your label or your street?" Because that's what the rapper does, it's about shoutin out. You're reppin a group. We used to go to the club and they would be like, "No rappers!" and we would slide them $500 and get the mic all night. So I had to say everybody's name and all that so when we did "6 'N The Morning" it was kinda like an homage to all the homies, "Bruce is a giant," Nat C, I talked to D-Bo, I said all the names, "Sean E. Sean was the driver," the "Louis [Vuitton] interior," it was very biographical. It was the closest record I've ever done to anything that was honestly the truth. When I did that I also created a kind of rap which I call 'fact-tion;' factual occurrences put into a fictional setting. So all those things happened, they didn't happen on that day. But I know niggas got caught with hand grenades, we went to jail, I got out of jail, I had the perm, you know we went through the cycle. So the key to Ice-T rap is anything I rap about has to have happened, it's just not created. It might not have happened to you, but it happened to somebody so that's why you've always got that texture of reality in the music. You know we're not gonna invent nothin. Why?

Around the time of "6 'N The Morning," and eventually my debut album *Rhyme Pays* there were already some rappers doing similar things. One of the first rappers I met was Too $hort. Too $hort was sexual, he was doin "Freaky Tales" and he didn't know shit about me, so you know, he's original as they get and he was makin little tapes. To me, Too $hort was kinda like Toddy-T. Toddy-T was a guy out in LA who made a record called "Batterram" and used to do rap parodies. He would take "The Freaks Come Out At Night" [by Whodini] and make "The Clucks Come Out At Night," talking about:

The dopeman don't open till after dark
And it ain't till 12 till the smoking really starts

He would rhyme over the original record and they were street hits. So there were other people doin hardcore stuff. I'll always remember I met the Honorable Louis Farrakhan and when he speaks he says, "In the words of the Honorable Elijah Muhammad," and I asked him, "Why do you say his name?" He said, "Because that's where I got the game from. For me to use his words as if they're mine, I'd be worse than a thief." Bishop Don 'Magic' Juan used to teach me, "All a player wants is a little credit." So whenever I say something that somebody taught me, you got to give credit, I mean how corny can you be?

So I was influenced by Schoolly and the Beastie Boys, but at the time I think the quickest similarities to me in LA came from [Ice] Cube and [World Class] Wreckin Cru. I mean we did "Reckless," they made a record called "Surgery," and if you play them side-by-side it's very interesting. When you play "6 'N The

Morning" play "Boyz-N-The Hood" [by Eazy-E]. But the thing of it is Cube was my friend so I look at his music as inspiration. We used to all go out on tour together and I remember I used to do this intro to "6 'N The Morning" where I used to say:

You know the police tell me I can't play this song
And if I play this song I'ma go to jail

And the crowd would scream, and then I'd say:

Fuck tha police!

And then I'd say:

My name is Ice-T I got a rep like a killa

And it would echo, *"killa, killa:"*

No one gets wilder no one gets iller
I don't get high I don't drink Miller
But if your girls empty I'm sure I can fill her
I make stupid ass records cause I just don't care
Muthafuckas can't even play my shit on the air
But y'all know you like it you say you want more
Cause every time I leave my crib to go to the store
I hear "6 'N the morning police at my door..."

So that was my intro and I see Eazy and them sittin on the side of stage watchin me get this shit. Next time we left to go out of town Eazy had a record called "Fuck tha Police." So I was like, "You muthafuckas is on my ass in real way!" But it was all love because when I started off with NWA and Doc [the D.O.C.], those were the only muthafuckas that I felt really understood what we was doin, which was really tryin to cause problems. You know, I was a troublemaker. I was out to go out and just really bring the energy of LA to Omaha [Nebraska]. So we comin on stage bangin and saggin and you know it was just the whole thing of like, "You gonna feel what we are!"

It was so much fun back in the days when we were all together and it was a good vibe. I still love Cube and Ren and Dre and them today because when they came out with NWA it just became more powerful because I was just one guy. They came out and said, "We're a gang called Niggaz Wit Attitude." They came out as a gang and when I heard *Straight Outta Compton* I was fucked up! I was like, "Whoa! This shit is BANGIN!" So it's all respect, and I like to say 'influence' versus "Oh, you stole something." No, one thing makes somebody else think about how to do it a little different, so it was love. It was interesting, though, because Eazy never wrote a rhyme. But the funniest thing I'll never forget, I sat with Cube one day and Cube was bitchin because he was kinda disgruntled a lot, but he was like, "Man, shit, I wrote the rhyme where Eazy goes 'Ice Cube writes the rhymes that I say'" [on the Eazy-E song "8-Ball"]. And Cube said, "He said it!" Cube wrote it, but didn't expect for Eazy to rap it!

But Eazy was a very interesting cat to know. When we would go on the road I would do my interviews and Eazy was the rep from NWA and Eazy-E. And Eazy would go on the radio and tell people he was 15. Eazy was like 30 or some shit, but he was a funny muthafucka! He was a character, and if it wasn't for Eazy there probably wouldn't be no NWA so you gotta respect Eazy. He had his own little flavor. Also, I think the next group that was also very similar back then was Ghetto Boys. If you listen to Scarface, he is very similar to Ice Cube.

I think the trick behind West Coast hip-hop's wide ranging appeal was that New York hip-hop was very breakbeat oriented. To be a real hip-hopper from New York, music wasn't really part of it. It was more about breakbeats. You gotta listen to Gangstarr, you gotta listen to the early, real, what was considered true hip-hop. LA has a different life vibe. New York is more static, the world is more in your face so that works. But that doesn't really work when you're in a lowrider. So LA added musicality to it thanks to cats like Dre, and the musical aspect of it which made it a little bit more mainstream. "I'm Your Pusher" was the first West Coast rap record with a singing hook, and I thought it was too easy. When I did it and the record hit I was like, "Oh this shit's easy to do, it's kind of cheating." Hip-hop had always had these 'rules,' so I thought it was cheating to have someone singing on the rap record. Do you believe that? I thought it was cheating, I mean you know you had to have somebody scratch the hook. You can't have a singer, that's kind of turning you back on rap. We're not singers. So I kinda felt I cheated and got away with it, you know, with the Curtis Mayfield sample, but look at rap today.

Then when Dre and them started to break out the P-Funk, it just opened up and really, the first real mega New York star after Run-DMC, Run-DMC did it over beats and rhymes, but the first one was Biggie, and he really broke with West Coast music. "It was all a dream" [from the Notorious BIG song "Juicy"] and all that, that's more LA than New York style. So I think it was our addition of melodics and music versus just the traditional hip-hop, which is breakbeats.

I think that once LA did hip-hop, it made it global. When

something is so strong and it comes from the tri-state area, everybody that can break that bubble makes another person believe they can do it and I think that was important for it to be alive. I mean you've got German rappers, Asian rappers, you've got rappers from everywhere now. But it had to break out of New York for everyone to believe. It's kinda like I got to be on "Law and Order" for you to think you can get on "Law and Order." Obama got to damn near win the presidency for you to want to get into politics, to know it can happen. So this was a big boundary that had to be broken and, thanks to myself and some other people we proved it could be done. [Sir] Mix-A-Lot said you can rap from Seattle, so everybody who broke a boundary made the music that much bigger. You couldn't have told me 20 years ago that you could rap from fuckin North Carolina. Impossible! You've got to be from New York. So once LA was able to break it just started to break in more places. LA broke, then Luke [Skyywalker] broke in Miami, like I said, Mix in Seattle, [Rappin] 4-Tay and Dru Down came out of the Bay, and it just started to move and now you can rap from anywhere.

But when I actually got signed, I got signed in New York. By being at Radio I befriended Afrika Islam, and when you are part of hip-hop you know New York is where it comes from, so to me, when I met anybody from New York, it was very important. It's kinda like right now when I go out and meet gang bangers and they like, "Yo, you from LA? You really was in the Crips?" It's like some reverence cause they know you from the Mecca. So when I would meet New Yorkers I was like, very humble, like "I'm not gonna pretend like I know, I wanna learn." So I met Afrika Islam, but they were impressed cause I had money. They were impressed like, "You wanna rap, but you already got a Porsche, you already got the gold, you got bitches, what the fuck?" And I was like "Yeah, that's all cool but I wanna rap." And they were like, "Why you wanna rap? Ain't nobody even bought a car rappin yet!" And I was like, "Yeah, but I wanna do it!" But I was hustling, I had two beepers on, I was doin all kinds of shit. I was carryin pistols and I was doin something different that I didn't even teach them niggas about but everybody was like, "Rap about THAT!" And I was like, "Nobody wants to hear this shit."

I compare makin gangsta rap for me with me makin a peanut butter and jelly sandwich every day that I don't think I can sell and then you comin over sayin, "That's what you need to sell!" And I'm like, "You wanna sell this shit?" Once I figured out I could do that I was like, "Oh I can talk about this shit all day!" So it was just like it kinda fell in my lap, I got an unlimited supply of stories and game and shit I can teach. Then [Afrika] Islam took me to New York to get the record out and that's where I met Seymour Stein, who was the president of Sire Records. His unknowingness about hip-hop is how I got a record deal. He was so far out of the loop of rap, being a label that had signed Madonna and the Talking Heads and other alternative [rock] groups, he didn't know you 'couldn't' rap if you were from LA, he didn't know the theory. He told me I sounded like Bob Dylan, and I knew who Bob Dylan was so I took that as a compliment. But he was like, "Yo, do it!" so I got put on. I've always had allegiance to New York City; New York gave me a lot of love. The theory of making something happen, sometimes you gotta deal with somebody who just doesn't know it can't happen. He wasn't on that whole, "Oh, you can't rap if you from LA." If you from outer space and you don't know that a Black man can't skate you might put him on a hockey team. That's all the action we needed. I mean I felt I was giving inspiration doin *New Jack City*, I was like, "Yo, if I could pull this shit off they gonna let niggas act!"

If you really wanna know what I want out of it, I want people to listen to the words. I think a lot of people know my records, but never really studied them. I think if you take out my collection, have a drink and just sit back and just really get into it, and go into it not like its music, go into it like it's an Iceberg Slim book, you're gonna come out of it with a lot of game and a lot of information. That's what I always wanted to do because I kinda modeled myself after Iceberg Slim. I used to read his books and one day after tryin to live his life I said, "Well damn, this guys a writer. If I really admire him I shouldn't try to live the game, I should document the game." So I think Ice-T really documented the game. I mean I've got records like "The Rap Game's Hijacked," I've got records where I'll tell you what a nigga is. A straight up nigga. What is a bitch? Some of you niggas is bitches too. What is a hustler? Here's a hustler. What is a pusher? I mean it's like a dictionary to the game and that's what I wanted to be known for, like bein the rapper that gave out the most information about the streets. Not I'm doin it, but I mean really in detail explain to you some of the laws and theories, like on my new album I got a record called "The Code of the Streets" where it's like these are the rules, this is what can happen. One of my favorite records from Biggie is "10 Crack Commandments."

Those kinds of records to me are dope. Not this, "I got a car, I got a bitch, I got a house." How did you get the car? What did the narcs look like? How did your bitch rat you out? So the legacy is Ice-T is the most comprehensive musical documentation of the game. And then I think also that Ice was a guy who tried to do things we wouldn't try to do, and now we do it. You know, he was the cat that went out and did rock and roll, he was the cat that went out and did the movie, he's the cat that's on TV playin the cop telling everybody to suck his dick cause he's getting paid, he's that muthafucka that redefined hustling! Hustlin is getting your paper. If you workin at McDonald's, it's a hustle. And redefined a lot of these things so that it made it okay to do a lot of shit. Don't let any muthafucka that you don't admire tell you what the fuck to do. Set your own shit; only take advice from those you admire.

So I just tried to push it, and I'm still pushin shit you know, I might do stand up comedy man, fuck that. And I believe you can do it. If you're willing to fail you can do anything. You're guaranteed to miss 100% of the shots you don't take. I think the best quote I've ever heard about myself was when Chuck [D, of Public Enemy] said, "Ice is the only muthafucka I know that will do something to entirely jeopardize his career in order to stay awake." Everything will be going good, I'll be havin everything right and I'll be like, "You know what? I'm about to do this!" And everyone will be like, "What?" But my thing has always been this; I never ran with the hood. I ran with a group of elite individuals in my neighborhood who thought we were smarter than the hood. I can't go to the hood to tell me what the fuck is hot, the hood is dumb to me, I'm smarter, so I can only fuck with elite individuals that look beyond normal shit. If I was gonna wait on a broke nigga to tell me what to do, I mean why the fuck am I gonna listen to a broke muthafucka tell me what to do? It's like yo, first off, impress me with what you've done, with the caliber of your life, now I might listen. I'm not gonna listen to your broke ass tell who I should be, this that and a third.

Since I'm an orphan, I don't have no mother, I don't have no father, I don't have no sister, I don't have no brother. My video "I Must Stand" starts off with a little dot and it turns into me. I've always felt like: You know what? I ain't Black, I ain't White, I'm just a human and I'm not from LA, I'm from earth, dig it? So I'm a human from earth and I have no guidelines. Muthafuckas is like, "Oh, you married a White girl!" I would've married a Martian bitch if she coulda taught me the right shit. So it don't matter, I'm playin this game with all options and all potential scenarios available to me until I see otherwise. And when you live your life like that, you might be jet skiing, you may be snow skiing, you may be an equestrian rider, but when you allow culture and people to tell you what you shouldn't do, you gonna live in a little capsule. So whatever a player really wants to do, a player gonna do. You may tell me, "I hang-glide over the weekend." And I'm like, "Oh shit, I'm scared of that shit, but that's fly." If that's what a player wants to do, a player's supposed to go do that. Don't tell me, "Oh niggas don't do that." If you follow what 'niggas' is supposed to do I guess I'm supposed to be hangin out on the corner drinkin a 40, chillin. That's so easy, I mean come on, man.

I tell all my pimp buddies to watch the movie *The Usual Suspects*, Keyser Soze, "The devil's greatest trick was convincing people he didn't exist." So for me to be what you stereotype me as, how hard is that for me to do? It's easy to be who they say you are. To convince somebody that that's NOT who you are is the trick. So the game is really based around changing your perception of me. If you watch all the gangster movies, them niggas is wearin suits. Why they wearin suits? They not businessmen! Because it's stupid to look like a gangster if that's what you are. So you gotta learn the higher level, the Ph.D. levels of the game. When all of sudden you see this guy ain't saggin no more, well this muthafucka ain't flossin no more, what's really goin on? Oh, he's goin into the next level of the game. But they say tryin to teach that is like teachin astrophysics to a wino, so we just gonna keep it pimpin!

The Spread

The birth of hip-hop in New York during the 1970s created a culture that quickly traveled across the United States. As this culture spread, it began to reflect the flavor of the different places in which people were trying it out. From the beginning, evidence of hip-hop's mobility was found in the music's lyrical direction of the rhyme, and also in the production of the track. Starting around 1987, the West Coast made major musical contributions to hip-hop culture. In Los Angeles, several artists were mainly responsible for what would eventually become known as 'gangsta' rap. Meanwhile further to the north, the traditionally eclectic Bay Area was producing a variety of work that covered hip-hop's entire musical spectrum.

The five-year period between 1987 and 1992 on the West Coast was arguably the most important in the short history of hip-hop culture. Today hip-hop is the most influential element of popular culture not only in the United States but the world as well. Access and diversity have allowed young people in the post-hip-hop generation an opportunity to see that they share many common experiences, something previous generations did not have growing up. As a result, hip-hop has facilitated and normalized intercultural contact like no previous media or art form.

Considering its beginnings, the amount of mainstream play hip-hop has received is amazing. Equally amazing is the manner in which this acceptance was achieved. Ice-T summarized it in the movie *Rhyme and Reason* when he discussed his career, saying he did it with his "hat turned backward, tellin America to kiss my fuckin ass!" Russell Simmons described hip-hop as "the new American mainstream. We don't change for you; you adapt to us." Once the general public, and youth in particular, got a taste of that rebellious flavor, its appetite for hip-hop steadily increased. Since attention + controversy = $$$, heavy investment eventually followed. With more money at stake and more attention being paid, disapproval from parents and critics increased. This strategy backfired; young people have always tended to want what adults tell them they can't have. Early on, conservative and intolerant rap critics increased the desire of hip-hop's first generation, born roughly between 1965 and 1980, to be culturally affiliated with hip-hop music and culture.

The relationship between hip-hop and the mainstream also hugely shaped what has become known as the 'hip-hop nation.' Up to this historical moment the East Coast, and New York specifically, was still basking in the glow as the birthplace of hip-hop. However, the late 1980s brought about a change in the public image of the hip-hop artist. In the beginning he was a young street poet wearing shell-top Adidas, saying "Peace!" at the end of songs, an image based on the stereotypical East Coast artist. By the early 1990s he had evolved into a 'gangsta,' who wore khakis and Los Angeles Raider hats and rhymed on the effects of drugs and guns, an image mainly associated with artists from the West Coast. The West Coast's rise in artistry and popularity made the East Coast pay attention and give grudging respect to one of the first areas outside the northeast to establish a real national identity around hip-hop culture.

The western pioneers of this period took the next logical step from Grand Master Flash and the Furious Five's seminal 1982 song "The Message." This track is widely credited as one of the first socially conscious rap songs that made you bob your head while hearing about the horrors of urban decay:

"It's like a jungle sometimes it makes me wonder how I keep from goin under." Living in environments laced with crushing poverty, crime and drugs, many young inner city residents had in fact gone under. Instead of simply reviewing the problems, West Coast hip-hop was getting ready to share their anger with the world as well as tell what they were going to do about it.

Enter the Mainstream

By 1986, the door between hip-hop and the mainstream had been cracked open by the Beastie Boys. Mike D, King Ad-Rock, and MCA were White rappers who had credibility in early hip-hop culture. This was due in large part to their association with hip-hop management pioneer/record mogul Russell Simmons and the fact that The Beastie Boys debut album, *License to Ill,* was released on Def Jam, hip-hop's first great record label. The group also toured and performed with the biggest acts of the time such as Run-DMC, LL Cool J, Public Enemy, Slick Rick, Whodini, and DJ Jazzy Jeff and the Fresh Prince. The Beastie Boys' close association with the premier names in hip-hop allowed White kids to see someone who looked like them 'catching wreck' and getting 'props' within hip-hop culture.

If the Beastie Boys opened that door, then Run-DMC

kicked that shit in. Their album, *Raising Hell*, contained a remake of the classic Aerosmith song "Walk this Way." Rick Rubin, who co-founded Def Jam with Russell Simmons, developed an MTV-friendly angle to the project by not only having Run-DMC cover the song, but including the participation of Aerosmith. In the book *Life and Def*, Simmons explained:

> At that time Aerosmith was at a low ebb in their career while Run-DMC was on the rise. So Steve Tyler and the band were very cooperative and we all had a good time together. But did any of us think that this would be a landmark record? No. Much talked about? Yes. A massive hit? Only in our dreams. But it went on to become the biggest single on the album and the song that would resurrect Aerosmith's career.

Aside from the boost that this collaboration gave to Aerosmith, there was another significant aspect to the song. In the book *Rap Attack*, David Toop argued "Walk this Way" became "one of the breakthrough records of rap, its metal guitar riffs, rock chorus, hard beats and raps fusing into an ultimate in rebel music that

MTV and radio programmers, along with a lot of White rock fans, found impossible to resist." This exposure to the mainstream led more and more curious youngsters of various colors and backgrounds to explore and investigate this new, rebellious culture known as hip-hop. On the universal nature of youth experience, Simmons noted, "Even though rap was born in the ghetto, it addresses issues a lot of kids across America are dealing with – anger, alienation, hypocrisy, sex, drugs. All the basics."

The natural dynamic of youth rebelliousness certainly played a role in hip-hop's broad appeal, but there was something else at work as well. As an example, in my time teaching college level courses based around cultural issues, I have frequently assigned a paper that is essentially a cultural autobiography, requiring the students to think and reflect on their own cultural makeup and heritage. More times than I can count, I have had White students come up to me with puzzled looks on their faces saying something to the effect, "I don't really have a culture." Of course everyone is a cultural being; it's just that some people have been led to think that culture is something exotic and ethnic that only people of color have. In a sense, these young people felt culturally disenfranchised. Even though they may descend from the power structure that brought about the creation of hip-hop in the first place, millions of White kids identified with hip-hop culture in spite of this. Hip-hop's inclusive nature, evidenced by the success of the Beastie Boys and Run-DMC's collaboration with Aerosmith, served as proof that everyone was welcome to this party.

While there was an excited buzz among young people around hip-hop culture, there was an equally uncomfortable buzz among adults. Many adult opinions of hip-hop were informed by mainstream media coverage, such as an incident at a Run-DMC concert held at the Long Beach (California) Arena in front of an estimated 14,500 fans as part of their *Raising Hell* tour in August, 1986. An article about the incident in the September 1, 1986 edition of *Time* magazine began, "Its driving beat and chanted lyrics echo the pulse and pitch of inner-city streets. But rap music also draws out a meaner side of ghetto life: Gang violence." The story said that over 300 Black and Hispanic gang members "swarmed through the crowd, attacking everyone around them. Audience members struck back with metal chairs and whatever else came to hand, until police armed with batons broke up the concert." There were forty-five reported injuries, including a man who was stabbed. The article noted that this was the fourth "major outbreak of violence" on the tour, with earlier incidents in Pittsburgh, New York City, and St. Louis, leaving a total of 39 injured.

The *Time* piece also stated that the day after the Long Beach incident officials at the Hollywood Palladium canceled an upcoming Run-DMC show, "fearing another bloody melee." DMC was quoted defending the group, blaming lax security and saying, "Rap music has nothing to do with crack and crime... Check my lyrics, I'm a role model for kids, and I go out of my way to give them a positive message." While noting that some "rappers have produced songs that urge kids to stay in school and avoid crime and drugs," the article was dismissive, stating:

> The majority of rap lyrics are concerned with
> nothing more volatile than partying and macho
> boasting. Since rap became popular several years
> ago, many performances have been marred by
> brutality. Says Public Safety Commissioner John
> Norton of Pittsburgh, where teenagers went on a
> window smashing rampage after a Run-DMC

concert in June: "There is absolutely no doubt in my mind that rap music spurs violence."

The piece ended with a quote from Harvard University psychiatrist Alvin Poussaint. Poussaint, who is Black, rejected the notion that rap is inherently violent, saying, "Rap music really comes from inner-city street kids, some of whom are gang members immersed in antisocial behavior."

Even though the article explained that when security guards were trained to identify gang colors and keep potential troublemakers out of the venue rap concerts remained trouble free, the mainstream had seemingly made up its mind. Negative quotes from a Public Safety Commissioner combined with the general public's growing street gang hysteria, fueled by sensational media descriptors like "bloody melee" and "marred by brutality," convinced many that hip-hop was not to be trusted.

This Shit's Insane

Street gangs were a problem on the West Coast during the 1980s. The reasons behind them were varied and complex, but in the eyes of many the first 'gang' to make its presence felt was the Los Angeles Police Department. The culture of the modern day LAPD was shaped by William H. Parker, who was Chief from 1950-1966. Parker actively recruited White men from the south, usually ex-Army or Marines, to serve as officers. This was a deliberate attempt to set a tone for how citizens, particularly Black citizens, would be dealt with by law enforcement in Los Angeles. For example, the Central Avenue Vice Squad was notorious for harassing Black owned businesses on Central Avenue and surrounding areas. Eventually police involvement in crimes like racketeering and extortion, which are often associated with street gang activity, became just another added cost for Black business owners. Police shakedowns and payoffs siphoned millions of dollars out of the community.

As problematic as the police could be, integration brought about other challenges for Blacks in Los Angeles. Until the late 1940s, neighborhoods like Compton and South Central Los Angeles were virtually all White. Once Black families began moving into these areas ignorance, hostility, and opposition to integration led to numerous incidents of groups of White youths seeking out and assaulting Black youths. In response, Black kids began to form and travel in groups as a means of protection. While these Black youths did not necessarily view themselves as a 'gang' in the modern sense, they were up against groups of White kids, like those who called themselves the "Spook Hunters," that definitely did.

Like so many other places in the United States in the 1960s, the phenomenon of integrating urban communities led to another phenomenon - White flight. As more White families moved out of South Central and Compton, more Black families moved in. Consequently, the groups of young Black men that had originally been about self-defense began to grow and establish rival identities with names like the Slausons, the Farmers, the Businessmen, and the Gladiators. With the White gangs now largely gone, cramped quarters, rivalry and competition caused these Black groups to turn on each other. However, there were limits to these conflicts in that 'gang wars' of this time consisted primarily of fistfights. The only weapons used were generally sticks or knives.

A turning point in California gang evolution occurred in August, 1965. After a routine traffic stop of a car full of young Black males by the California Highway Patrol, the LAPD arrived on the scene. A crowd gathered and people fought back when the police tried to strong arm them. The situation quickly escalated into what became known as the Watts Riots. While this uprising resulted in the deaths of some 34 people, it also saw street youth come together to drive the Los Angeles Police Department out of their community. This series of events lit the fuse on radical politics and Black power in Los Angeles.

As a response to police harassment and economic hardship, Huey Newton and Bobby Seale had formed the Black Panther Party for Self-Defense in Oakland, California. In the aftermath of the Watts uprising, Alprentice "Bunchy" Carter met with Newton and Seale and soon started the LA chapter of the Black Panther Party. Widely portrayed in the mainstream media as a terrorist organization, the Panthers actually were extremely community focused. The book *Seize the Time* by Bobby Seale, first published in 1970, laid out the Black Panther Party's Ten Point Platform and Program:

1. *We want freedom. We want power to determine the destiny of the Black Community.*

   We believe that Black people will not be free until we are able to determine our destiny.

2. *We want full employment for our people.*

   We believe that the federal government is responsible and obligated to give every man employment or a guaranteed income. We believe that if the White American businessmen will not give full employment, then the means of production should be taken from the businessmen and placed in the community so that the people of the community can organize and employ all of its people and give a high standard of living.

3. *We want to end the robbery by the White man of our Black community.*

We believe that this racist government has robbed us and now we are demanding the overdue debt of forty acres and two mules. Forty acres and two mules was promised 100 years ago as restitution for slave labor and mass murder of Black people. We will accept the payment in currency which will be distributed to our many communities. The Germans are now aiding the Jews in Israel for the genocide of the Jewish people. The Germans murdered six million Jews. The American racist has taken part in the slaughter of over fifty million Black people; therefore, we feel that this is a modest demand that we make.

4. *We want decent housing, fit for shelter of human beings.*

We believe that if the White landlords will not give decent housing to our Black community, then the housing and the land should be made into cooperatives so that our community, with government aid, can build and make decent housing for its people.

5. *We want education for our people that exposes the true nature of this decadent American society. We want*

education that teaches us our true history and our role in the present day society.

We believe in an educational system that will give our people a knowledge of self. If a man does not have knowledge of himself and his position in society and the world, then he has little chance to relate to anything else.

6. *We want all Black men to be exempt from military service.*

We believe that Black people should not be forced to fight in the military service to defend a racist government that does not protect us. We will not fight and kill other people of color in the world who, like Black people, are being victimized by the White racist government of America. We will protect ourselves from the force and violence of the racist police and the racist military, by whatever means necessary.

7. *We want an immediate end to POLICE BRUTALITY and MURDER of Black people.*

We believe we can end police brutality in our Black community by organizing Black self-defense groups that are dedicated to defending our Black community from racist police oppression and brutality. The Second Amendment to the Constitution of the United States gives a right to bear arms. We therefore believe that all Black people should arm themselves for self-defense.

8. *We want freedom for all Black men held in federal, state, county, and city prisons and jails.*

We believe that all Black people should be released from the many jails and prisons because they have not received a fair and impartial trial.

9. *We want all Black people when brought to trial to be tried in court by a jury of their peer group or people from their Black communities, as defined by the Constitution of the United States.*

We believe that the courts should follow the United States Constitution so that Black people will receive fair trials. The Fourteenth Amendment of the U.S. Constitution gives a man a right to be tried by his peer group. A peer is a person from a similar economic, social, religious, geographic, environmental, historical, and racial background. To do this the court will be forced to select a jury from the Black community from which the Black defendant came. We have been and are being tried by all-White juries that have no understanding of the "average reasoning man" of the Black community.

10. *We want land, bread, housing, education, clothing, justice, and peace. And as our major political objective, a United Nations-supervised plebiscite to be held throughout the Black colony in which only Black colonial subjects will be allowed to participate, for the purpose of determining the will of Black people as to their national destiny.*

When, in the course of human events, it becomes necessary for one people to dissolve the political bands which have connected them with another, and to assume, among the powers of the earth, the separate and equal station to which the laws of nature and nature's God entitle them, a decent respect to the opinions of mankind requires that they should declare the causes which impel them to the separation.

We hold these truths to be self-evident, that all men are created equal; that they are endowed by their Creator with certain unalienable rights; that among these are life, liberty, and the pursuit of happiness. That, to secure these rights, governments are instituted among men, deriving their just powers from the consent of the governed; that, whenever any form of government becomes destructive of these ends, it is the right of the people to alter or to abolish it, and to institute a new government, laying its foundation on such principles, and organizing its powers in such form, as to them shall seem most likely to effect their safety and happiness. Prudence, indeed, will dictate that governments long established should not be changed for light and transient causes; and, accordingly, all experience hath shown, that mankind are disposed to suffer, while evils are sufferable, than to right themselves by abolishing the forms to which they are accustomed. But, when a long train of abuses and usurpations, pursuing invariably the same object, evinces a design to reduce them under absolute despotism, it is their right, it is their duty, to throw off such government, and to provide new guards for their future security.

The inclusion in point #10, "We hold these truths to be self-evident," was an intentional quote from the United States Declaration of Independence. In addition to demands for basic civil rights, the Black Panthers tested thousands of children for sickle-cell anemia, established free community medical clinics, and created no cost breakfast and lunch programs for local school children. But in spite of their stated goals and community involvement, the group's choice to exercise their second amendment right to bear arms in public led many people to see the Panthers as little more than hoodlums and thugs. Spiro Agnew, then Vice President of the United States under President Richard Nixon, called them "...a completely irresponsible anarchistic group of criminals."

Although the Black Panthers ushered in a period of increased consciousness and unity in the Black community, politics were still present. Bunchy Carter was a Slauson, and initially many early members of the Los Angeles chapter of the Panthers were Slausons as well. Flyers for parties, which were also used as recruiting events, had headlines like "From Slausons to Revolutionaries." People from rival sets formed alternative Black power groups like the US Organization started by Ron Karenga. While a big part of the Panther's approach was challenging authority, the US Organization took a less confrontational stance by focusing on organizing and changing the system from within.

Friction between the Black Panthers and the US Organization, already present because of the various affiliations of the different members, increased as the federal government implemented a counter-intelligence program, or CO-INTELPRO. The government considered the Panthers to be more dangerous than the Communist party or the mafia. As a result, an FBI directive called for "imaginative and hard-hitting counter-intelligence measures aimed at crippling the Black Panther Party." These measures included propaganda of various kinds. One example was an FBI-produced drawing that depicted Ron Karenga sitting in a chair with his feet on a desk. In his hand was a piece of paper with the heading, "Things to do today," and below that was a list of names, including John Huggins and Bunchy Carter, both of which were crossed out.

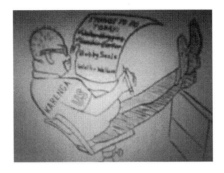

Whether that cartoon was drawn before January 17, 1969 is unclear, but on that day Bunchy Carter and John Huggins were shot and killed as they attended a student election meeting at Campbell Hall on the campus of UCLA. The murders were initially blamed on the US Organization, but subsequent documents and admissions by former FBI agents indicated that the shooter was actually a mole planted by the government to create dissent amongst the young Black radical political organizations. A *New York Times* article dated May 9, 1975, with the headline "Senate Staff Report Says FBI Incited 'Gang Warfare' and Killings In Plot To Destroy The Black Panther Party," stated that although the FBI didn't pull the trigger on Carter and Huggins, they "did cause the unrest that preceded it."

As the Panthers began to fade in the 1970s, a new group of leaders began to assert themselves. The Community

Revolutionary Inter-Party Service, started by Stanley 'Tookie' Williams, Jamel Barnes, and Raymond Washington originally sought official recognition from the city of Los Angeles as a community organization, complete with a constitution. According to the documentary film *Bastards of the Party*, the Crips went as far as to send a letter of introduction to then Mayor Tom Bradley. Apparently alarmed by the radical potential of the organization, the city requested the group change the R in CRIP from Revolutionary to Reform.

Things began to shift on the night of March 25, 1970, when a young man named Robert Ballou was beaten to death at the Hollywood Palladium for his leather jacket, allegedly by a group of Crips. A media frenzy ensued and the perception of the group was changed forever. The Crips grew in membership, but some people and communities refused to be recruited, such as Eugene "Taboo" Battle in the Athens Park neighborhood, and banded together as Bloods. Bobby Lavender, an original member of the Bloods, explained it this way in the documentary film *The Fire This Time*:

When you take something away from a

community or people, the community will
replace it with something. When you took away
the leadership in the 60s, the youth replaced it
with something. We seeked our own leadership.
We felt the leaders of the 60s failed us because we
didn't quite comprehend what they stood for.
Also, the act of violence totally on a people
without people fighting back didn't make sense
to youngsters. So we formed our gangs and we
dealt with our own brand of leadership. Today
they're called Bloods and Crips.

In his book *City of Quartz* Mike Davis argued that the Crips and
the Bloods were the "bastard offspring" of the Black political
parties of the 1960s. Deindustrialization in places like Southern
California meant the adolescent labor pool faced a transition to
adulthood without the steady middle-class manufacturing jobs
their parents and grandparents worked in the past. Perhaps not
coincidentally, plans were already being drawn up in California
for several new state prisons like Mule Creek, Corcoran, Wasco
State, and Pelican Bay that would open by the mid-1980s.

Without a doubt, the single biggest factor that accelerated

the rise of Los Angeles street gangs like the Bloods and the Crips

in the 1980s was crack. President Ronald Reagan had considered

the drug problem important enough to declare a national 'war

on drugs.' Crack was seemingly available on a majority of inner

city street corners. In Los Angeles, it appeared that the

government's war on drugs was ineptly handled or purposefully

negligent. The question was: If they knew it was coming, why

didn't the government stop, or at least slow down, the cocaine? A

series of newspaper articles a decade later suggested a sinister

reason why crack was so successfully imported to urban centers

in the United States.

On August 22, 1996, *The San Jose Mercury News*

published the first in a Pulitzer Prize winning series of

investigative articles by reporter Gary Webb. The first stanza of

the first article stated:

> For the better part of a decade, a San Francisco
> Bay Area drug ring sold tons of cocaine to the
> Crips and Bloods street gangs of Los Angeles and
> funneled millions in drug profits to an arm of the
> Contra guerrillas of Nicaragua run by the Central

Intelligence Agency, the San Jose Mercury News has found.

This drug network opened the first pipeline between Colombia's cocaine cartels and the Black neighborhoods of Los Angeles, a city now known as the "crack" capital of the world. The cocaine that flooded in helped spark a crack explosion in urban America - and provided the cash and connections needed for LA's gangs to buy weapons.

It is one of the most bizarre alliances in modern history: The union of a U.S.-backed army attempting to overthrow a revolutionary socialist government and the "gangstas" of Compton and South-Central Los Angeles.

The army's financiers - who met with CIA agents before and during the time they were selling the drugs in LA - delivered cut-rate cocaine to the gangs through a young South-Central crack

dealer named Ricky Donnell Ross. Unaware of
his suppliers' military and political connections,
"Freeway Rick" turned the cocaine powder into
crack and wholesaled it to gangs across the
country.

This series of articles came to be known as "Dark Alliance."
Although serious factual questions about the articles were later
raised, this was not the first story linking the United States
government to the rise and spread of crack in inner city
communities. Soon after "Dark Alliance" Peter Kornbluh wrote:

> Although many readers of the *Mercury News*
> articles may not have known it, "Dark Alliance" is
> not the first reported link between the Contra
> war and drug smuggling. More than a decade
> ago, allegations surfaced that Contra forces,
> organized by the CIA to overthrow the
> Sandinista government in Nicaragua, were
> consorting with drug smugglers with the
> knowledge of U.S. officials. The Associated Press
> broke the first such story on December 20, 1985.

The AP's Robert Parry and Brian Barger
reported that three Contra groups "have engaged
in cocaine trafficking, in part to help finance
their war against Nicaragua." Dramatic as it was,
that story almost didn't run, because of pressure
by Reagan administration officials (see
"Narco-Terrorism: A Tale of Two Stories" *CJR*,
September/October, 1986). Indeed, the White
House waged a concerted behind-the-scenes
campaign to besmirch the professionalism of
Parry and Barger and to discredit all reporting on
the Contras and drugs.

Many community members who witnessed the crack epidemic
up close did not need media validation to believe that the
government was involved, at least on some level. Enough
mistrust had developed over the years between
African-Americans and the government that stories like "Dark
Alliance" made sense.

In the late 1980s, the West Coast, like much of the United
States, was just beginning to come to grips with crack's
destructive force as it swept through urban communities. The

drug fueled gang culture on two levels. Economics was first. Companies paying decent, living wages abandoned urban areas and populations; in comparison, crack cash was a bonanza. The 1970s set the stage for the urban economic devastation of the 1980s. Globalization, economic restructuring, social dislocations, gentrification, and loosened trade restrictions, led to the loss of large numbers of manufacturing jobs. The social rollbacks enacted by the Reagan Administration were the final blow. Increasingly, the option of moving away from these poverty and drug stricken neighborhoods was open only to those who could afford it. Drug sentencing guidelines disproportionately targeted communities of color, although data would later confirm that only about 25 percent of crack users were African-American. As crack addiction and drug related crime increased, legislators passed disparate sentencing guidelines, e.g. the 1986 100 to 1 rule, for crack and powder cocaine offenders. Under the rule, an individual charged with possessing 5 grams of crack would receive the same amount of prison time as someone who was caught with 500 grams of powder cocaine. Not surprisingly, these sentences disproportionately affected Brown and Black youth. In 2010, Congress reduced this ratio to 18 to 1.

Secondly, the 'war on drugs' actually intensified the damage that crack did to families. Police actions and harassment, combined with the desperation of addicts dismantled families sometimes overnight. Crack addiction created smokers, or 'baseheads,' who were hollow shells of their former selves. For the local crack dealer, the desperation of their customers and competitors along with the availability of automatic weapons, combined to make it a profession where every day could be your last. Death, prison, and addiction, dealt a crushing blow to already strained family units in urban areas. As a result, young people, particularly young males, looking for family found it in the streets. Statistics from this period revealed that nearly one-third of African-American males between ages 18 and 35 in California were either in jail or on parole. The hellish environment so many young people were growing up in and around was fertile ground for the development and style of hip-hop music that was about to emerge.

Verbal Tradition

Toasting is an African oral folk tradition that has become absorbed into mainstream commercial entertainment. One of the early, publicly recognizable examples of toasting was the verbal beatdowns that boxer Cassius Clay (later Muhammad Ali) gave his opponents. However because they were often televised or recorded, and because the 1960s and 70s were a different time, Ali's legendary linguistics were pretty tame. In their rawest form, toasts could take on a very different sound. David Toop, in the book *Rap Attack* described toasts as narrative poems that are "rhyming stories, often lengthy, which are told mostly amongst men. Violent, scatological, obscene, misogynist, they have been used for decades to while away time in situations of enforced boredom, whether prison, armed service or street corner life."

In a sense toasting represents a form of conversation that occurs in homogenous groups and not in the presence of 'mixed company.' Sometimes drawn along racial or gender lines, conversation topics and the language used within these groups is very different depending on who is or who is not around. For instance, a group of men might discuss topics and say things to each other that they would not say if a woman were present. Some might call this 'locker room talk.' In addition, the people saying these things may not necessarily feel that way inside. The pressure within a group dynamic to conform can be intense, and the desire to be seen as a worthy member of the 'in-group' can drive people to go way over the top just to prove themselves.

This in-group/out-group dynamic has been around since the beginning of human interaction. Yet the in-group discussions of young, disenfranchised, urban African-American males had never had a public forum. If each style of music can be viewed as an expression of a segment of society, this demographic had been unheard. Very soon the young Black male's style - machismo, misogyny, insecurities, politics, homophobia, anger, fears, hopes and dreams - would be on display for all to bob their heads to.

First Person Account: GREG MACK

I first encountered hip-hop music in California in August of 1983, which is when I moved to California, and I started working at a radio station called KDAY [1580 on the AM dial]. A lot of people were playing rap then, Sugar Hill Gang, Run-DMC, and I think Kurtis Blow was just coming out at that time. People in California were playing it, that's why I started playing it on the radio. When I first moved to LA, I was living in South Central, which, for those that don't know, was kind of a rough part of town. You didn't even have to open up your window to hear it [rap]; they would vibrate or even shatter your window with the car stereos. They were playing a lot of hip-hop, but I noticed no one was really playing that music on the radio and that's how I kind of transformed it to radio because I was the Music Director at KDAY.

When "Rapper's Delight" came out, I was working in

San Antonio, Texas, and I didn't think much about it. I liked it, I
thought it was different, but you also had "Disco Duck" by Rick
Dees, out which was blowing up. I was just thinking, "Okay, well
I kinda like this but this is another novelty record that's kind of
catchy." I didn't think much about it to be honest with you. But
when I got to LA and you had more [hip-hop] groups coming
out, it was kind of like, "Okay..." I should mention that before
this, when I worked in Houston, and there we started playing a
lot of Sugar Hill stuff, only at night though. But when I got to
LA, it was so big there already that I felt like it needed to be heard
all day long.

This is where ideology comes in; I've always been the
kind of programmer that would much rather support a mediocre
local artist than a really big national artist. So some of the local
acts that started to come out at that time out of the West Coast
were more what I would call techno hip-hop. You had the
Wrecking Cru, which was produced by Dr. Dre, and that had a
lot of techno sound to it. I remember one day I was riding
around with Run-DMC and we were listening to KDAY, and we
played Wrecking Cru and Egyptian Lover records, and they were
telling me how that music made them nervous, it was just too
much! They didn't like that techno/rap thing, as they called it,

because New York rappers were on a different tip. But LA rappers at that time had a different vision of what they thought hip-hop was, at least until Ice-T came out with "6 'N The Morning."

By that time we were already playing a lot of east coast and local techno rap groups. Earlier, Russell Simmons had come to me and said, "Hey I've got this new kid coming out and it would be great if you guys would play this and we're going to bring him out here to do schools and all kinds of appearances." The guy's name was LL Cool J and the song was called "I Need A Beat," so that song had kind of exploded on the West Coast. But the beginning of when the West Coast started to change its style a bit was when "6 'N The Morning" came out, which I consider the first 'gangsta' rap song. We did not play it right away because it was a little hard for our audience. We did end up playing it later, I don't remember if we got a different version or if we edited it, but we got it to where we could play it on the air. It was not a gigantic record for us, although we did get a lot of response off of it, which I think is what laid the blueprint for NWA to come along later on. But you have to go back a few years from 1987 to understand where all this came from. When I first got to

LA, there was a kid that started mixing for me named Dr. Dre, and he was at that time was doing the techno rap but he always had a vision of doing something a little different. Apparently Dre had gotten into some trouble and was locked up, I'm still not clear on what exactly happened, but a kid named Eazy-E had gone to bail him out. Eazy said he would bail Dre out, but wanted Dre to join his group, which he did. But I remember Dr. Dre bringing Eazy to a dance I was doing at a club called the Casa Camino Real, Dre tells me the story and says, "Greg, I'm gonna be working with him [Eazy], he's gonna let me get loose and do what I enjoy doing, I'm going to show the style I've been wanting to show, and we've got this song that we want you to hear." We went out to the car and that song was "Boyz-N-The Hood." Now mind you, this was like a year after "6 'N The Morning." So they let me hear it and I was like, "Well I like it, it's got potential, but I can't play that on the radio. You've got to clean it up for me." So 24 hours later they had a radio version, as we used to call it back then. But when we said 'radio version' we meant radio version where it wasn't just words turned backwards or edits, they actually changed the lyrics for us. Within 24 hours it was my most requested record. So [19]87 was actually not the starting point for 'gangsta' rap, it might have been the starting point for the first gangsta rap song, but it was an evolution of what started in [19]83 with Dre. In fact, the guy who produced "6 'N The Morning," DJ Unknown, was my drinking buddy back then. I never knew what songs he produced because he never liked to say who he was, but it was DJ Unknown.

I can tell you when I first noticed the effects the music was having on the larger mainstream culture. At that time I had a girlfriend that went to UCLA. I went to visit her and this White guy pulled up a in a big pick-up truck and he was blastin the crap out of NWA. At that point I said, "Okay, we've made it." It's kind of funny because the White guys were checking it out and they loved it. The Hispanic people were checking it out and they loved it. Also, you have to remember that during those years the major record stores wouldn't even carry it. All the record companies hated me because by me playing the rap records, we weren't playing the traditional R & B songs that they were putting out. So we were kind of looked down upon, I learned later that I'd pissed off a lot of record people because they felt like I was playing all this novelty bullshit when I should be playing Freddy Jackson or Luther Vandross, which we did, but we didn't play it enough for them because we were also playing some rap music. So I was really looked down upon by the industry at that time, and a lot of people thought I was nuts. But the way I looked at it was with the R & B artists, because we used to do a lot of promotions back then and I would always try and get the R & B artists to go out and do stuff with the radio station, they were just too big or they didn't have time or they're above that. Shoot, the hip-hop artists? Oh man we were doing schools every day of the week and we had major artists going out to appear at these schools and they won these kids' hearts over. They were just accessible and the kids felt like they were in tune with what they were dealing with.

For example, our street team, or what people call street teams nowadays, back then our street team was Dr. Dre, Ice Cube, Eazy-E, LA Dream Team, Egyptian Lover, LL Cool J, Run-DMC, Big Daddy Kane, Biz Markie, just about every name in hip-hop from the mid-80s was part of our street team. We went out to schools every day. EVERY DAY! High schools, junior high, elementary, basically in the hoods where people said, "Don't go there, you're crazy for going in that neighborhood." What I always did was, whenever we did things, I tried to do them in different areas, meaning we would do certain things for the Blood area of town, the Crip area of town, the Mexican gang area of town, we did neutral areas of town, we also did the White

areas of town and the Hispanic areas of town. We tried to show

the folks that were in the gangs that, "Hey, we're not down with

anybody as far as gangs but we're down with everybody as far as

going to the different neighborhoods to show you that we're not

down with anybody." So we exposed all these artists to the

different areas of town. I didn't understand when I first got to

LA that I couldn't wear a blue hat in a red area or a red hat in a

blue area, I didn't know all of that. You're talking about a guy

that pretty much still had a Texas twang coming into town not

knowing all these things, and I think that the genuine naivety of

me is what made them trust me, because I didn't know. And

that's probably why I didn't get capped later. These guys, I built

a relationship with them. And the thing about me is that they

knew they could bring their song to me whether it was a cassette,

it didn't matter. They also knew that they didn't have to pay me,

I was very proud of the fact that I never ever took payola. If you

had a good record, and especially if you were local, if you had a

halfway decent record they knew I was gonna give them some

love. So we just built that kind of relationship and that

partnership.

I think what a lot of people don't realize is that the majority of people that were buying this music were not Black people. I would guess that 60-70% of the people that were buying it were White kids, even in the beginning. I think that the White kids picked up on it right away because they didn't quite understand what was going on in the Black neighborhoods, so they had to hear it through music, and also they liked the beat. I truly believe the most important years were 1983-87 because that's when it was all developing. By the time you got to '87 you were seeing the fruits of the labor that we had put in, and it's kind of interesting because we didn't look at it in those years like we were doing something innovative or that we were groundbreaking. We didn't look at it that way because we were too busy doing it. It was a passion, it was a vibe. I'd lived that life, and also I understood what they were rapping about. Now one of the misconceptions about a group like, say, NWA, was that these guys were gangbangers and were rapping about what they lived. That's not true! These guys were good kids. They were really good kids and I look at them that way; I look at them like my kids. But none of them were gangbangers, at least to my knowledge, because they knew that if they were gonna be around me they just couldn't be doing that; I just didn't roll that way.

But they had so many friends that would tell them stories and tell them about things that were going on. While they were experiencing the same things that I was experiencing, like getting pulled over by the cops for no reason other than the fact that I had a nice car and my first wife was Hispanic, so they thought I was a pimp. So when NWA came out with a song like "Fuck Tha Police" and everybody else was like, "Oh my God," I knew exactly what they were talking about. But a lot of those things that were happening, when they were happening, we didn't look at it like as groundbreaking. It was fun and it was a reflection of what was really going on in LA at that time. It really was a reflection of it.

In terms of legacy, there was a gentleman that used to be the president of A & M, president of MCA, president of Motown named Jeryl Busby. I heard him explain the legacy of what was going on at that time better than I could have said or I've ever heard it said. What was going on, what I was doing there was giving these youth a way out. It also changed a lot of things for the mom and pop record stores. All of sudden they were making a killing because Warehouse wouldn't carry it, and none of the other major chains at that time would even carry the music. So the mom and pop record stores were making money, you had kids that were growing up in the hood and had no way out that all of a sudden were making all of this money. It just really created a whole different change for Black youth, and I was very proud of that. I tell people all the time, and I really feel this way, I don't feel like it's so much what I did but what they did and because they were successful it made it look like I knew what I was doing. But I didn't look at it that way, that I knew what I was doing, I looked at it like, "Wow, these kids are good I'ma give them a shot," and they just one right after another kept blowing up. So I think the legacy of it all was the artists themselves, not so much me or KDAY, but the artists themselves. They had the creativity, they had people like Jerry Heller, and Jerry will argue with me about this, but he was basically feeding off of who I would develop. He'd be over at Macola Records, "Oh, KDAY's playing you? I wanna sign you, I wanna manage you!" If I played it, they signed them up. Basically I was a conduit. I tell people all the time, not that I'm a crazy Christian, although I am a Christian, that God used me to allow them to grow. That's kind of the way I look at it.

I feel very blessed that I had a great general manager by the name of Ed Kirby and a program director named Jack

Patterson. When I got there KDAY wasn't doing very well, and they gave me the chance to turn it around; the minute I got there I got that chance. What I tried to do with KDAY was take the experience I had gained at Magic 102 in Houston and at KYS in Corpus Christie. I took the programming skills I learned from those guys and was able to take what I was hearing in the streets and make it a reflection of what was really going on out there, and KDAY allowed me to do that. In doing that, and again I have to go back to the idea that I don't think KDAY even recognized the strength of what was happening until a few years later, but nobody in the world was doing that at that time. We realized the Hispanic population in LA even back then was huge and I knew I had to reach out to them as well. So we eventually brought in a gentleman by the name of Tony G, Tony Gonzales. I told him to call himself Tony Gonzales because I wanted the Latin people to know that they were being represented, and he ended up becoming one of my most popular mixers. We just tried to be mass appeal, and I think what we were doing had mass appeal as is evidenced by what is called today the CHR [Contemporary Hit Radio] rhythmic format; KDAY was doing that back then. But we weren't just all hip-hop, we played R & B, some of the dance groups, we broke Lisa Lisa and Cult Jam; we were the first station to ever play them, months before they ever came out. We started breaking groups like Expose, Cover Girls, Debbie Deb, that Florida/Miami sound that was happening, and we mixed that all together. What we didn't know was that we were creating a whole new format, the CHR rhythmic format which is still huge today. It's not as big as it was because hip-hop isn't as big as it was, but back then it was just gigantic.

The very first [radio ratings] book after doing this, out of the five Black stations in the market at that time in LA, KDAY went from 5th up to 2nd. So we didn't exactly know that it was that strong, and the reason I keep saying we and I is simply because of this: At that time I don't think KDAY, Jack and Ed, really appreciated me because when the ratings would come out I would always hear them partying and celebrating and poppin' bottles of champagne, but nobody ever came down to say, "Hey Greg thanks, good job." I look back on that and, I wouldn't say it bothers me, but it did amaze me that I was the one pulling the strings on that but never got a pat on the back, so to speak.

I just think it's important for people to realize that we set the world on fire, with no idea we were doing it at the time. We were just having fun, and I think that the first FM station to ever

do it was WUFL Power 99 out of Philly. They were the first East

Coast station. I remember being on the air at KDAY one day and

I had a call from a gentleman by the name of Jeff Wyatt who was

the program director there and he said, "You know, I kinda like

that format you're doing. What is that called?" I said, "It's called

'playin the hits!'" He says, "But you put a lot of rap music in

there, what's that about?" I said, "Those are the hits to the

listeners here." Next thing I know he's doing it out there, and it

kind of blew up in Philly, then just snowballed from that point. I

would say that they were the first FM station that did it. Power

106 did come on board years later and that was the demise of

KDAY. KDAY was still doing well but if you could hear the

same music on FM, that's tough for an AM station. The people

that owned KDAY at the time were looking at making $10

million a year and all of a sudden it dropped down to $6 million

a year because the FM was taking away a lot of the advertisers.

That's why they ended up selling the station, I tried to buy it

when it went down but just couldn't raise the money. I went to

Russell Simmons, I went to Clarence Avon, I went to Jeryl Busby

but couldn't get anybody to lend me the money to do it, and you know what? It was probably good that they didn't because with the rise of FM it probably would have been a losing proposition.

There was some initial resistance to hip-hop on KDAY. When I first started, they would only let me play it at night, but then when the ratings showed how strong nights were, they decided to loosen that up a little bit and spread some of the stronger rap songs throughout the day. So what we ended up doing was playing the songs that were major hits during the day and then the ones that were marginal we still played only at night. 'Day partying' is what we called it and a lot of stations do that today. As far as the listeners, there was no West Coast bias. LA, unlike New York, which only wanted to play East Coast rappers, was wide open to the East Coast rappers, the West Coast rappers, as well as the sound that was coming out of Florida, like Newcleus and Pretty Tony that were doing some big things. But LA was more open to different areas of the country being played, unlike say, Texas, which only wanted to hear East Coast and only some West Coast. Now eventually Texas came to like the West Coast a little more, but LA liked different areas as opposed to some other cities, and New York definitely hated West Coast rap. It took Dre forever to get up in there. Took Snoop forever, too. They just did not like the West Coast music and none of the earlier Wrecking Cru or Egyptian Lover stuff ever got played on the East Coast. The people in New York were just a little bit different, but I also look at it like the pioneers of the East Coast side, my friends, and I would call them friends because they were, Marley Marl, Mr. Magic and Red Alert, they weren't feeling the West Coast sound and so if they weren't feeling it, it wasn't getting played. That doesn't necessarily mean that New York people didn't like it, but they weren't getting exposed to it so it didn't do as well.

But again, we were way receptive to the East Coast because of people like Russell Simmons. Russell and I had a great friendship, still do as far as I know, but his whole thing was that he had a plan. His plan was not only for us to play people like LL [Cool J], Whodini, the Fat Boys, and some of these other popular groups on the radio, but for them to come out to LA and be in the community. So whenever we did stuff for the schools or fundraisers, even our own events, he made sure that his groups came there and shook hands, hung out with folks and signed autographs. All the stuff, like I said before, that the R & B singers wouldn't do. Russell had a vision, and his vision is what helped me a lot as far as getting the West Coast people access to the East Coast rap artists.

If They Ask You If I'm Def Don't Front
and Say Kinda

Ice-T was born in New Jersey, but grew up in Los Angeles and graduated from Crenshaw High School. He gained some mainstream exposure in 1984 with a single called "Reckless" that appeared on the soundtrack for the movie *Breakin*. Ice spent most of that song rhyming about the DJ, Chris 'The Glove' Taylor:

> *He moves like a madman as he spins his disc,*
> *He's the number one scratcher on the DJs list,*
> *He's reckless!*

By 1985, an active hip-hop scene had developed in the greater Los Angeles area. In the book *Rakim Told Me*, Brian Coleman noted:

Even up through the mid-'80s, the hip-hop scene
in Southern California had taken its time
building a real foundation. Ice had a couple of
records out, and so did local legends like [Kid]
Frost, Egyptian Lover and Uncle Jamm's Army,
World Class Wreckin Cru, Bobby Jimmy and the
Critters and the LA Dream Team. But much of
the LA scene was localized before 24-7 rap radio
stalwart KDAY started to rev up in 1983 and
1984.

While "Reckless" got his name out there, the song that would
distinguish Ice-T was "6 'N The Morning," which was actually
released in 1986 as a b-side to the single "Doggin The Wax." "6
'N The Morning," named after the LAPD's practice of using a
battle ram to raid suspected crack houses at 6 am, was at least
partially inspired by the Schoolly D hardcore jam "P.S.K." P.S.K.
stood for Parkside Killers, a Philadelphia gang that Schoolly D
claimed to have once belonged. A remixed, extended version of
"6 'N The Morning" would appear in 1987 on Ice-T's debut
album, *Rhyme Pays*. However, it was this initial version that still
vividly represents the defining musical soundtrack to the

atmosphere and events of the period. A hard 808 kick drum, a dramatic synthesizer, and Ice's "Word!" at the end of each bridge combined with his tales of escape from the police, assault, seven years in prison, release, and murder, brought life on the streets to a conscious level. In the midst of everything going on in the song, the substance of the streets was balanced by the hip-hop sense of style from that time. The first lines of "6 'N The Morning" display this:

> *6 'N the morning police at my door*
> *Fresh adidas squeak across my bathroom floor*

Worth noting is the fact that both the brand name and condition of the kicks are central to the lasting image left by these lines. Adidas, specifically the Superstar, or shell top model, were standard b-boy foot gear placed in the consciousness of the early hip-hop nation by Run-DMC. Additionally, athletic shoes had started their journey to becoming high fashion apparel, leading to the hip-hop proverb, "The kicks make the (out)fit." Also it was not enough to simply have these shoes, you needed to have a 'fresh' pair.

Ice-T had grown up a student of authors like Iceberg

Slim, aka Robert Beck, and Donald Goines. The name Ice-T was inspired by Iceberg Slim. Iceberg Slim was born in 1918 in Chicago, Illinois. In the 1930s he briefly attended Tuskegee University, and shortly thereafter began living 'the life' at age 18, back home in Chicago. After several stretches in prison, Slim decided to 'square up' and moved to California in the 1960s. He published his first autobiographical novel, *Pimp: The Story of My Life*, in 1969. His gritty depictions of street life had a universal appeal that helped him sell over 6 million books. Slim's work was included in a literature course at Harvard University and has been translated into German, Spanish, and French. Iceberg Slim died in 1992 at age 73.

Donald Goines (1936-1974) was a prolific author who wrote 16 books in 5 years. He also depicted street life in his writings and was criticized for glorifying the lifestyles of murderers, pimps, hos, thieves, and drug addicts. Goines was not known for 'ride off into the sunset' happy endings, and works such as *Dopefiend* and *Black Girl Lost* fill a literary gap in American literature, which became part of the vernacular of West Coast hardcore rap.

In high school, Ice-T would memorize lines of Slim's

poetry, and recite them for friends and classmates. Other influences included comedians such as Rudy Ray Moore, Redd Foxx, and Richard Pryor. Firmly rooted in this 'blue' tradition, Ice-T wove brutal, explicit stories of Los Angeles street life into "6 'N The Morning:"

> *Posse to the corner where the fly girls chill*
> *Threw action at some freaks till one bitch got ill*
> *She started acting silly simply would not quit*
> *Called us all punk pussies said we all wasn't shit*
> *As we walked over to her ho continued to speak*
> *So we beat the bitch down in the goddam street*
> *But just livin in the city is a serious task*
> *Bitch didn't know what hit her didn't have time to ask*

This graphic description of violence against a woman was an early example of the misogyny that has continued to exist within rap music. Though violence against women may have been a fact of life for those who influenced Ice-T, the inclusion of it within the rap music spawned the 'reporting' vs. 'glorification' discussion. Were these kinds of lyrics just an acknowledgment that things like this happen, or did they simply serve to celebrate and normalize misogynistic attitudes?

By 1987, Ice-T was one of the predominant faces of rap outside of the greater New York area. This was due not only to the success of "6 'N The Morning," but also his earlier mentioned soundtrack work and a brief appearance in the movie *Breakin*. However, Ice-T's debut album *Rhyme Pays*, raised the profile of non-New York based hip-hop music in the national consciousness. The album's cover intentionally expressed a West Coast vibe that would inform the flavor of the music. *Rakim Told Me* author Brian Coleman noted:

> Of course Ice, the savvy, flashy LA player, knew
> that the album cover would be important. For
> that, he enlisted one of hip- hop's most
> important photographers: Glen E. Friedman.
> "Glen gave me that album cover for *Rhyme Pays*
> that made me stand alongside the big cats," Ice
> says, of the image: Ice scowling from behind the
> wheel of his purple Porsche, with a fine female
> standing tall in the passenger seat, DJ Evil-E in
> the back, and a palm tree hovering strategically
> above their heads. "He made sure that we got the
> girl, the Porsche and the palm tree in it. He said:

'The palm tree is the most important thing in this shot.' LA was very important to the image I was getting across. And images were very important back then for an album cover. At that time there was only like 10 or 15 albums out in total, so people were definitely going to see your cover.

The content of *Rhyme Pays* addressed a variety of topics, but rarely strayed far from Ice-T's street origins and fixations. Songs such as "Somebody Gotta Do It (Pimpin' Ain't Easy!!!)," "Sex," "I Love Ladies," and "6 'N the Morning" certainly fulfilled the obscene and misogynistic qualities present in toasting, but there was more to his concept. A song like "Pain" was a decidedly dark track that chronicled the agony often associated with street life:

> *Deuce-deuce revolver was my problem solver*
> *Had a def girl really didn't wanna involve her*
> *In the life of a gangsta used to rob banksta*
> *But now I'm locked up I'm just a punk low ranksta*
> *Jail cells know me too damn well*
> *Seems like I've built on earth my own personal hell*

"Squeeze the Trigger" was a socio-political joint that called out the hypocrisy of those who criticized Ice-T but ignored the issues he attempted to address:

> *Cops hate kids kids hate cops*
> *Cops kill kids with warning shots*
> *What is crime and what is not?*
> *What is justice I think I forgot*
> *We buy weapons to keep us strong*
> *Reagan sends guns where they don't belong*
> *The controversy is thick and the drag is strong*
> *But no matter the lies we all know who's wrong*

In the future Ice – T would be attacked repeatedly for the explicit and violent content of his music. However, it was precisely those things that helped *Rhyme Pays* generate a consciousness that would continue to influence hip-hop artists for years to come.

The Dope Fiend Beat

Around this time, roughly 400 miles north in the Bay Area, another up and coming artist was making his mark with a unique concept. Oakland native Too $hort was devising his own raw, toasting masterpiece that would become known as a pioneering work in the ever developing cultural landscape of hip-hop. $hort had been active in the West Coast hip-hop music scene since 1983. He released his first album, *Don't Stop Rappin,* on a local label called 75 Girls. After a couple more album releases over the next few years, $hort formed his own label, Dangerous Music. It was during this time that his song, "Freaky Tales," was recorded. Three main features combined to distinguish this song from everything else at the time. First was the lyrical content; $hort spent the entire time telling graphic stories of all the women he'd had sex with. Names were mentioned, specific acts were described, and locations were given:

I met this freak named Yolanda
Rode baby doll like a brand new Honda

This in itself may not have been a very big deal, except that it ties into the second distinguishing characteristic of the song: It was nine minutes and twenty-eight seconds long. In a world where most songs lasted anywhere from three to four minutes, the fact that anyone would make a ten minute song that talked over and over about essentially the same thing was either highly visionary or really stupid. Given the response to the song, Too $hort would appear to be the former.

Still, the ability to listen to any song, and particularly a song of this length and subject matter, is rooted in the musical production that laces the vocals, the third unique trait of "Freaky Tales." The song was set to a distinctly West Coast bassline reminiscent of maple syrup. $hort rode a synthesized beat that was simultaneously slow, sticky, dripping and sweet. The fresh sound was wildly popular yet simple enough that tuba players in high school marching bands would sample it as a crowd favorite during athletic events and pep rallies. The song appeared on $hort's major label debut album, *Born to Mack*, along with several other similarly themed songs, most of which contained that distinctive slow, synthesized sound that would eventually

influence producers not only on the West Coast, but everywhere.

Most notable among these were the tracks "Partytime" and

"Dope Fiend Beat." "Dope Fiend Beat" particularly stood out

because of its unique sound and trademark $hort nastiness:

> *But I'm so fresh I'm so down*
> *I'll tell you bitches the other way around*
> *If you do me first well I'll do you*
> *So the game jumps off when the bitch is through*
> *Soon as I cum all in her mouth*
> *I smooth get dressed and roll out*
> *I'm Too Short baby fresh fresh again*
> *One MC one bitch broke in*

Beyond the controversial lyrics, $hort made an important

business move that was largely overshadowed by the content of

the rhyme. $hort's already extensive experience in the rap game

led to his behind the scenes involvement on *Born to Mack*. He

was listed as the album's executive producer and received credits

for keyboards, production, mixing, writing and arrangement.

$hort was an early role model for future successful

MCs/executives who sought artistic, financial, and copyright control of their material.

In his visual representation, Too $hort could easily be identified as a player straight out of Iceberg's street game and philosophy. The cover of *Born to Mack* features $hort sitting up on a drop top Cadillac Eldorado Barritz with a white leather interior and gold trim sitting on Trues and Vogues, with a white leather covered fifth wheel on the back. This image derives from the Iceberg Slim/Donald Goines vibe, but there is some Bay Area influence as well. *The Mack* was a 1973 movie about a pimp named Goldie who lived in Oakland. It was released during the so-called Blaxploitation era of movies, but was viewed as somewhat unique in the genre. Unlike the spectacular exploits of Dolomite and Shaft, *The Mack* was credited with providing a more realistic, everyday version of street life. And macking was clearly what $hort's early music and overall image were all about.

First Person Account: DAVEY D

In the Bay Area during this time there were a number of records that were starting to bubble up from local artists. Too $hort was the most prominent, but there were others that were coming up and just starting to make a little bit of a buzz like Digital Underground, Rappin 4 Tay, Huey MC and Mac Dre. I think people were starting to get their own voices, not that they never had a voice, but the game started to pick up in terms of it being a business. People started to see that there was an avenue for them to rebirth themselves and be heard.

I would make the case that by this time New York was not the beacon that it had once been, but I would also make the case that New York never was a beacon for the Bay Area. I think the Bay Area was kinda like its own thing and it prided itself on being that. A lot of it had to do with Los Angeles being so close by, and definitely not trying to be like LA. Being the home of the

Panthers and that whole situation, there was kind of this pride of never being under someone else's wing.

You also have to consider that this is around the height of the crack era, so you now have a lot of money that was startin to flow to a lot of cats. That underscored this independence even more. The Bay didn't have to get into a New York thing because whatever New York was showing, we had already created our own. So you have "Soul Beat Television" down here, which in many ways predates "Yo! MTV Raps." You already had radio stations that were playing hip-hop music; LA had KDAY, we had KPOO.

So you have a lot of superstardom in the hood, and to the degree that rap allowed that to be enhanced was a tool. But I think they were looking at it as coming into an arena where they were going to be valued without New York having to cosign. So people like Hammer were coming out about this time and they were all doing independent stuff and starting to bubble over that way.

Every city has its own personality. LA, for instance, is an industry town. There are some cities that are step-brother and little brother to big cities. They look at the standard and they try to either replicate New York or try to be right alongside. For example, we can go to some cities and be like, "BET is comin to town!" and everybody will be excited like, "Oh man, BET!" That means it's they time to shine and get on. You come to Oakland and cats be like, "Fuck BET! We got our own BET here!" Detroit is kinda like that. Detroit is not too far from Chicago. Chicago is the Mecca, but if I go there Chicago will kinda be like "BET is in town!" because to an extent it validates who they are. Detroit ain't like that. Detroit is like its own thing. They'll be like, "Yeah it's cool that BET is here, but we're Detroit." Houston is like that on a certain level. New Orleans is definitely like that, and Oakland is like that.

In terms of content, from day one, references to the city were being made. People talked about Oakland. Too $hort had his accent, showing immediately there was no "Let me try and do somewhere else." Now to the degree that LL Cool J, or somebody else who was out at that time and was popular, might have influenced somebody's rhyme flow, I would say that was the case. I remember Paris sayin he was influenced by LL. But it wasn't because they felt like they needed to appeal to New York, it was just more like, "Yo this sounds kinda fresh, that's how we gonna do this." If you really study it, Hammer didn't sound like New York, Too $hort didn't sound like New York, Rappin 4 Tay certainly never sounded like New York, Chilly MC didn't sound like New York, and Illmatic Posse didn't sound like New York. But Shock G, who comes from New York, sounded like New York and he did his thing. Sway and King Tech had records out at that time and I remember when I used to see Sway I didn't believe he was from Oakland because he had a New York flow, but I think that was more natural to him as an MC than it was him tryin to impress New York. I never really saw those guys tryin to win New York over, but they had a big hit record out here at that time. There was "Red, Black and Green" [radio show] down at Stanford, they tended to have a New York show, but most of those guys were from New York. But that sound that people associated with New York had more to do with a certain type of hip-hop, you know, you can call it a 'boom-bap' influence or more of a 'pure' thing. For some of these cats who were deep in the hood, they had already been makin music, and as hip-hop came along they just added what they was already doin on top of some new tools. They might've kept the bassline and that funk vibe and then just added the vocalization of rap to it.

In comparison to what was happening in LA, you have to ask which LA are we talking about? LA from the hood, or LA that's Hollywood? By this I mean like Egyptian Lover, Arabian Prince, Rodney O and Joe Cooley, Toddy-T, them dudes didn't try to be like New York at all. But because there was an industry influence, sometimes you can get caught up thinking, "Now that I've signed with label, let me see what I can do." Now Ice-T was from back east, so I could see him doin that, and he was hangin out with Bambaataa and Zulu Nation, so he was around New York cats. So I think there was gonna be that influence more directly to him, but if you think about it, you didn't really see no New York flows for the sake of tryin to be New York comin out of LA. I mean LA Dream Team? You know that was the shit! They had they own shit but it was like the most popular stuff, and there was a lot of up-tempo stuff comin out. So I wouldn't say that LA was tryin to be like New York, but there was a lot more New Yorkers in LA than there was in the Bay that were into hip-hop and was gonna bring their flavor with them. There was more of a cross-country colonization at that time between LA and New York than there was between New York and the Bay.

But specifically in the Bay Area, there was a very conscious effort by cats to be its own thing. There were cats who prided themselves on that. If you got into NWA coming out and then move up into the early 90s, every city on the West Coast had Crips and Bloods hittin them. But Oakland and San Francisco didn't have it. In fact a bunch of songs came out talking about how there ain't no Bloods and Crips in the Bay, like "Nah we didn't let nobody come off of I-5 and set up camp here." The couple of times that was tried, folks got their butt handed to them and sent back home, which just emboldened people and it became even more of a "LA is gangsta, but we ain't havin it," that's pretty much the best way to describe it.

The Bay Area had an interesting interaction with 'gangsta' rap as it became more popular. We were among the first up here to interview a lot of those cats. I mean, we liked it like everybody else, you know, they was talking about stuff that was in the streets and they were good. But the shows that I was doin was also playin a lot of Malcolm X, but then we got challenged by the folks over at KZSU at Stanford, and they was like, "Yo, what's up with this? How you play Malcolm X and then play," we didn't call it gangsta rap at the time, "all this stuff where they talking crazy right afterwards?" So we did two weeks of interviews with an open mic on our show. It involved some guys from Digital Underground like Money B, there were stories written about it, and the deal was if the majority of the community didn't want us to play these songs on the air, we won't play them. A majority of people in the hood was like, "Nah, we don't really need to hear that on the airwaves," so we didn't play it. So we basically put a boycott on them for about 2 or 3 years, we just wouldn't play them. We did big interviews with people like Eazy-E and Ice Cube around that, and that was our reaction being on the radio. Now, everybody knew their songs. NWA was very popular, people liked what they were doing, they thought it was good, but they started to bring the gangbang stuff. When they came up and did their concert at the Oakland Coliseum, the Bay came together to put it down and was like, "Yeah we like that, but that ain't gonna happen here."

In terms of 'gangsta' rap's influence, I think it gave people license to tell their own hood tales. Cats was like, "Well shoot let me do this!" The only difference was young cats that knew was like, "There's this dude and that dude, they real gangsta. The other one, well I don't know. They tell a good story and they can rap good, but they ain't really bout it-bout it like that." But then you had cats that was really about it get into the game and they was like, "Well yo, why am I fundin you to do your thing? Let me just jump on and do my own rap!" Then you started to get a mixture of people from drug dealing rappers to Caucasians, doin songs and it wasn't necessarily that they were trying to be like NWA, but it was more just, "Let me tell you about my hood." So it just opened the door for hood stories to be told. NWA was the pinnacle, obviously Schooly D and Ice-T preceded them, but they took it to a whole new level. After that it became, "Let me get up and I'ma tell you what's goin on." Pimpin, hoin, hustlin, whatever you felt like conveying to the world.

A couple of things really kind of spread this approach. One was the movie *Colors*, in terms of the whole gang mentality goin into other cities. The other thing was "The Box," which is what really made the regionalization jump off, because everybody was able to see each other on TV. It was like, "Oh, this is how they get down in Detroit. OK, this is how they do it in Arkansas." "The Box" really networked a lot of people around the country really quickly, but then it got bought up and it was done. It became a major label thing. You had "Yo! MTV Raps" comin out and they was doin their thing and it gave you a glimpse, and it was more sophisticated, but MTV wasn't gonna be playin LA Dream Team or America's Most Wanted.

One of the main points here is that this time corresponds with exposure. There were more outlets that didn't exist before that came into play. I mentioned "The Box," you had the rise of Premier Radio with KMEL in San Francisco, which was the first time you had hip-hop topics on the morning show. Those sorts of things were taking place, and that predates Hot 97 by a number of years. The epicenter, in terms of being on another level, existed in California. You went to New York you were still doing mix shows at night. In California, you had folks like myself and others with access to the airwaves. Sway and King Tech started doin "The Wake Up Show," you had Summer Jam concerts, the Gavin was there, so there was a lot of things going on. All those things played important roles in terms of the evolution of exposure, and that was a good thing. The fact that you had music that was coming out at that time from California and other areas added to it. Some of it is right place, right time; if you live in California you don't have a lot of Black people like you do back east, so there was going to be a natural crossover. There's gonna be a lot of Asians hangin out at the party. There's gonna be a lot of Mexicans hangin out at your party. There's gonna be a lot of White folks that are going to come a lot more quickly than they would back east. They gonna come across it and at least see what you're doing and be like, "Oh, OK what's this?" and they gonna check it out and be a part of it.

Another thing I'd mention is the second wave, because the first wave of that crossover was in the early [19]80s with punk rock and new wave, and then Run-DMC doing their thing with "Rock Box." So in some ways hip-hop was more commercialized. It was commercially packaged and available to the masses. During the new wave/punk rock days, if you was a White dude, you was gonna have to go on a hunt to go get that hip-hop. You'd have to get on the train and come uptown, maybe in LA you'd go down to Radio or something, you couldn't get it like that. But once you get to the late 80s, you just turn on the radio to get it.

By then hip-hop is becoming more exclusively connected to rap than its other elements. You're sayin hip-hop and then what comes up in your mind is the rapper. The dance had disappeared. The DJ damn near disappeared, at least as far as the mainstream was concerned. You went from Jazzy Jeff and the Fresh Prince to Fresh Prince and no longer Jazzy Jeff. You're moving into this direction where hip-hop is becoming more of a commerce thing. With that came the opportunity for artists, especially outside of New York, to gain exposure appeal above and beyond to those large audiences of people.

California always had a say in mainstream culture, because the Meccas in America were always California and New York, which are the two largest marketplaces. On a street side, the West Coast got put on the map because people discovered that Hollywood wasn't all sunshine and beaches. There was real ghettos and cats out here that would hand you your ass if you stepped out of pocket wrong. For a lot of people that was a wakeup call because you didn't necessarily associate California with that. Take San Francisco, "Yeah, they got a bunch of gay dudes who are just gonna run away and talk all funny" and all that, and you get up in Frisco there's places you'll get rolled up, and then cats are like, "Yo, I didn't know!"

Just like when I was in New York, people thought Staten Island was the suburbs, then when they get out there it's like, whoa, they got hoods here. So California kind of put itself on the map by letting folks know that not only was it a music Mecca that had its own culture and stuff jumpin off, but it was also certified as a place where it wasn't gonna be some cornball stuff. And if they did call those cats cornballs, which many people did, you found out that once you stepped in they hood all that cornball conversation shut right up. You didn't see a whole lot of people comin to LA and start mouthin off about who's corny in LA.

Then you also had groups that were doing phenomenally well: Spice-1, gold; Too $hort, platinum; Digital Underground, platinum; Hammer, 14 million, and NWA it was just like hit factory after hit. There was no denying it, it was like, "Yo I went platinum, what'd you do son?" So the other 48 states woke up and realized they didn't have to go to New York to get they shine. That there was a conversation goin on between the Bay Area and Kansas City, Kansas City and St. Louis, St. Louis into Chicago, Chicago into Houston, and Houston into Louisiana. You didn't have to go to New York to get that validation, and we could see each other and be like, "Well you know that's cool what they do there, and you know what? You keep that, I'm just gonna do what I do here," and that became important. This was the time where people were realizing that they didn't have to go to this one watering hole to get money, fame, and fortune.

By the time you get into this period, New York in some
ways had played itself. There was a club called the Latin Quarters
in the [19]80s where a lot of people went out there, Hammer
went out there, Egyptian Lover went to the New Music Seminar,
and I was there and they was kinda like, "We don't know who
y'all are" and they just didn't get that love. So by then people
kind of realized like, "Man every time we go to New York they
gonna be on some not really respectin you type stuff." Hammer
went to Latin Quarters, and they tried to dis him. He was at the
New Music Seminar and just felt like these cats weren't respectin
them, and what they realized was that there was an industry that
was kind of dictating stuff.

California put out undeniable music and was a center
unto itself. You couldn't really make it unless you went to LA.
Economically you had to deal with it because people bought
records out here. New York kinda got this reputation, it's kinda
like the U.S. is now: You think people in France care about
comin to the United States to make it? Hell nah! In Germany
and these other places, they couldn't care less. There used to be a
time, but I think cats kind of realized that the United States is
gonna be one of those places that cats couldn't even tell you the

country that's next door to them, so people just stopped trippin and they did they own thing. I know cats that go on 40 city tours, goin through North Africa, through the Middle East, down to New Zealand, Australia, and not even think about comin to the U.S. Meanwhile we're running around talking about nothing, but they got they own stuff jumpin off. They couldn't care less, they're not thinking about us. And the only people that think they're thinking about us, is us. Show up in some of these places talking bout, "I'm from America" or "I'm from the hood," muthafuckas will whup your ass and keep it movin. I've been to Africa where Black people look at you and call you colonizers, sayin you tryin to act like White boys. We're like "I live in the hood," no, where THEY live is the hood. You ain't really seen hood, 13-year-old child soldiers, I mean the world is rough and rugged. We're just now goin through this economic recession and movin in a direction that the rest of the world has been living for centuries. People are like, "Aw man, we might not have electricity." These muthafuckas is like, "Yo, we get blackouts every day! What you talking about? We might not have food to eat!" I mean, welcome to the world.

So I think what they [West Coast rappers] found, and what people outside of New York found, were their own voices.

They used this as a communication tool to talk to other people and they do what they do. But for us, we became American without the power and the economic benefits that we should have for somebody that would support a country that doesn't really give us a fair shake.

New York was and is still a beast. I look at it like this: It's not so much geographic as much as it was a lot of middle men who represented something that didn't necessarily click. A grimy cat from Brooklyn will get along with a grimy cat from LA because grime is grime and hood is hood. But the difference is that somebody from LA was really from the hood when he traveled and somebody from New York wasn't always that person. Like when Suge [Knight] left, Suge was a G, he was that guy. When Short and those people left, their crew was that crew, they really came from those places. Hammer and them came from those places, so there was a lot of people who were really close to those situations. So when they came there they kind of represented, were maybe closer to the streets, than somebody who was from New York. They could sense, "You're not that grimy guy from Brooklyn. You're not MOP or Freddie Foxxx," where you know, they walk in and they got a hood pass everywhere. I think that's what it was, hoods started to talk to each other.

Hood is hood, and people in the hood only want to get their just due at the end of the day. Especially because the conditions of living in the hood dictate that you create stuff at least half the time. Rap is music that's indigenous to the hood. There's an Oklahoma style of rap and there's a Dallas style of rap. People stick to their realities in ways that are gonna reflect certain types of music, pace, slang, and I think for a long time the media in New York did not reflect it. I just don't think they were really connected to what it meant when you were comin up like that. If a cat comes up from Baltimore and you know he's been struggling, yeah his stuff might not be all that poppin but game recognize game, so you can embrace it and you can build around it, and you can be like, "Man, I can understand where you comin from. You're tellin your story." But somebody else, these guys that were on the media side were kinda dismissing everybody's story. So I create other avenues to tell my story, and I think that's what was happening at the end of the day.

See, I'm not a thug. I don't pretend to be, I don't try to act like one. I'm in the media, I'm on the radio, etc. If I all of a sudden, because of my position, I started trying to dictate what it means to be a thug, real thugs can see through that. They'd be like, "Man, he's a square!" They would know, your way of being or your mannerisms, I would miss certain things if I tried to play that role. And that's what was happening around that time. You had people that were gatekeepers that was trying and saying those things but they weren't that dude. You could just look and be like, "Nah, not you." So there was a time when you could just see and recognize what was going on in these other places, but you could respect it.

What also was going on was the Afro-centric stuff that was coming out; KRS-1, Chuck D, and X Clan, all of which were popular in other cities because they was real, they wasn't comin across thug, but they was real so people could recognize and be like, "OK, these cats is talking about uplifting our stuff, so I can get with that." By the end of that era, they themselves were being marginalized out by the rise in gangsterism. But there was still some tension in that within groups like NWA, who early on had internal debates about whether or not they should qualify some of the stuff that they were doing. Eazy and them was more like, "Let's make this money and do our thing," Cube was more like,

"Maybe we should let people know where we're coming from," and the rest is history. What NWA ultimately should have done was what Cube did when he did his first solo album, *AmeriKKKa's Most Wanted.* There's always gonna be a struggle, that's what made the group good, but they definitely had their discussions around that and I think they was just like, "Let's just do this music, we don't need to be explaining to everybody what's going on in that way." I remember Cube telling me, "Look man, I wanna let people know why we're doing this," and he told me that he was basically overridden by the group.

It Was Once Said By a Man Who Couldn't Quit

While 1987 marked the release of *Rhyme Pays*, it also coincided with the release of another record from Los Angeles. *NWA and the Posse*, by the group NWA, who claimed to represent Compton, California. Though still undergoing personnel and artistic changes that would eventually form the core members and influential message of the group, the name was firmly in place and would soon go down in history. Naming their group NWA, short for Niggaz Wit Attitude, immediately sent a message that most listeners would not be able to ignore. The inclusion of the word nigga, with all of the cultural baggage this term carries in the United States, was a sure attention grabber. In addition, their use of the word as a means of self-definition and empowerment was confusing to many Black and White folks alike. They also claimed proudly that they were 'niggaz' with an attitude, and immediately tapped into something that was simultaneously a source of great excitement, entertainment, and fear for mainstream culture.

As a marketing tool, the name NWA was a stroke of genius and stirred interest from different parts of the population. Recall Dr. Todd Boyd's quote from his book *Young, Black, Rich & Famous*: "Black culture has always been positioned between the poles of fear and entertainment in its relationship to the White mainstream." At the same time he noted, "The mainstream often pigeonholes Black culture, forcing the culture to accommodate whatever perceptions might already be in place as opposed to allowing it to exist on its own terms and give off its own representation." The anti-establishment, defiant stance implied by the name NWA appealed both to the righteous side of a core urban, young African-American audience, as well as the curious, culture-starved, middle to upper-class suburban demographic. NWA's active self-definition, regardless of whether it fit within the confines of mainstream culture, appealed to young people from all sections of America society.

NWA and the Posse initially received relatively limited attention after its release. However, the record included several

songs that laid the critical groundwork for what would become
the predominant pioneering West Coast hip-hop sound and
message. The continuing historical importance of these initial
songs is evident when you consider that one of them,
"Boyz-N-The Hood," was reissued on the Eazy-E album,
Eazy-Duz-It, and two others, "8 Ball" and "Dopeman," were
reissued on the hugely influential second NWA album, *Straight
Outta Compton*. Eazy-E, who was rumored to have started his
record company, Ruthless Records, with drug profits and Dr.
Dre were the de facto founders of NWA. Eazy's vocals on
"Boyz-N-The Hood" rode a beat that was made to pound the
15-inch speakers which had begun to appear in the cars of mostly
urban residents:

> *Cause the boyz-n-the hood are always hard*
> *You come talking that trash we'll pull your card*
> *Knowin nothin in life but to be legit*
> *Don't quote me boy cause I ain't said shit*

Eazy-E was also largely responsible for popularizing a couple of
cultural markers within West Coast hip-hop. One was the 1964
Chevrolet Impala that he made famous in the song "Boyz-N-The

Hood" ("cruisin down the street in my 6-4..."). The other more controversial Eazy favorite was the 40 ounce bottle of Old English 800 malt liquor, which became the unofficial alcoholic beverage of choice for hip-hop headz looking to 'get the party started.' The song "8 Ball" was an ode to cheap beer that incorporated a simultaneously liberating yet self-destructive approach that refused, as Boyd noted, "to act in accordance with the straightjacketed rules that society often imposes on its young, Black, urban male citizens:"

> *Rollin through the hood to find the boys*
> *I kick dust and cuts crank up the noise*
> *Police on my draws I have to pause*
> *40 ounce in my lap and its freezing my balls*

Along with the illmatic nature of life on the streets, NWA also found a space for humor. The song "Fat Girl" featured Eazy-E rhyming about his experience with an overweight woman who just loved her some Eazy. He apparently didn't remember her, but as she explained in the song:

> *'Remember the time when you was drunk at the party?*
> *We were slow dancing I gave you all this body!'*

When she said that she loved me I was in shock
Oh my God I gotta fat girl on my jock

"Dopeman" was by far the most powerful album cut for two
reasons. First was the unblinking narrative about the devastation
that crack created in both communities and individuals.
Newsweek magazine called it quite possibly the most powerful
anti-drug song of all time. The song used graphic street life
stories to illustrate the reality of the crack economies that had
become well established in urban centers and actively chastised
those who chose to smoke crack. "Dopeman" even introduced
new slang to describe these people:

If you smoke caine you a stupid muthafucka
Known around the hood as the school yard clucker
Doin that crack with all the money you got
On your hands and knees lookin for a piece of rock

"Dopeman" also dealt with other drug fueled issues such as
Strawberry (a woman who trades sex for drugs), sexually
transmitted diseases, conflict resolution in the crack era, and
other related crimes present in the crack economy:

Strawberry just look and you'll see her
But don't fuck around she'll give you gonorrhea
And people out there not hip to the fact
That Strawberry is a girl sellin pussy for crack

"Dopeman" introduced a groundbreaking performance by Ice Cube, an NWA member who would swiftly distinguish himself and go on to solo success and movie stardom. Cube had written extensively for Eazy-E, including "Boyz-N-The Hood," and would become the group's lyrical backbone. Cube and Eazy met after Cube and a partner, Sir Jinx, formed a group called CIA (Cru In Action) and rapped at parties DJd by Dr. Dre. Cube's strong delivery and overall microphone presence on "Dopeman," combined with his wordplay and flow, granted the listener access to drug life from the comfort of home:

You're robbin and stealin buggin and illin
While the dopeman's dealin what is healin your pain
Cocaine this shit's insane

NWA and the Posse was certainly a powerful influence on the style of hip-hop music, which was moving more and more toward a full on embrace of the violence and misogyny that were present not only in underground toasting, but now, also, the crack era. As a group, NWA's core ultimately became five main members: Eazy-E, Ice Cube, Dr. Dre, MC Ren, and DJ Yella.

The Los Angeles hip-hop music scene had started to gain the attention of both hip-hop and non-hip-hop media around the country. However, there was still tangible resistance, particularly from New York City. In a February 7, 1988 *Los Angeles Times* story, Nelson George, the New York based Black music editor of *Billboard* magazine talked about how in the early 1980s, "New Yorkers considered Los Angeles 'too soft' to be a factor in hip-hop." The story went on to state that "the Los Angeles hip-hop contingent is faced with some serious obstacles: Not being taken seriously by the important New York market, lack of exposure and what some feel is an unsubtle brand of racism." LA record executives complained how hard it was to sell records in New York because of "lingering anti-LA bias." One East Coast record executive even commented, "Where it originated will always have more respect, and I don't know if LA rap will ever be as big. A lot of rap is about lifestyle. When you're living it, it makes it better somehow." Even before these sentiments appeared in print, the Los Angeles hip-hop community undoubtedly sensed them. Very soon you'd be able to call the LA hip-hop scene a lot of things, but soft wasn't going to be one of them.

First Person Account: JERRY HELLER

I knew very little about the hip-hop scene in New York, which

was mostly an art scene in the 1960s and 70s and then what

evolved in hip-hop around 1985-86. It's ironic that the album

that I consider to probably be one of the two or three most

important albums of the second half of the twentieth century,

which was [The Beatles'] *Sergeant Pepper,* set the bar so

impossibly high for all of the other rock and roll people in the

world that it changed the focus of the whole business and really

led to what I feel is a real down period in rock and roll. Because

people started to try to emulate that album so enthusiastically

that they start spending way too much money on records, and

when they start spending way too much money on records then

they had to spend way too much money promoting the records.

So really people were involved with music just because they were

trying to protect their jobs rather than the fact that they loved the music, and I just feel that it's ironic that an album as influential and important as *Sergeant Pepper* would be the cause of all that. The other was *Straight Outta Compton.*

But during that period of time around 1985, when I feel that the music business was really in a very bad place, a friend of mine called me and told me about a little scene that was happening down in old Hollywood on Santa Monica Boulevard at a pressing plant called Macola Records. For a thousand dollars you could get five hundred copies of your record pressed up and this guy would send it out to four or five different guys around the country that did what he did. The records themselves cost so little that the actual tape [the music was recorded on] cost more than the record cost to make. So we had this scene at Macola where there were a bunch of artists not only from Los Angeles but from Seattle and the Bay Area pressing their records. There was Jay King and the Timex Social Club, MC Hammer, Ice-T, the LA Dream Team, Egyptian Lover, Rodney O and Joe Cooley, Sir Mix-A-Lot, and the World Class Wrecking Cru. After thinking about it for a while, I finally got over to Macola and met this guy Rudy Pardee who was from Cleveland, where I'm from, and he had a group called the LA Dream Team and also signed to him was JJ Fad. I listened to what he had and I liked it a lot more

than I liked what was happening on the East Coast because not
only was it more musical and melodic, because I've always been a
melody kind of person, but it had a sense of humor which I
didn't think the East Coast music had. So I started to get
involved there and was managing Egyptian Lover and Bobby
Jimmy and the Critters, Rodney O and Joe Cooley, LA Dream
Team, and JJ Fad and I was really liking what was happening
there because to me the music business is a win-win business. In
the music business, the more the artist makes the more
everybody makes. In any other business, the more one person
makes, the less someone else makes, so it's really one of the few
win-win businesses that I've ever seen and I liked it a lot because
if you sold ten or fifteen thousand in vinyl you could split up
some money and everybody made some money, and that's what
the music business is supposed to be about.

During that time, when I was managing World Class
Wrecking Cru who were on Cru Cut Records which was owned
by a guy named Alonzo Williams, who I feel never really gets the
credit that's due him. He really was one of the great early
pioneers of the West Coast hip-hop movement. In the World
Class Wrecking Cru were Yella and Dr. Dre, and in one of his

other groups, which was called CIA, Cru In Action, were Ice Cube and Sir Jinx. So he [Williams] was a very influential guy, and he owned a club called Eve After Dark, where when I used to go down there I was literally the only White person in the club. So he kept telling me about this guy that wanted to meet me, and his name was Eric Wright. This went on for a couple of months and I was real busy and I had sort of checked up a little bit on him and he was a reputed drug dealer from South Central, he had some money and he was getting involved in backing other peoples records, so nothing about it made me really want to meet him. Alonzo was never really comfortable with the portrayals of violence and misogyny in our inner cities. If you look at the early Wrecking Cru records they were sort of The Temptations of the West Coast hip-hop movement. They had choreographed dance steps and they wore glittery outfits and make up. But finally Alonzo said to me, "You know this guy Eric Wright offered me $750 to meet you," and I said "Okay," and agreed to meet Eazy-E on a Tuesday, which was March 3, 1987. I meet him over at Macola and he drove up in this tricked out Suzuki Samurai with MC Ren. I was certainly impressed with his charisma and I said to him, "Do you have anything you want me to hear?" First of all he reached in his sock, pulled out a wad of money and paid

Alonzo the $750, and he just said to me, "Yeah," and handed me
a cassette.

That was very impressive to me because most of the
music business, at least the music business that I grew up in,
there's a lot of bullshit. Everybody's got this guy, it's all hype,
and they got this song, it wasn't that way with this kid. This kid
just said to me "Yeah" and handed me a cassette, so obviously he
was willing to let the music do the talking for him. So we went
inside, put Ren in another office where he proceeded to carve his
initials into the owner of Macolas desk with his knife, and I heard
"Boyz-N-The Hood," and I thought it was the most important
music that I had heard probably since the mid-1960s. Being older,
these guys were all in their teens, I was of course in my mid-40s
already, I had been there at Berkeley and grown up with Bill
Graham and Mario Salvo, and the Panthers and Gil-Scott Heron,
and the Rolling Stones, so I was able to relate to what they were
rapping about. For the first time I felt that maybe this is some
music that all of America is going to be able to relate to, it's going
to show people in Kansas, Nebraska, and Minnesota exactly what
it's like to grow up in a place like Compton, California. I heard in
this music the rebellion of the Rolling Stones and Gil-Scott

Heron and the Black Panthers, and having been there for that I felt it was really important for everyone to understand the angst and oppression that minorities in our inner cities have always felt. I grew up Jewish in Cleveland, in fact I grew up on the same block as Bone Thugs-N-Harmony, but being Jewish in Cleveland was very restrictive. For example, I literally went to college in Ohio with girls that were not allowed to go out with Jews, so I was also able to relate to where that was coming from.

But I knew that this music was important, and maybe my goals weren't totally altruistic, I mean I had been at the forefront of every musical movement in America. I was in rock and roll at the beginning of rock and roll, I was in new wave at the beginning of new wave, I was in punk at the beginning of punk, so I had been involved with some of the most important artists of our generation. I was involved with Creedence Clearwater, I brought Elton John to this country, Pink Floyd, I represented Journey, Styx, REO Speedwagon, Marvin Gaye, The Four Tops, Van Morrison, Boz Skaggs, Joan Armatrading, ELO, I'd been involved in most of the important music of my generation so I just felt that this was important. I'm not sure if it was from a monetary point of view because I tend to think of things being measured in success, and I'd certainly been successful in my

career and my artists had been successful, so I just felt that this
was going to be the next big move in American music.

Knowing that the music was good, and Eric Wright
didn't need me to sell records at swap meets, my problem then
became a marketing problem rather than a musical problem. I
recognized that the music was there, so the issue was how to get
the rest of what we call White, middle-class America to listen to
these songs and relate to them. So I went to where I felt the
hotbed, in California at least, of people that were on the cutting
edge, which were the surfers and skateboarders in Huntington
Beach. These guys are always on the cutting edge. So after
spending some time down there I said to myself, "Look, who do
they like?" At the time they liked Guns-N-Roses, they liked
Metallica, they liked Suicidal Tendencies, and I felt anybody that
ever bought [the Guns-N-Roses album] *Appetite for
Destruction* certainly would buy *Straight Outta Compton.* So if
you look at any interview or video that any of those groups did
from 1987-91, you'll see them wearing *Straight Outta Compton*
hats and t-shirts, and their favorite group became NWA. So I
approached it from a marketing point of view and obviously it
worked because the original members of NWA wound up doing

to this date probably $15 billion between their writing, producing, and record sales. And Ruthless was a company that Eazy and I started that day, March 3, 1987, when I didn't even know what NWA stood for. I said, "What's it stand for, No Whites Allowed?" and Eazy just laughed and said, "That's pretty close!"

Eazy-E was a real visionary. He was a good guy, and it was hard for me to relate to why or how he knew that somehow our futures would be linked together like that. I mean there were no two people that were more diametrically opposed: I was tall, he was short, I was White, he was Black, I was old, he was young, I was from Cleveland, he was from Compton, I was educated, he dropped out of high school in 11th grade. There was nothing about us that would ever portend to the two of us building this incredibly successful company, except the music. Although it wasn't true with Eazy because he and I were such close friends, he was like my son, I've always said with most of my artists I've always only had one thing really in common with them: We both like what they do. Other than that, Van Morrison, if I saw him on the street I would turn my back because he's a bad guy. So most of the artists that I represented over the years, when our business relationship was over our personal relationship was over. There are some exceptions with artists that I'm still fairly close to, but really it's the exception rather than the rule. I've always felt that was really a true-ism; we only like what they do, and you know something? That's usually enough. That's all you have to have. All you have to do is have respect for what the other one does.

Eazy and I built this incredibly successful company, and within a short period of time we were doing $10 million per month. I think that probably at that time Russell Simmons had a singles deal at Columbia. Although I've never really been a big fan of his, I think that Rick Rubin was certainly, musically, one of the most important guys in rock and roll. But Eazy came to me and was able to put this group of artists together; Eazy always said that he was the conceptualizer, Dre was the musicalizer, Ice Cube was the verbalizer, and I was the financializer, and that was NWA. At first everybody was saying, "Aw man Jerry, it's great that you can do this," then of course when we started being successful they came out of the woodwork to say to Eazy, "Aw man, why are you with this White Jewish guy? You should be with brothers keeping the money in the community," all that stuff. Right to the very end he stood up to a lot of peer pressure to stick with me. I had made a deal with Irving Azoff for Dre to have his own label and [that] was like $20 million upfront or something like that, and then Mo Ostin refused to fund it because he was having his own problems at Warner Brothers with all that heat over "Cop Killer" by Ice-T, and C. Delores Tucker and all these people putting them under pressure when Warner Brothers at the time was really in the cable business, not really in the music business. Ostin ended up getting forced out at Warner Brothers, which was one of the great record companies of all time, it's not anymore but it certainly was when he and Joe Smith were there. In fact, one time I later went to see Joe Smith when he was the chairman of the board at Capitol [records], he was an old friend of mine. I played him one of the songs that started off, "What the fuck is up, who the fuck is he, comin on the mic its Eazy-motherfuckin-E," and he looked at me and said, "Jerry, you really gotta stop getting high! You're trying to tell me that people will listen to this garbage? That anyone will play it on the radio?" He said, "Jerry forget it! I love the name Ruthless. I'll write you a $2 million check for the name right now. But this music, just forget it, man, it's just not happening." I said, "Joe, I remember when radio stations wouldn't play 'Let's Spend the Night Together' by the Rolling Stones, and now Mick Jagger is

Frank Sinatra." Times change and this was the music of the future because besides being musical, besides having a sense of humor, besides being important music, obviously someone like Rodney King wasn't the first Black guy to get beat up by a bunch of cops on the freeway. So when we wrote "Fuck Tha Police," that had come from years and decades of police oppression in the inner cities, but that was just the first time anyone had ever videotaped it, that's all. If not for that videotape, who knows? Just like who knows what would have happened if Bobby Kennedy wouldn't have been assassinated? I mean here's a guy that was talking about this stuff in the 1960s. Who knows if there wouldn't have been a video camera that day [of the King beating] how things would have been different?

Eazy was actually in that courtroom every single day when those cops were on trial in Simi Valley. He just had this insatiable quest for knowledge, he wanted to know everything about everything. Eazy was a unique individual and they don't come along often like him, I mean a true, true visionary. I think nothing portrayed it to me more than a time when he and I were in New York at a party that Bill Graham threw. Bill Graham was an old friend of mine and he had a party at the Parklane Hotel

and Eazy and I were coming down the elevator. Diana Ross and
Chaka Khan were in this elevator talking, and then these other
three big Black dudes. Now this was before *Straight Outta
Compton* was ever released, we were selling it at swap meets out
of the trunks of our cars, so we're not talking about tremendous
exposure yet. But these guys on the elevator went into
"Boyz-N-The Hood" and rapped every line of it, word for word.
Eazy and I stepped out of the elevator and I don't think he
understood at that particular moment the impact of what that
meant. I said, "Do you realize, here we are in New York, no radio
stations are playing the record and those guys on the elevator
knew every word to 'Boyz-N-The Hood?'" And he said, "Oh,
you mean Run-DMC?" So I'm thinking to myself, "Well
nobody's playing this music, so how are people hearing it?", and
I've never really been able to answer that question to my
satisfaction. I can say that it had something to do with the mall
becoming the social center of urban America, it had to do with
people beginning to have cell phones, always talking on the
phone in cars or wherever they were, and it had something to do
with a social change that was going on in America. When we
finally did get some airplay, there was only one station in the
country that played our record. That was a five-thousand watt

station on the top of Alvarado Street called KDAY. Greg Mack
and the Mack Attack, the Mix Masters Tony G. and Julio G.,
these guys were instrumental for us. These guys played our
music. They were the only station in America that played our
music. A couple years later there was a station in Dallas that
started to play it, but KDAY was really the only station in
America that would play West Coast gangster rap. I've just
[always] had a tremendous affinity toward Greg Mack, we're
very close friends to this day. Julio G, Tony G, the Mix Masters, I
mean these were important guys. We would go over there and
play a record for them, we had a promo guy named Doug Young,
we would go over there and play the record for them, they'd say,
"Aw man, we can't play this, you gotta take out this, you gotta
do that," we'd go back to Eazy's mother's garage and beep it or
reverse it or overdub it, come back two hours later and it would
be on the air. Then we'd get orders for 40 or 50 thousand units
the next day.

If you look back to the East Coast, Hollis, Queens, and
you're talking about Kool Herc, the Jamaican influence,
"Rapper's Delight" and some of that early stuff up to Afrika
Bambaataa, that's one set of circumstances that I'm not familiar

with and wasn't involved in and really wasn't interested in because it's not real musical and actually had no sense of humor. I call it the era of big dicks and gold chains because that's all they were talking about. When we started on the West Coast, there was some humor in the music, plus it was real musical. Eventually we started to pave the way for people to listen to it and dance to it and have fun with it, and even though we were talking about very serious subjects, we were doing it in a way that was a little more palatable.

Along with a guy who I consider, and even though he's my neighbor he's no friend of mine, you know, I think of the 20 best or worst dis records of all time listed in *XXL* magazine and six were about me, but certainly Andre Romel Young [Dr. Dre], who did the song "Dre Day" and a couple of other dis records about Eazy and I, is the most important musical influence of the entire rap era. Starting in 1986, just look at what his body of work is. He started with the World Class Wrecking Cru with "Surgery" and "Juice," then he did a song called "Turn Out the Lights" with Michel'le, who sang the lead on that, who he brought out of nowhere, of course he did the music and production for every song that ever came out on Ruthless so that means he did the D.O.C., Penthouse Players with DJ Quik, NWA, he did World

Class Wrecking Cru, the Michel'le album, he does *The Chronic* for himself, he does Eminem, 50 Cent, and The Game. I can only say one thing: This guy has been doing this since 1986 and he's still at the very top of his game. I gotta say that this guy is the most important musical factor of the entire hip-hop era.

I used to always tell Eazy that he was our biggest asset, and that was the one place where Eazy had a little blind spot was with Dre. Because Eazy had started the company and we built it together, he never felt that Dre was that instrumental and it just reinforced it after Dre left when we came out with Bone Thugs-N-Harmony. If Eazy wouldn't have died and I wouldn't have left the company, Bone Thugs-N-Harmony today would be the biggest group in the world. They were just so self-destructive and very difficult to deal with. But you know, we had Dr. Dre. That's 25 years, and show business years are like dog years. These guys come and go, they burn out, they're like the flavor of the month. I like some of the stuff Pharrell did, I like all those guys for a period of time, but I can't really say that I really like everything. Except for that first Aftermath album [he did] after he [Dre] left Ruthless, [along] with 'Mr. Evil'/Suge Knight I would say that I really just love his entire body of work. For me he's the number one guy and then I think Rick Rubin, who has done it in a lot of different genres, not just hip-hop. But that early stuff that Rick Rubin did with the Beastie Boys was just great material.

I don't know if a legacy has to be good or bad, but I tend to look at it both ways. Number one, hip-hop re-established the economic integrity of the music business because we cut *Straight Outta Compton* for 12 thousand dollars, we cut *Eazy Duz It* for 8 thousand dollars, we did the first D.O.C. album for 30 or 35, the first Michel'le album for 30 or 35, so that's what the music business is supposed to be about. It supposed to be about win-win, establishing the economic integrity of the business and I think that's one of the things hip-hop did. The other thing it did was unite the country. I don't see any of the kind of discrimination that we used to see - I know that as a Jewish person I certainly don't. But I don't think that we see the extent of discrimination coming from the time when I grew up and went to college. So I think that it brought that change, and NWA became the audio documentarians of their time. Politically you would certainly have to give that mantle to Public Enemy, but sociologically you'd have to give it to NWA. They are the two most important factors of that entire era, and on the other side of the coin I think that the music business now is a shell of what it was before. Everybody is talking about how downloading has ruined the music business. I don't believe that. I believe that the downfall of the record business came from the greed of the executives at all the major companies who then imposed their scope of economic integrity on the business, because to do a Snoop Dogg record now costs the same as a Whitney Houston record. They do three minute videos now that cost more than it took to make [the movie] *Easy Rider*. There's just something basically wrong with that, and the same stations that play a Whitney Houston record play a Snoop Dogg record. So the business has changed and hip-hop has become, I'm not even sure it's hip-hop anymore, but that form of music has become the rock and roll of the past generation. It's different now and I attribute the downfall to the greed of the major labels who become married to these business plans that are doomed to failure. Anybody that's ever read Karl Marx can see that's it's just a traditional cost-push downward spiral, and I blame guys like Jimmy Iovine for the downfall of our business.

I think Jerry Heller is an enabler, I don't wanna make too much of my part in it. But I think if you talk to anybody that was in high school or college between the years 1987 and 1992, they can tell you exactly where they were the first time they heard *Straight Outta Compton.* I think that its affected people all over the world in so many different ways, just for example: In 1988, maybe three or four months into *Straight Outta Compton,* we did a 10-page spread in foreign *Elle* magazine called "Gangster Chic." Half the people that take my class at UCLA are in the fashion business, so I just think it affected the world in so many different and positive ways, it's unbelievable. We got a letter from the head of the FBI saying that we were responsible for the deaths of something like 80 police officers and law enforcement personnel in 1988, it just affected the world in so many different ways, it's just astonishing to me.

Look, I found Creedence Clearwater when they were the Golliwogs playing in a small bar in San Francisco. The Grass Roots, the Guess Who, I represented Marvin Gaye, Journey, Styx, REO Speedwagon, ELO, Boz Skaggs, Van Morrison, Joan Armatrading, The Four Tops, The Miracles, I've represented all those people, but of all the things that I've done in my life the most important period of my life was from March 3, 1987 until March 26, 1995, when Eazy-E passed away. I think that was certainly the most important period of my life, and that's the

period that I am the most proud of. Jeff Chang was doing a
speaking tour with his first book, *Can't Stop Won't Stop*. I heard
that he was speaking in Los Angeles so I went to see him at some
hip little book store in Echo Park or Eagle Rock or one of those
areas that's really becoming very hip now, and a bunch of people
were there in suits and ties sitting on these little chairs on the
floor. The place was packed and he's doin his speaking thing; I
got there late and walked in, then people started to ask questions.
I raised my hand and said, "I read your book and I certainly think
it is the definitive work on the hip-hop nation and I just love it.
For the first time I saw a book on the music business on the front
table at Barnes and Noble!" So I said to myself now's the time for
me to write my book [*Ruthless* published by Simon & Schuster]
to establish Eazy's legacy and reconstitute my own reputation a
little bit because I was very naive and very stupid as far as that
went. A friend of mine named Big Regg, who's in prison now,
said to me, "You know man, you know what you know, and I'm
just tellin you I know the streets, and if you don't deny the things
that Dre and Ice Cube are saying about you and Eazy, then
because you don't deny them, in my world people are going
think they're true." I thought that was the stupidest thing I'd

ever heard, I mean come on, that's just impossible! You wanna know something? He was 100% right, and I was the one that was arrogant and naive in my thinking. So it just came to a point where I wanted to right those wrongs. Eazy had died, I saw Jeff Chang's book on the front table of Barnes and Noble, which I had never seen before, and thought the timing was right. So I said to Chang at his talk, "I don't know you, but once again, like all of you jive-ass New Yorkers, you've totally relegated the West Coast to almost insignificance in your book!" He says back to me, "First of all I'm from San Francisco. Second, I gave NWA six whole chapters," and then I asked him a couple of other questions and then someone in the audience whispered, "Man, I think that's Jerry Heller!" because I've always been a behind the scenes kind of guy. It just got electric in the room, and Chang says, "You're Jerry Heller?" I said, "Yeah." He said, "Come up here," and in my copy of his book he wrote: "To Jerry Heller: The man who's responsible for all of the important music in my life." In closing, this Saturday [March 26th] is the anniversary of the death of my friend and business associate, "The Little Big Man," Eazy 'Muthafucking' E. Rest in peace my brother.

The Hip-Hop Thugster

The level of attention paid to West Coast hip-hop music would only increase during 1988 as NWA looked to build on their success from the year before. This would be achieved by the release of two projects: The Eazy-E solo album, *Eazy-Duz-It,* and the second NWA album, *Straight Outta Compton. Eazy-Duz-It,* with its 'remix' version of "Boyz-N-The Hood," also featured more stories about the crime and posturing that were rampant in places like South Central Los Angeles. MC Ren was another vocal presence on the album, making strong contributions in songs such as "Nobody Move," "Ruthless Villain," and "2 Hard Mutha's." Ice Cube received writing credits on three songs, while Dr. Dre and DJ Yella were named as producers. It was clear even though this was an Eazy-E album (complete with Eazy listed as executive producer), *Eazy-Duz-It* was a product of NWA, full of objectionable material for critics to have a field day with. Take the lines from "Nobody Move," the story of a take-over style bank robbery gone bad:

One hostage got brave and got off the floor
But I smoked his ass before he got to the door

While there certainly were plenty of upsetting lyrics for adults to protest, there was something else as well: A commercial sensibility on the second side of the album. Side two almost completely avoided profanity and seemingly broached more mainstream friendly topics. A prime example was the track "We Want Eazy," which was a rework of the P-Funk classic "Ahh, Bootsy's the Name, Baby." It featured crowd noise in the background as well as a call-response bridge between Dr. Dre and the audience. In addition, the track "Radio," with its cameos by Greg Mack, then music director and disc jockey at legendary Los Angeles radio station KDAY, and 'Nasty' Nes Rodriguez, a Seattle radio DJ who hosted the first all-rap radio show west of the Mississippi River, was clearly an attempt at mass appeal with an NWA touch. The song's creation of the fictional KEZE was most certainly a shot at the numerous radio stations that continued to resist playing hip-hop music. You don't want to play me on the radio? I'll play myself on the radio.

Also impressive was the masterfully executed "No More ?'s." The song was set in an interview format with the reporter asking questions and Eazy replying with verses describing his life of crime and overall ruthless attitude. Written by Ice Cube, and featuring various beats for different answers, this was arguably the high point for Eazy-E the MC:

> Ruthless my style as a juvenile
> Ran with a gang slanged in the meanwhile
> Bankin I specialize in gankin
> Whites Mexicans brothers and others

Eazy himself attracted additional attention when people began to speculate about his age. This 'controversy' was born out of a brief outro Eazy performed at the end of the song "Eazy-Duz-It:"

> From around the way born in '73
> Hardcore b-boy named Eazy-E

It was hard to believe that Eazy-E was doing all he was doing at only age 15. However, this little curve only added to the mystique and speculation surrounding NWA and Compton, California.

Turned out he was born in 1964, which actually made him closer to 25. The group poked fun at the whole situation in the song "We Want Eazy," with Ren posing as someone in the crowd yelling at Eazy, "Man you wasn't born in no '73! Why you be lyin about your age?" Eazy's response: "Man, why you gotta bring that up? Yo! Get this fool outta here!"

Often overlooked was the clear allegiance to hip-hop that Eazy-E found necessary to emphasize. The end of the song "Eazy-Duz-It" found him referring to himself in the third-person as a "hardcore b-boy." A b-boy, though technically defined within hip-hop as one who breakdances, was also a loose term often adopted by some who considered themselves members of the hip-hop nation, even though they may not necessarily have danced. Eazy's insistence on defining himself in this manner indicated a time when the hardest of the hardcore still verbalized a conscious connection with hip-hop culture.

You Are Now About to Witness the Strength of Street Knowledge

The release of the album *Straight Outta Compton* in late-1988 proved to be a moment of truth in the journey of NWA. Artistically, their formula was becoming more refined as they became more familiar with themselves and their vision. As a group, these individuals played beautifully off of one another. Dr. Dre's production talents, already close to brilliant on *Eazy-Duz-It* were confirmed as such on *Straight Outta Compton.* Ice Cube's equally genius lyrical tours of duty rode Dre's beats to some deep, dark places. MC Ren was the perfect role player coming off the bench. Good enough for a solid verse here and there, yet also able to hold it down by himself on a cut or two. Eazy-E played his part as the 'boss' well, getting the last verse on collaboration jams, and he was clearly at his best with someone else writing his rhymes. NWA presented an album that featured tales of the streets from the bottom looking up, with beats that reflected the grime, grit, introspection, and celebration associated with that life. It was a 13-song expedition into a place that, before hip-hop came along, society had largely managed to silence and push out of view. For some young people, the album reflected relevant aspects of their day-to-day environments. For others, it introduced these issues for the first time. Adults who attempted to hate on culture like *Straight Outta Compton* just made their children want to hear more about it.

Several songs on *Straight Outta Compton* helped NWA push themselves into the national consciousness and dialogue. The first attention grabber was the song "Straight Outta Compton." The video for the song was very publicly banned by MTV as the network, according to David Toop in *Rap Attack,* attempted to "prohibit videos that glorify violence and/or show gratuitous violence." In response to this, Dr. Dre positioned NWA in the now familiar role of 'reporters' within the culture of hip-hop, which has been described by Chuck D, of the group Public Enemy, as the 'Black CNN.' Dre pronounced, "We're not on the good side of violence, we're not on the bad side, we're in the middle." Indeed, throughout society in general it seemed tougher than ever to distinguish between news as information and the thrill of voyeurism. Predictably, MTV's decision to ban "Straight Outta Compton" sent thousands of young people out on a mission to buy it.

Second came the song and video "Express Yourself." Lyrically this track seemed somewhat preachy. For instance, Dr. Dre disavowed marijuana smoking:

> *I still express yo I don't smoke weed or cess*
> *Cause it's known to give a brother brain damage*
> *And brain damage on the mic don't mange nothin*
> *But makin a sucka and you equal*
> *Don't be another sequel*

This stanza is ironic, given that Dr. Dre would later define his career and public image as a chronic smoking lowrider. It says a lot about the state of the hip-hop nation at the time that Dre wasn't necessarily seen as corny, but instead trying to remain clear-headed and sharp in order to maximize microphone potential. "Express Yourself" also called out rappers who "forget about the ghetto and rap for the pop charts," musicians that "cuss at home but scared to use profanity when upon the microphone," and those who "say no to drugs and take a stand, but after the show they go lookin for the Dopeman!" The lecture-like, almost parental tone of this song was a bit of a departure from the image NWA was developing for itself. However, it spoke to the diverse, effective, and varied artistic nature of NWA, all of which would make the group a controversial success on their own terms.

The beat of the song featured in the video was different than the one that appeared on the album. The remix version contained a high pitched, screeching hook that would later become a signature of the West Coast 'G-Funk' sound. Remixing and re-releasing songs with new and improved beats was something that was then still an emerging marketing strategy in hip-hop music. "Express Yourself" was convincing evidence that it could work.

The video for this song began with the group bursting through a sign that read, "I Have a Dream." The use of a quote from Dr. Martin Luther King, Jr., a famous advocate of non-violence, by a group that was widely perceived in the general public as the exact opposite was a clever twist.

The video also tellingly juxtaposed past and present injustices done to the African-American community throughout

U.S. history. The scenes shifted alternately between a slave-era cotton field and the present day streets of Los Angeles. The overseer in the cotton field and the police officer harassing the group in LA were clearly the same White man. As a priest, this same individual also gave Dr. Dre his last rights while Dre was shown being executed in an electric chair at the end of the video. NWA was making a clear statement regarding their views on how White males in positions of authority destroyed the lives of African-Americans throughout history.

On the album *Eazy-Duz-It*, the NWA production brain trust had displayed a commercial sensibility with songs such as "Radio" and "We Want Eazy" that were more radio friendly. *Straight Outta Compton* also contained a commercial dance track, the fast paced, techno-based "Something 2 Dance 2." It stuck out from tracks such as "Gangsta Gangsta," "Parental Discretion Iz Advised," and "Compton's N the House," like a sore thumb. While Ice Cube was stirring the pot on male-female relationships in "I Ain't the 1," "Something 2 Dance 2" was talking about:

This is what I want you to do

Feel the groove bust a move
Yo yo I'm tired what about you?
Man this is something 2 dance 2

In the end, it was song number two on *Straight Outta Compton* that created the greatest controversy. Following its release, the album rode a wave of underground buzz, which saw *Straight Outta Compton* sell 500,000 copies in six weeks with no video or radio play. This unprecedented grass roots level of success raised NWA's profile and brought increased attention from mainstream critics and pundits. It wasn't long before law enforcement agencies began to hear about one NWA song, "Fuck the Police." The song was essentially a statement against police brutality, racial profiling, and harassment. It featured members of the group as court officials in the trial of a police officer:

Right about now NWA court is in full effect
Judge Dre presiding
In the case of NWA vs. the Police Department
Prosecuting attorneys are:
MC Ren, Ice Cube, and Eazy Muthafuckin E!

This time NWA's attempt at self-definition put them at direct odds with law enforcement. Almost on cue, the track generated a letter of protest from the FBI. According to David Toop in the book *Rap Attack*, the note "accused the group of 'encouraging violence and disrespect' towards police. Police forces used their fax machines to warn other departments in cities due for a visit from NWA." The group held the letter up like a badge of honor in front of the hip-hop nation, and anyone else who happened to be looking. For a younger generation, facing the FBI and refusing to back down was inspiring. After all, 1988 was less than two decades removed from a time that, given the United States government's track record with young black male social agitators like Bunchy Carter, could have brought about deadly consequences for NWA.

Straight Outta Compton established several important precedents within hip-hop music. First it showed that it was possible to produce angry, funky music, and still have significant record sales. Second, it appeared that the more controversial you were the more the mainstream media, which was beginning a lengthy flirtation with hip-hop music, would begin to pay attention. Finally, NWA had begun to transcend rap in the traditional sense of the group simply being some MCs and a DJ. Instead of rhyme-writers they had become entertainers, their image as public figures becoming almost separate from their work as hip-hop musicians. This would open the door for other artists who would take the idea of transcending hip-hop to the proverbial 'next level.'

First Person Account: SASSY C of JJ FAD

There was this venue in downtown LA called The Casa, and at
that time nobody had really made it. This was a place where
everybody just came and did their thing. Tone-Loc would always
be there, Eazy-E, Dr. Dre, Yella, and MC Ren, prior to them
becoming NWA, would be there. It was really cool and it
reminded me of the movie *Brown Sugar* when the main female
character was saying how she and her friend would always go out
and hear hip-hop, it was kind of that vibe, you know everybody
would go to The Casa on Friday night. If you mention The Casa
now it's really funny because everybody got their start there. Our
group was already together at that time, but we hadn't put out
"Supersonic" yet. As a matter of fact the initial discussions that
eventually brought us to Eazy's label [Ruthless] happened there.
He saw us at The Casa, and originally we were on LA Dream
Team with Rudy Pardee, who actually put us together. From

there Eric saw us and said, "You guys need to be with me," and that's how the opening discussions got going that eventually brought JJ Fad to Ruthless Records.

Everyone had heard "Supersonic," it was a local hit but hadn't gone national at that point, and we were on Rudy's label as he was trying to follow that single up with an album. So we would go to The Casa and perform all these songs that he had done and they were pretty much wack! We were saying stuff like, "We're JJ Fad" in like a Dream Team song and I remember everyone was teasing us about it! They was like, "For real? That's how y'all gonna come back out? That's how you gonna follow up 'Supersonic?'" We kind of felt it too, but when it's your first shot you're just excited to be out there and having someone liking you and picking you up. We were met with open arms, people respected us for who we were when we got up on stage because we definitely brought it. I think that's what's funny now even to this day, people are like, "Wow, you guys still bring it!" We have always been performers and they respected our showmanship, so it was just a matter of getting with the right people and getting the right material out. I'm glad that Eric stepped up to the plate because I know we would not have been as successful as we have been if we would have stayed under

Dream Team's tutelage. Not that Rudy wasn't a great person or anything like that, I totally respect him for putting us together. But the material that he had for us just wouldn't have done as well.

Honestly, we got our props because as female MCs we rocked it. It wasn't like we were just going up there saying, "Hi! We're cute, check us out!" They respected us for what we were trying to do because we really had showmanship, we brought it. So folks were like, "Its garbage what you're doing but we recognize your talent." That's how we ended up at Ruthless, Eric really wanted us on his label. They never really gave us a hard time in that respect, I think they just recognized that these girls got it and how can we make these girls more marketable? I mean, real talk, dollars were definitely thought about. They knew that they could make money off of us because "Supersonic" was taking off all over the country, more so than it was even here in California. It was just so crazy to me; we would go and literally be stars in other states and then come back to California and people would be like, "Yeah, whatever." It took a long time for "Supersonic" to catch on in California or for us to get recognized in our own area.

Something that really stands out for me was one time when we were on tour with UTFO. The Kangol Kid was saying how he had not realized how hip-hop had come so far because he was from the East Coast so, of course, they thought they were the kings of it all, everything was centralized around them, they were the hub and that anybody that was going to be anything had to be either affiliated with them or sound like them. This is what was in his mind, but one day in the dressing room he was like, "You know what? I'm going to have to give you guys your props because I didn't even look at 'Supersonic' as a hip-hop song." He went on to say that in doing shows with acts like LA Dream Team and Two Live Crew, whom UTFO had never really heard of, there would be arenas full of people going crazy and knowing every word to their songs, Kangol realized he had to change his thinking because clearly this non-New York music was coming from a different place. And it took a while because hardcore hip-hop people never really considered "Supersonic" a hip-hop song because it crossed over to so many different musical tastes. Lots of different people liked it, and because of that we would get harassed about that when we did hip-hop shows. We would just laugh and say, "Okay, you call it what you want, but we'll meet you at the bank and see who's account is looking a little bit different."

But then you look at what started happening after that: People started trying to emulate and get that sound in the hope of crossing over. All of a sudden it became the thing to do, whereas before you were considered a sellout if you crossed over, and that was the silliest thing I ever heard in my life. Wouldn't you want your music to appeal to people? Wouldn't you want whoever you could touch to hear what you're saying? I just thought that that was the craziest thing ever.

At that time if one record label had a really successful group, another label would go out and try to mimic what the first label had in the hopes of trying to capitalize on what was hot at the time. For example, we come out, and then L'Trimm came out. So many people thought that we were them and they were us, even to this day I get, "Oh, we love 'Cars That Go Boom'!" [L'Trimm's biggest hit] and I'll say, "Yeah, but that wasn't us." I'm sure they [L'Trimm] get it too, and they're cool girls. I like them a lot. But what I'm saying is that was Atlantic's [Records] answer to us, their attempt to cash in on that particular market at the time. That's what we started seeing; all these girls coming out with similar songs or similar styles, or the dis record as another way to try to make something off of us.

I don't feel like we modeled ourselves after anybody, as a matter of fact, I think that we were original in the sense that we pretty much coined biker shorts. Girls were wearing the little half-shirts in our style, if you will, because we were known for the biker shorts and the stretchy pants so we kind of did our own thing. We had a stylist originally, and personally I didn't like where it was going, but when you're in a group you have to come to an agreement on what was going to be portrayed.

We definitely took sex appeal to a different level because we were more feminine. With the exception of Salt-N-Pepa in New York, the girls were harder in terms of lyrics and attire. I think that they felt in order to be taken seriously in this business at that time they had to come like the guys. We set the stage to say "No you don't," and we took all the flak for it. Now Nikki Minaj and Lil Kim can come out and be the bomb because we already took all the, "Oh you guys aren't real rappers," or "You're not hip-hop." MC Lyte, Latifah, Sweet-T, these women didn't wear mini-skirts or things that we wore. They wore jeans and slacks and things that made them look more street, which is fine, that was their style, that's who they were. I loved it and I respected what they were doing, it's just we came a little bit different. You have to remember hip-hop was still in its infancy, it was just starting. In fact, some people felt that it shouldn't have even been around this long. But because of acts like ourselves and other people that brought our own creativity to it, that's what has gotten this longevity.

From our perspective, we would talk to our fans and moms in particular. We had such a vast following, so many different types of fans that came for the music, the beat. Music is universal. Like this talk about Prince William and his wedding, dissecting everything about it, including what type of music will be played, and they alluded to the fact that he likes hip-hop and R & B, and that's crazy to me! You have this royal in England who loves hip-hop. So, music is universal. It's not restricted to any one race or group or anything like that, and I think "Supersonic" kind of served as a segue for that. What we heard a lot were mothers being really happy that their kids can listen to rap without cussing in it. Will Smith was another one. We toured with him a lot because we had the same type of music. Those types of artists packaged together made a popular tour, and parents were excited about that because they could appease their kids. Rap had a negative connotation at first; it was street and rough and what have you. So for them to be able to listen to 'good' rap without cussing and degrading women was important, and "Supersonic" was a fun song, it was a dance song, it was cool. It's still that way, I mean we still appeal to young kids. The funniest thing ever is my children! They were not born when we were at the height of our career so it blows them away when they come to a show and they see all these thousands of people cheering and wanting my autograph. They're like, "You're kidding, that's my mother! Are you serious? There is no way you want my mom's autograph!" It just blows them out of the water but they love the song. My eleven year-old, he knows it from forward, backward, sideways, every kind of way.

California became a force to be reckoned with, where before it was pretty much a joke to them [the East Coast]. I was saying about how at first Kangol was like, "What? California? Yeah right!" But then during that time when all these artists started coming out and being successful and making music that even the East Coast liked, it started being recognized. I wouldn't necessarily say rap from California was more musical because you had artists like NWA that were comparable to some stuff that was coming out of the East Coast. But there were definitely different types of rap that made California popular, and this opened the door; it broadened it if you will. Whereas before hip-hop was just considered New York and that one sound with everybody trying to have that dialect and put that in their rap. But then it was like, "Really? You're from California? Why are you talking like that? Why are you rapping like that? It doesn't have to be that." This was the beginning of putting California on the map.

When did I start to get some perspective on what we were doing? Towards the end of what I didn't realize at the time was the end of our careers, we went to the Philippines and "Supersonic" was like the national anthem over there. Everybody knew "Supersonic," they knew who we were from the time we touched down, it was the most mind blowing experience I've ever encountered. This little girl, couldn't have been more than two, singing "Supersonic," that's when I knew. We were in a whole different country and it seems like the whole country knows us. Here I'm thinking we're going over there for the servicemen or something like that, we'll do a couple of shows in an arena. I had no idea, I was totally blown away.

Cause We Are the Homechicks That Are Rockin Your World

Although male dominated, West Coast hip-hop in the late 1980s did have female MCs that made an impact on the culture. One example of this was a group of three women, MC JB, Baby-D, and Sassy C, who collectively were known as Just Jammin Fresh And Def, or JJ Fad. JJ Fad's debut album, *Supersonic*, featured a single by the same name that would define the group's career. Produced by NWA associate Arabian Prince and released on Ruthless Records, the song "Supersonic" began with MC JB and Sassy C rhyming over Baby-D's beat box:

> *We're JJ Fad and we're here to rock*
> *Rhymes like ours could never be stopped*
> *See there's three of us and I know we're fresh*
> *Party rockers non-stoppers and our names are def*
> *See the J is for Just the other for Jammin*

The F is for Fresh A and D Def

Behind the turntables is DJ Train

Mixin and scratchin is the name of the game

Now here's a little somethin bout nosy people

It's not real hard it's plain and simple

Baby-D!

Loosely based around the concept of people who like to get in other's business, "Supersonic" mentioned several core hip-hop concepts such as beat making, scratching and cutting by DJs, and biting (the practice of one rapper stealing rhymes from another). Simple, yet fun and definitely made with a pop feel, the mainstream was entranced by the song and visual of three attractive women asserting themselves within the emerging hip-hop climate of the West Coast, and specifically Los Angeles.

The album *Supersonic* achieved platinum status and stayed on Billboard's Pop and R & B charts for four months, peaking at number 49. The song "Supersonic" was a top 30 pop and R & B hit that crossed even the most extreme gender boundaries, including the manliest of all places, the sports locker room. In *Young, Black, Rich and Famous*, author Todd Boyd recalled the scene when he was a reporter covering an NBA game between the Chicago Bulls and Detroit Pistons in the late 1980s after Michael Jordan had just torched the Pistons for 59 points in Detroit:

> When I arrived in the Bulls locker room, the deafening sound of JJ Fad's 'Supersonic' was engulfing the entire space. Charles Oakley, Jordan's valet in those days, and Horace Grant were deeply into the music, as no one wanted to speak with them or anyone else on the team for that matter on this particular day. Jordan was the man, without a doubt. He was the front, back, and center of attention.

After spending time with the media, Boyd noted, "Jordan – now clearly tired of answering questions – turned toward Oakley and Grant and began bouncing to the music with them."

The single "Supersonic" achieved the ultimate mainstream validation when it was nominated for the first Grammy Award in the Best Rap Performance category. Other nominees that year were Kool Moe Dee's "Wild Wild West," LL Cool J's "Goin Back To Cali," Salt-N-Pepa's "Push It," and the eventual winner, "Parents Just Don't Understand," by DJ Jazzy Jeff and the Fresh Prince. Although this would be the high point of JJ Fad's existence, their accomplishments were further evidence of the diversity within the hip-hop music scene on the West Coast during this time. The crossover success of a West Coast group of female MCs revealed the growing numbers of new hip-hop listeners, both male and female, from all over the country and the world.

I Am a Nightmare Walkin

The interrelation of crack and the rise of gang activity, combined with sensational coverage by the mainstream media, meant it was only a matter of time before Hollywood got involved. Any combination of drugs, poverty, violence, Black people, and the police, has long been a screenwriter's best friend. What Hollywood delivered was a movie directed by Dennis Hopper called *Colors*. Sean Penn and Robert Duvall played the lead roles as two Los Angeles Police Department officers. A summary of the plot listed on the International Movie Data Base stated:

> A confident young cop is shown the ropes by a
> veteran partner in the dangerous gang-controlled
> barrios of LA about to explode in violence in this
> look at the gang culture enforced by the colors
> that members wear.

Some of the taglines used in trailers and advertisements for
Colors included:

> "70,000 gang members. One million guns. Two
> cops."

> "Two cops. Two gangs. One hell of a war."

> "In the heart of our cities people die for wearing
> the wrong colors."

> "It's the movie that forced America to choose a
> side... Now it's your turn."

> "Gangs. The war is here. The war is now."

Another look at these lines provides a clear view of the approach
mainstream media brought to their skewed perceptions of Black
urban existence. Four out of the five taglines contain either the
words "guns," "war," or "die." And while terms such as
"dangerous" and "explode in violence" may have been accurate
given the homicide rates for young Black males in Los Angeles
during this time, they do not speak to the contextual issues that
created these conditions. This could just be promotion for a
movie or an example of the mainstream's failure to think broadly
regarding issues in urban culture. Repeated criticism of a

situation without proper consideration to the social and economic factors that help create it is a simplistic, non-critical approach.

The movie itself focused mostly on the police officer's perspective, delving into the family life of Officer Hodges (Duvall) and the love life of Officer McGavin (Penn). There were other notable actors who probably could have given *Colors* additional substance if they had been given the chance. The 'featured' gang members included Glenn Plummer ('High Top'), Don Cheadle ('Rocket'), and Damon Wayans ('T-Bone'). For most people around the United States, and the world, the film was the first view of African-American and Latino gang culture in California. In addition, Ice-T recorded the title song for the soundtrack.

The theme song for *Colors* was set to a jumpy drum track, sprinkled with gun shot sound effects, some scratching, and a high pitched whistle reminiscent of Public Enemy. Ice-T's voice was sampled for the break and inserted at different speeds between verses.

Lyrically, the song was fairly tame considering some of the content on *Rhyme Pays*. This shouldn't have been too much of a surprise; the song worked as a message but also as promotion

for the movie. It couldn't be too explicit if it wanted to get

mainstream airplay. Ice-T still managed to explain the situation

from the gang member's perspective within the bounds of these

restrictions. In fact, the song "Colors" probably did more to tell

their story than the movie did:

You don't know me fool you disown me cool

I don't need your assistance social persistence
Any problem I got I just put my fist in
My life is violent but violent is life
Peace is a dream reality is a knife

Ice-T's direct challenging and questioning was an effective

emotive method to involve the listener in urban problems and

life. Was it discomfort or indifference that made those in the

mainstream not want to have to think about what was really

being asked?

Tell me, what have you left me? What have I got?
Last night in cold blood my young brother got shot
My homeboy got jacked my mother's on crack

My sister can't work cause her arms show tracks

The video version of the song "Colors" contained additional vocals during the breaks. These monologues were almost speech-like, featuring Ice-T as the gang member giving his point of view. The messages were clearly anti-gang and urged young people to avoid the lifestyle:

> *Listen to me man no matter what you do*
> *Don't ever join a gang you don't wanna be in it man*
> *You're just gonna end up in a mix of dead friends and*
> *   time in jail*
> *I know if I had a chance like you I would never be in a*
> *   gang man*
> *But I didn't have a chance you know I wish I did*

While Ice-T did make it clear others should make a different choice, he also made it clear that his reality was his reality:

> *See the wars of the street gangs will always get to me man*
> *But I don't wanna be down with this situation man*
> *But I'm in here if I had something betta to do*
> *I think I'd do it but right now I'm just out here boy*
> *I'm trying to get money cause I'm smart*

I'm gonna get paid while I'm out here

I'm gonna get that paper you know what I'm saying

If I had a chance like you maybe I would be in school

But I'm not I'm out here living day to day surviving

And I'm willing to die for my colors!

And just when it seems that the song will end in contradiction, the final words seal the bottom line.

> *"Yo please stop, cause I want y'all to live. This is Ice-T, peace."*

Colors was another marker in the mainstream's gradual feeling out of hip-hop culture. From a critical standpoint, the movie did an injustice to the stories of young people in the streets of Los Angeles during the late 1980s. Some redemption came as the song held its own in attempting to counter the shallow bias of the movie. Still, the marketing dollars and sensationalism of the movie made its mark on the general public. *Colors* became the reference point for gangs, and by extension hip-hop, for many in the mainstream.

A Mind Full of Rhymes and a Tongue of Steel

As the rebellious side of hip-hop music in Los Angeles began to attract attention, another side of the culture, from the Bay Area, was about to rise and would parallel the popularity of what was becoming known as 'gangsta' rap. If West Coast hip-hop was to be commercially successful it required an MC who could transcend hip-hop and cross over onto commercial hit radio and video. It was at this juncture in the evolution of West Coast hip-hop music that MC Hammer came along. Hammer was a product of Oakland, and had worked as a bat boy for Major League Baseball's Oakland A's in the 1970s. He got the nickname "Little Hammer" from players who thought he looked like home run king "Hammerin'" Hank Aaron. Hammer self-released his debut album, *Feel My Power*, in 1987. It sold over 50,000 copies, which led to a deal with Capitol Records and their re-release of the album in 1988 with a new title, *Let's Get It Started.*

Musically and lyrically, Hammer positioned himself as
sort of a 'medium core' b-boy. Not hard enough to fill his album
with profanities, but edgy enough to claim 'true' to hip-hop
status. Due to his later fame, it is largely forgotten that MC
Hammer, like Eazy- E, went out of his way to explicitly align
himself with hip-hop culture in his early work. For instance, the
song "Let's Get It Started" contained lots of high energy,
shouted choruses and references to beats, parties, honeys, and
other things that were relevant to hip-hop kids about that time:

> *Now you're party wasn't jumpin and your DJ was weak*
> *Instead of dope beats he was spinnin up ZZZs*
> *All the fly girls who came with the beat in mind*
> *They all up against the wall like a welfare line*
> *It also included a shout-out to b-boys:*
> *Makin lots of money from top to bottom*
> *Whatever's in effect yo b-boys have got em*

The album began with an intro called "Turn This Mutha Out,"
an example both of Hammer's toeing the commercial language
line (instead of "Turn This Muthafucka Out"), and his hip-hop

vision of starting the party and rocking the crowd (aka 'turning it out'). Other song titles such as "Cold Go MC Hammer," "You're Being Served," and "They Put Me In The Mix," all employed standard hip-hop slang that would have been recognizable to those familiar with the culture at the time.

MC Hammer started attracting widespread attention with the release of the video for the single "Pump It Up (Here's the News)." While he had danced in earlier videos and was developing a reputation as one of hip-hop's premier entertainers, this performance laid the groundwork for his eventual rise to mainstream cultural icon. Hammer and Oaktown's 357, his group of three female back-up dancers, put it down performance wise like it had not been done in hip-hop before. Nelson George wrote at the time, "His 'Pump It Up' suggests that this super-nimble dancer, backed with a crew of female and male dancers, is bringing new ideas and energy to hip-hop performing."

Hammer's early self-generated image was consistent with his desire to be associated with more traditional aspects of hip-hop culture. There were several examples of this in the inset photo for the album *Let's Get It Started*, for instance the number of people who appear in the picture. Besides Hammer himself, there are ten other people in various poses surrounding him. The scene is similar to the image on the *NWA and the Posse* album cover. Both are examples of artists wishing to portray themselves as having a 'posse,' an urban philosophy of strength in numbers.

The second significant aspect of the photo is the way that Hammer is standing. He is striking what is commonly known within hip-hop culture as a classic b-boy stance. He is not smiling, which gets the point across that this is a serious matter. His arms are folded and he is leaning back slightly, which indicates that he is waiting for you to make the next move. Finally, the sunglasses on does not allow you to get a good read on exactly what or who his eyes might be looking at.

The third notable hip-hop visual connection was the gear being sported in the picture. Several people wore Troop sweatsuits. During late 1980s, Troop was one of the most recognizable clothing brands within hip-hop culture. Often featuring loud colors and oversized lettering, Troop was an early example of brand name hip-hop fashion and an easy way to promote yourself as a 'true' b-boy.

Hammer also displayed the brash confidence often associated with hip-hop culture, which is frequently labeled as arrogance by the mainstream. Indeed, it would have been hard to argue that he wasn't arrogant when he stated in the 'Special Thanks' section of the album liner notes:

> ...and all the Old School Rappers and to
> whomever think they're the King, Prince or
> whatever of Hip-Hop, MC Hammer is in effect
> and will take all titles one at a time, or all at once,
> now what's up? Yeah boy!

No question Hammer had his sights set on a large identity early on, as these were clear shots at two of hip-hop's top acts. Run-DMC was known as the Kings of Rock and/or the 'Kings from Queens,' while LL Cool J had dubbed himself the 'Prince' of hip-hop. The beginning of the video for "Pump It Up" featured three men dressed suspiciously like Run-DMC, saying things like, "Oh man Hammer, why you dethrone us like that?" As things turned out, Hammer would indeed find himself with plenty of titles, not all of them flattering.

Think I'm Fakin But I'm Takin All You Sucka MCs to the End of the World and Push You Over

When Too $hort came to be recognized as a leading voice of West Coast hip-hop, he began to reorient his style toward potential larger audiences. While still keeping one foot firmly planted in the controversial underground style he grew up with and developed, he began to dabble in the mainstream. He created an ethical tension that critics of hip-hop are still unable to reconcile. The mainstream standard was unambiguous: Hip-hop artists were either positive or negative, period. Mass appeal, money, and radio friendly hip-hop helped merge rawer, underground album material into the mainstream while still provoking it.

Life is... Too Short was the name of the album, the debut

single, and video all demonstrated Too $hort's stylistic shift. The song "Life is... Too Short" was radio friendly, with his trademark synthesizer and a choppy scratch. It stood as a profanity-free, cautionary tale told from the perspective of Too $hort, now a veteran of the rap game:

> *Then the new style came and the bass got deeper*
> *You gave up the mic and bought you a beeper*
> *Do you wanna rap or sell coke*
> *Brothas like you ain't never broke*
> *People wanna say it's just my time*
> *Brothas like me had to work for mine*
> *8 years on the mic and I'm not jokin*
> *Sir Too $hort comin straight from Oakland*

While he did make a play on mainstream sensibilities with "Life is... Too Short," Too $hort used other songs on the album to demonstrate that the connection to his underground roots remained strong. He alluded to the issue at the start of "Cusswords," where he half asked/half stated, "So you muthafuckas thought I was gonna change my style!?" In an atmosphere of growing mainstream paranoia about the content of hip-hop music, this particular song went out of its way to provoke the establishment:

> *Ronald Reagan came up to me and said 'Do you have
> the answer*
>
> *To the U.S. economy and a cure for cancer'*
>
> *I said what are you doin in the White House if you're
> not sellin cocaine*
>
> *Ask your wife Nancy Reagan I know she'll spit that
> game*
>
> *Like one night she came to my house and gave me a
> blow job*
>
> *She licked my dick up and down like it was corn on the
> cob*

The news reports that would later surface regarding CIA involvement in the spread of crack into cities across the United States made Too $hort's question to Ronald Reagan ironic at best, and prophetic at worst. As for his reference to then First Lady Nancy Reagan in "Cusswords," Too $hort was clearly interested in seeing how far he could push the envelope in the midst of a growing censorship/first amendment debate over urban flavored music.

The continued rise of crack still flavored the environment for many urban residents, whether they smoked it or not.

Depending on circumstances, drugs could become the centerpiece of existence. A song like "City of Dope" reflected this experience. A dark track with an acoustic guitar lick, it was Too $hort's commentary on the level of chaos engulfing inner city America, in which he famously stated, "I'm from the town called the City of Dope, it couldn't be saved by John the Pope."

The Night I Retired Would be the Same
Night That My Whole Life Expired

West Coast hip-hop was marketable; and the success of a song
and video like "Colors" proved it. Like Too $hort, Ice-T dropped
an album laced with both mainstream appeal and the raw.

Power, Ice-T's second album, featured a cover that set the
tone for the record, and was most certainly meant to stir
mainstream paranoia over sex and violence in hip-hop. Set
against a completely white background, Darlene (also featured
on the cover of *Rhyme Pays*) stood in a white swimsuit and red
high heels holding a shotgun in her right hand. Ice-T, sporting an
Africa necklace, was in the middle, while DJ Evil E stood to his
left. Both men had their right hands hidden. The back cover of
the album presented a view from behind that showed each
holding an automatic weapon.

Ice-T's evolution as artist and social commentator developed into a style that played on double meanings. The single and video for the song "I'm Your Pusher" moved in several directions at once. Most obvious was Ice-T's word play and sound in substituting music for drugs.

"I'm Your Pusher" was based on the 1972 Curtis Mayfield song "Pusherman" from the *Superfly* movie soundtrack, and was a strong anti-drug song, though not always recognized as such. The introduction to the song featured a dope fiend character asking Ice-T for drugs:

> **Dope Fiend:** Yo what's up man I need to get high man I need to get hold of some big time dope man you know where I can get a key?

> **Ice-T:** I know where you can get an LP.

> **Dope Fiend:** LP man have you went crazy man I'm talkin bout some dope man I need to get high right now man why don't you hook me up with a 5-o!

> **Ice-T:** I can hook you up with a 12-inch.

Ice-T repeatedly emphasized his anti-drug stance, for instance:

> *I'm the kingpin when the wax spins*
> *Crack ya smack ya take you to a show-n*
> *You don't need it just throw that stuff away*
> *You wanna get high then let the record play*

The dialogue between Ice-T and the dope fiend character exchanged the basis of the fiend's addiction from drugs to hip-hop music. He eagerly pressed Ice-T for more hip-hop to satisfy his need for a 'fix:'

> **Dope Fiend**: Aww Mr. Dope Man I'm lovin you man you got it goin on man, what else you got?
>
> **Ice-T**: I got some of that Kool Moe Dee.
>
> **DF**: Aww yeah man I want some of that man.
>
> **IT**: Got some Doug E. Fresh.
>
> **DF**: Aww gimme an ounce of that man I want that all night long.

IT: Got some Eric B. and Rakim.

DF: Aww that is some real dope right there.

IT: Got some of that LL Cool J.

DF: Naw, naw man I don't want none of that man, you can keep that man.

IT: Got some Boogie Down Productions/KRS 1.

DF: Aw now you talking man, come on.

IT: Public Enemy.

DF: Yeah, don't stop, don't stop.

IT: Biz Markie.

DF: Make the Music with Your Mouth Biz! I love it!

The hip-hop nation clearly understood Ice-T's shot at LL Cool J, one of the top MCs in the hip-hop game at the time. As such LL had become a target of New York rap pioneer Kool Moe Dee, among others. Kool Moe Dee made his feelings about LL Cool J known by showing a red Kangol hat, an LL trademark, under the tire of his jeep on the cover of the Kool Moe Dee album *How Ya Like Me Now*. Ice-T, it appeared, was also unhappy with the self-proclaimed 'prince' of hip-hop.

When discussing the true 'dope' that hip-hop had to offer, Ice-T mentioned seven artists, all from New York. This was perhaps a window into a West Coast hip-hop inferiority complex that was seeking East Coast approval. The development of West Coast hip-hop would soon break free of this need for validation from its East Coast 'big brother.'

A compliment to "I'm Your Pusher" was "High Rollers," another radio/video friendly song. "High Rollers," similar to "Life is... Too Short," was a cautionary tale of urban street life that cast Ice-T, now a veteran of the hip-hop game, as the wise man giving advice:

> *Speed of life fast*
> *It's like walkin barefoot over broken glass*
> *It's like jumpin rope on a razor blade*
> *All lightning quick decisions are made*
> *Lifestyle plush*
> *Females rush*
> *This high profile personality*

Who earns his pay illegally
Professional liar
Schoolboys admire
Young girl's desire
Very few live to retire

Also, like Too $hort, Ice-T balanced mainstream friendly material on his album with songs that would incense the general public. The socially positive end of his expression was a song like "Radio Suckers" which sampled Chuck D's voice from Public Enemy's song "Rebel Without a Pause." It spoke to hip-hop's continued lack of radio play, as well as, the simplistic nature with which rap was characterized by the mainstream.

Conversely, a song like "Girls L.G.B.N.A.F" (Let's Get Butt Naked And Fuck) represented Ice-T raunchy and humorously doing what he had done before more mainstream friendly songs like "Colors," "I'm Your Pusher," and "High Rollers." West Coast hip-hop artists became business savvy, they threw potential hit single and videos into the album mix in order to gain mainstream access. Once they became a subject of discussion within the general public, the furor and controversy generated by the deeper album cuts would provide even greater exposure and cultural discussion.

Why Would You Ask Me a Question
Knowin You Knew the Answer

As *Straight Outta Compton* officially reached gold status
(500,000 copies sold) with little or no radio and video play, the
NWA production team prepared, in 1989, to build on their
increasing popularity. With Eazy-E as executive producer and Dr.
Dre and Ice Cube as musical and lyrical point men respectively,
the group was poised to become a brand name and corporation
that had options, whether it was producing/recording their own
music or working in collaboration with other artists. NWA's
collaborative smarts set the stage for the release of a project that
had historic implications for hip-hop on many levels.

Originally from Texas, the D.O.C. had a history with
NWA. He first appeared on the album cover of *NWA and the
Posse*, and had been active behind the scenes as a writer for the
group. On the album *Eazy-Duz-It,* he wrote "We Want Eazy"

and co-wrote "Still Talkin" with Ice Cube. The D.O.C. made his NWA debut on wax with doing the intro for "Parental Discretion Iz Advised" on *Straight Outta Compton*. In that verse, he gave a taste of what was coming:

> *Cause upcoming is my album*
> *And for the record meaning my record*
> *Check it listen to the single*
> *And you'll be like 'Yo, I gotta get it!'*

As an extremely skilled lyricist with styles that were as sophisticated as they were diverse, the D.O.C. was able to balance the extra hardcore approach of NWA with a diverse hip-hop sensibility. His writing combined with Dr. Dre's production to create *No One Can Do It Better*, an album that stood out for a number of reasons. The biggest of them was that a star had clearly been born. Given a chance to shine on a solo album, the D.O.C. had risen to the artistic challenge.

While he was down with NWA, from the start of his solo career the D.O.C.'s image had a little different feel to it than his mentors. On his album cover, he wore two necklaces with leather Africa pendants on them. These were popular items at the time and represented a growing consciousness regarding Africa's significance to and connections with African-Americans and hip-hop culture. This was a sharp contrast to the album cover for *Straight Outta Compton*, which showed the members of NWA standing over the camera, presumably after a beat down, with Eazy-E pointing a revolver.

The first single from *No One Can Do It Better* was called "It's Funky Enough." It featured the D.O.C. riding a funky Dr. Dre beat with a Rasta inspired delivery that had instant mass appeal. Numerous jewels revealed themselves over repeated listening to the album's tracks. "Mind Blowin" was, and still is, a classic example of blending MC vocals and DJ scratching that reflected the true essence of early hip-hop music.

"Let The Bass Go," "The D.O.C. And The Doctor," and "No One Can Do It Better," all captured that creative chemistry present when the D.O.C. and Dr. Dre were together in the studio. A lighthearted vibe was featured in a couple of 'commercial' skits, as well as the song "Portrait of a Masterpiece," where the song (and his delivery) is so up-tempo that the D.O.C. rhymes himself breathless. In the middle of the song, with the beat still playing, he suddenly stops in mid-verse and says, "Hold on Dre! Stop the beat, lemme catch my breath!"

Dre: Ay yo man, why you stoppin? That was funky!

D.O.C.: To catch my breath!

Dre: Alright, you got it?

D.O.C.: Yeah!

Dre: Kick it!

Of all the songs on the album, however, one elevated the D.O.C. to elite MC status. Musically, "The Formula" was Dr. Dre at his finest. An easy listening Marvin Gaye sample, with drums, bells and a synthesized horn, combined with the rhymes to deliver the science fiction concept of the D.O.C. as a 'superhuman' MC, created through the combined efforts of Dre and the D.O.C:

> *High energy flowin with the wisdom*
> *Sense of a rich man knowledge and the rhythm*
> *This is what I'm usin to come up with a style*
> *So I'll interact altogether better with the crowd*
> *Nervous for a second then the record starts spinnin*
> *And I fall into the state of mind of what I've just created*

The video for the song was even based on a Frankenstein concept, complete with Dr. Dre as a mad scientist carefully working on constructing the perfect MC. After much studying and mixing of laboratory chemicals in vials and tubes, Dre unveiled his engineered creation, which turned out to be the D.O.C.

No One Can Do It Better delivered enough standout material to establish that Dr. Dre was now the best producer in the hip-hop game and the D.O.C. had created incredible expectations for his follow-up album. His voice sounded like it could cut steel, and his rhymes were witty and insightful enough that he distinguished himself as something much more than just an NWA associate or clone.

Fate, however, had something much different in mind. The D.O.C. was involved in a severe traffic accident and his injuries included, of all things, a crushed larynx. In the immediate aftermath of the accident, it seemed possible that the D.O.C. would never rap again. Eventually he could speak again, but he never regained the vocal tones that made him famous, he had been reduced to a gravelly rasp that did not sound very good on a microphone.

The D.O.C.'s impressive artistry on *No One Can Do It Better,* developed in collaboration with Dr. Dre, promised unlimited artistic and commercial potential, and made the debilitating accident a personal and professional tragedy. In a way, this situation was similar to what would later happen to Bo Jackson. Bo was the first athlete named to play in the all-star games of two major sports. In 1989 he made Major League Baseball's All-Star Game and in 1990 he was selected for the National Football League's Pro Bowl. However, in 1991 he injured his hip while being tackled during a playoff game with the Los Angeles Raiders. The subsequent deterioration of his hip forced Bo to undergo replacement surgery in 1992. For such a great athlete, it seemed a shame that a relatively freak injury ended his athletic career so early. The D.O.C.'s accident was similarly tragic and ironic. But the artistic tragedy that resulted from his car crash has since become somewhat overshadowed by other tragedies. In the 1990s, the losses of Tupac Shakur and the Notorious B.I.G. robbed hip-hop of two of its greatest voices. The difference, while not insignificant, is that while his voice was essentially silenced the D.O.C. remained alive. Still the cruel twist of fate that claimed his voice could be viewed, at least artistically, as an equally great loss. While the D.O.C. continued to ghostwrite for Dre and others, and even released some new material years later, the self-proclaimed "kid with the golden voice" was never the same.

The other news on *No One Can Do It Better* was found in the final song on the album, "The Grand Finale." Although it seemed from all appearances that NWA was ready to enter the 1990s as the premier force in hip-hop music, this was not to be the case. Behind the scenes Ice Cube had been questioning NWA's management team of Eazy-E and veteran rock manager Jerry Heller regarding compensation practices that had surfaced after *Eazy-Duz-It*, and remained unresolved through *Straight Outta Compton*. By the time *No One Can Do It Better* came out, Ice Cube, now unquestionably NWA's lyrical leader, had all but left the group. His appearance on "The Grand Finale" was vintage Ice Cube:

> *My medley is deadly as a pin in a hand grenade*
> *5 seconds before you get sprayed*
> *You can't throw me I guess you'll blow up*
> *Ever see a sucka scattered it'll make you throw up*

This song marked the last time Ice Cube would perform as a member of NWA on wax. His departure was effectively the beginning of the end of NWA and raised other relevant issues. First, this was not going to be a pretty divorce, multiple insults and controversy between the embittered participants were expected to escalate into a war of words and sound. Second, and most relevant to future artists, the situation became an early example of how feuds and 'beef' could be used as marketing tools to stir up publicity and sell records. Although they would eventually settle their differences for the most part, the aftermath of Ice Cube's exit from NWA played a defining role in the evolving cultural landscape of hip-hop.

Here Come the Suburbs

Run-DMC's platinum album and NWA going gold revealed
cultural trends percolating inside and outside their popularity.
Hip-hop music was proving wrong those who had labeled it a
fad. The premier of "Yo! MTV Raps," in 1988, was the highest
rated program in the network's history. Hip-hop music and its
lifestyle were economically and culturally infiltrating America,
which meant people besides young, urban African-Americans
were buying hip-hop records. Who were they? David Toop in
the book *Rap Attack* argued that "rap was drawing White kids
into Black music by virtue of its fierce energy, its promulgation
of an exclusive, if downbeat, lifestyle." Toop referred to an article
in the June 25, 1989 edition of *The Los Angeles Times* entitled
"Call of the Wild," which stated:

> In the past year or so, young people who would
> seem to be at no risk of becoming gang members

have begun to imitate gang behavior. Their

inspiration comes in part, youth workers say,

from the movie *Colors*, with its graphic depiction

of inner city gang life. Another factor, they say, is

the growing popularity of rap music.

For many in the mainstream, the NWAs and Ice-Ts of the world had solidified their perception of gangs and rap music as synonymous terms. Toop decoded the language used in the article, pointing out that these 'young people' were "the White sons of affluent Agoura Hills and Westlake Village residents, who spend good money on keeping Crips and Bloods out of their neighborhoods." Offering comment on the trend of these youngsters wearing beepers "in imitation of crack runners," a Los Angeles County Sheriff's deputy said, "The only time they'd get beeped is when their mothers wanted them home for dinner." Toop called this phenomenon a "challenge to musical and attitudinal (if not geographical) apartheid," and in fact it represented a large-scale demographic shift in the population of those who considered themselves citizens of the 'hip-hop nation.'

You Thought That You Could Do Dope and Still Stay Cool? Fool!

With two albums to his credit, Ice-T was continuing to spread his influence by serving as a bridge for new groups of young people looking for a way to access hip-hop culture. With *The Iceberg/Freedom of Speech...Just Watch What You Say*, Ice-T continued to push the toasting envelope while at the same time drawing listeners to his serial social commentaries. One of Ice's greatest skills was his ability to emotionally reach millions of mainstream youths who imagined themselves culturally disenfranchised and whose infatuation with the form would soon overrun hip-hop.

Keeping with the trend of illustrated album cover art, *The Iceberg* had a picture of a young man in a Los Angeles Raiders hat with a shotgun barrel in his mouth and pistols to either side of his head. A tear was falling from the young man's

right eye, and the black gloved hands holding the guns looked
menacing and official. The image was symbolic of the tension
between hip-hop's social agitation and the power structure's
reactive force.

The album intro, "Shut Up, Be Happy," was a graphic
illustration of Ice-T's approach. Punk rock legend Jello Biafra
delivered a speech announcing that the United States was now
under martial law. In addition, a curfew was now in effect and a
government official would be by soon to collect urine samples.
The whole thing was set to a slow, ominous electric guitar riff
complete with church bells, rain and thunder. As political activist
and lead vocalist of the punk rock band the Dead Kennedys,
Biafra may have seemed an odd match with Ice-T at first glance.
But as individuals within the outsider cultures they represented,
their collaboration made artistic sense.

Both Ice-T and Biafra engaged in what much of the
mainstream considered 'radical' or 'fringe' politics. Added to the
mix was Ice-T's interest in hard rock and roll, visible on *The
Iceberg* with the song "The Girl Tried To Kill Me." Ice-T later
formed his own heavy metal band. Finally, there was the
rebellious and marginalized ethos that the hip-hop and punk

rock cultures shared. Before they were co-opted by the mainstream, the general public disregarded both hip-hop and punk rock or viewed them with disgust. Similar to their misunderstanding of hip-hop, the general public was unwilling or unable to recognize the influence punk rock culture played for a generation of disaffected youth.

On this, his third album, Ice-T was humorously determined to remain on the toasting offensive with tracks like "The Iceberg:"

Out with the posse on a night run
Girls on the corner so let's have some fun
Donald asked one if she was game
Back Alley Sally was her name
She moved on the car and moved fast
On the window pressed her ass
All at once we heard a crash
Donald's dick had broke the glass
Toasts aside, Ice-T relished his position as an agitator of
    America's 'moral police' and elder generations:
Yes I'm the rhyme kicker the hard liquor
Parental guidance sticker?
Yeah, I'm the nigga

Triple X is how I rate

I'm the one your parents hate

The Iceberg also worked to balance emerging West Coast 'gangsta'ism in with a street smart, socio-political intelligence displayed in the work of many hip-hop artists of the time. Given his outsized media image, many assumed a song titled "Lethal Weapon" would be about some kind of firearm. Instead, Ice-T challenged the listener:

You think I'm violent

But listen and you will find

My lethal weapon's my mind

On the song he even goes as far as to issue the following outro:

I got my jammie with me at all times

They can't take this one thing away from me that's got more power

Than any gun in the world

I'm talking about brain power home boy they can't mess with me

Cause I'm too smart for them out there

Fully strapped always packed go to the library and get some more ammo

While that type of message seems almost foreign by current standards, it represented a period that saw hip-hop increase its ability to flex intellectual muscles.

By the time Ice-T had released a couple of albums, he had been around long enough to become the target of high profile mainstream critics. "Freedom of Speech" mixed street and academics into a forcible response. A young man led off by asking:

Ay yo Ice man I'm workin on this term paper for college, what's the First Amendment?

Cast as the Constitutional authority regarding what 'freedom of speech' actually means for those on the margins, Ice-T didn't hold back:

> *Freedom of speech that's some muthafuckin bullshit*
> *You say the wrong thing they'll lock your ass up quick*
> *The FCC says profanity=no air play?*
> *They can suck my dick while I take a shit all day*

Besides the profane response to the FCC, Ice-T mentioned being 'locked up' for saying the wrong thing. It wasn't just hyperbole, political organizations like the PMRC (Parents Music Resource

Center) tried to label, censor, and/or prevent distribution of recordings they deemed sexually explicit and/or violent. The PMRC was founded in 1985 by twenty wives of powerful U.S. politicians, the most public face being that of Tipper Gore, wife of future Vice President, Al Gore, as an opposition to what they decided were alarming trends in popular entertainment. The organization received instant mainstream credibility because of who its founders were married to. Due to PMRC political and social pressures, several record store retailers were arrested for selling 'obscene' music. It didn't play well with Ice:

> *Think I give a fuck about some silly bitch named Gore?*
> *Yo PMRC here we go raw*
> *Yo Tip what's the matter you ain't gettin no dick?*
> *You bitchin about rock and roll*
> *That's censorship dumb bitch*
> *The Constitution says we all got a right to speak*
> *Say what we want Tip your argument is weak*
> *Censor records TV school books too*
> *And who decides what right to hear you?*
> *Hey PMRC stupid fuckin assholes*
> *The sticker on the record is what makes it sell gold*
> *Can't you see you alcoholic idiots*

The more you try to suppress us the larger we get

The PMRC argued that rock and hip-hop music contributed to the decline of the nuclear family and overall social decay by encouraging and glorifying sex, drugs, violence, and crime. The PMRC actually had it half right: An increasing number of families in America during this were unemployed and/or impoverished. As for the PMRC's contention that rock and rap were responsible, *Rap Attack* author David Toop argued "music may be powerful and influential but no music is strong enough to create this kind of social decay." Still, the PMRC succeeded in pressuring the Recording Industry Association of America (RIAA) to place parental advisory stickers on all records containing explicit material.

Many within hip-hop viewed the PMRC and other

organizations like it as little more than tools of oppression, which are always available to the establishment. However, Ice-T demonstrated shrewd cultural awareness by recognizing the efforts of folks like Tipper Gore were bound to backfire. The irony, Ice understood, was that groups like the PMRC were actually causing more young people, including the children of their constituents, to buy these records and learn more about artists like Ice-T.

I'll Make You See Why Stevie Had to Wonder

Mainstream music always finds a way to blow off the pressure of its formative social extremes. With all the economic and artistic activity, success, and mainstream attention West Coast hip-hop music had generated, the time was approaching when all of these factors would come together to produce a big-time crossover song. NWA, while one the biggest acts in hip-hop, was too raw for the mainstream to immediately or completely embrace. If rap was going to break out commercially, what was needed was something that could strike a balance between being naughty yet still palatable to the general public. The man with the answer was Tone-Loc.

The name of his debut album was *Loc-ed After Dark*, but Tone-Loc rode a tidal wave of success generated by one single in particular. In retrospect the song "Wild Thing" was a cross-over ideal for its time. It was naughty, since doing the 'wild thing' was

urban code for sexual intercourse, but contained no profanity

and therefore was radio ready. *Rap Attack* author Toop

described the song this way: "The most distinctive feature of this

thumping, sleazy track with its Van Halen guitar riff and

distinctive drum roll was Tone-Loc's unique testosterone

growl." Indeed, Tone-Loc's voice was distinctive, almost

unmistakable. But perhaps most important was the way he

approached the subject of sex in this song from a humorous

angle, removing all threatening vibes from the situation:

> *She looked at me and smiled and said*
> *You have plans for the night?*
> *I said hopefully if things go well I'll be with you tonight*
> *So we journeyed to her house one thing led to another*
> *A key in the door I cold hit the floor*
> *Looked up and it was her mother*
> *I didn't know what to say I was hangin by a string*
> *She said hey you two I was once like you*
> *and I liked to do the wild thing!*

By this time, MTV was firmly involved in the promotion and

growing popularity of rap music. The right video could now

push the right song to previously unimagined cultural resonance and sales, exactly what happened in the case of "Wild Thing." The video itself used a concept borrowed from Robert Palmer's "Addicted to Love," which was a number one song in 1985, and the video for it featured Palmer performing in front of a 'band' of beautiful women who all looked exactly alike. They had the same make-up on and wore identical clothing as they pretended to play instruments. Tone-Loc's version was done in black and white, allegedly cost $500 to create, and was embraced by MTV. "Wild Thing" went on to sell 2.5 million copies, surpassing 1985's "We Are the World" to become the bestselling single of all time.

As the attention around "Wild Thing" increased, the song's status as a crossover darling was challenged by another race driven incident. When news of the infamous Central Park jogger case broke, "Wild Thing" was pulled into the aftermath. In 1989, five young men, four Black and one Latino, were arrested, charged, and convicted in the assault and gang rape of a young White woman while she was jogging through New York City's Central Park. The convictions were overturned in 2002, but at the time mainstream news outlets frantically sought connections between the case and rap music. The media claimed that a 'new phenomenon' known as 'wilding,' supposedly named after

"Wild Thing," in which young men roamed the streets in search of rape, beat down victims, looting, and even murder, had been responsible for the Central Park case. This was a media imaginative stretch. Indeed, as David Toop noted in *Rap Attack*, "The more that mainstream America got to know about rap through its pop hits, the more convenient the genre became for shouldering the burden of urban collapse."

Tone-Loc rode the formula of rock based guitar riffs and sexual subject matter for another hit single, "Funky Cold Medina." Tone-Loc's vocal chords sounded like they could grind cactus, which made him both urban and exotic and rock and roll palatable at the same time. But it was also the non-threatening nature of his rhymes, especially when compared to the likes of NWA, which attracted the general mainstream to Tone-Loc.

> *"Funky Cold Medina" was a 'love potion' given to*
> *people in order to make them want to have sex:*
> *It's better any alcohol or aphrodisiac*
> *A couple of sips of this love potion and she'll be on your*
> *lap*
> *So I gave some to my dog when he began to beg*
> *And then he licked his bowl and he looked at me*

And did the wild thing on my leg

In later years, this concept would receive large amounts of negative attention as numerous reports of sexual assaults linked to date rape drugs became common news fodder.

All of the attention generated by Tone-Loc's "Wild Thing" and "Funky Cold Medina" obscured another significant song on *Loc-ed After Dark* that was never released as a single. "Cheeba Cheeba" was a song with an underground vibe that was about buying and smoking marijuana, getting the munchies, writing rhymes under the influence, what the sex was like between him and his woman, and watching late night television after a smoke session. It was one of the first high profile pro-marijuana songs in the evolution of West Coast hip-hop music, and would subsequently be followed by a flood of tracks and artists that would eventually echo, expand, and solidify the cultural ties between hip-hop culture and marijuana smoke.

First Person Account: YOUNG MC

I was a New Yorker so to be blunt New York is very, I don't
know if myopic is the right word, at least it was that at the time,
but essentially when I was growing up in New York you could
look at the entire hip-hop world on a subway map. You could
say, "This artist came from here, that artist came from that
borough," maybe some people came from New Jersey, but
basically the five boroughs and Jersey, maybe a little upstate New
York, but that was it terms of all of hip-hop. So coming out to
LA, we just felt that nobody rhymed as well as anybody from
New York, so we just felt LA rappers weren't as good. They had
their own style, but it wasn't something that anyone felt would
rival what was going on in New York. So that was the image I
had coming to LA. Then when I got here and I actually saw
where the music was coming from and I would play at Skateland
and World on Wheels, The Casa, and the Stock Exchange and all

clubs downtown, converted restaurants and that kind of thing, I would see so many different aspects of it.

Not just the street aspect, but also the suburban White crowd that loved hip-hop but wouldn't necessarily go to a World on Wheels to enjoy the music. They were hoping they could pick up the KDAY signal in their neighborhood. Seeing that dichotomy, I didn't see as much of that in New York. New York it just seemed that it was an urban thing and that was pretty much it. There wasn't, at least back in the day, early to mid-80s, there wasn't really a crossover element to it. Run-DMC, a little bit, but it always identified with the urban crowd in terms of New York. So I was able to see from an artist standpoint the real crossover potential that rap had, not "Bust a Move," but my underground stuff, "My Name is Young," "I Let em Know," I would perform that in front of totally White crowds and kill it! And that was something different for me to see. I got to college [at USC] in 1985, I started working with the Delicious [Vinyl Record Company] guys in '87, so we're essentially talking 1986-87.

You had "Batterram," you had "6 'N The Morning," but I came onto the scene a little bit after [World Class] Wrecking

Cru, at least in terms of my influence, so I knew who they were but their musical influence didn't really touch me when I was on the campus in 1985 and '86. It was only when I got to the label in 1987 that I started going out see more and hearing more and I would look up see Ice-T, Toddy-T, the beginnings of NWA and cats like that. To me, New York was always breakbeat based like vinyl, like "Get the beat rockin and have the dude rhyme over the top of it." The LA stuff was more synthesized and music-based, and I think that came more from the funk influence and stuff like the Wrecking Cru, Egypt[ian Lover], Rockberry Jam, and Rodney O and Joe Cooley. All that stuff seemed a lot more musical, some of it was faster, and we didn't have as much up-tempo stuff in New York. I like the up-tempo stuff because I like rhyming fast so that was one of the things that appealed to me right off the bat. I also liked the music end of it because it seemed like there were more possibilities of what you could do musically. Rap in New York had gone back to the DMX drum machine so you had "Sucka MCs" and "It's Like That" [by Run-DMC] with a couple of hits on top of it, you had "What People do for Money" [by Divine Sounds], you had that kind of sound that didn't have a lot of instrumentation to it, and then you come out to LA and its either a full band sound or layered synthesized sound. Or something like King-T's "Act a Fool," even that to an extent was more musical than what you would find in a lot of New York stuff.

My decision to not go the hardcore route in terms of subject matter was because that wasn't my life, and also the people that knew me knew that wasn't my life. So I met all the guys that would do all this hardcore music and people from the outside would assume, "Oh they probably can't stand Young MC, they think he's a sellout," whatever whatever, but a lot of those guys would come up to me and say that they're thankful for me because my rap skill combined with the fact that I embraced being based on the West Coast not only motivated them to start rhyming and rhyming better, but also showed people outside of California that people in California could actually rhyme. That was a big thing because a lot of cats would say that they were from California and people wouldn't even give them a second look because everybody thought that California rappers couldn't rhyme. So my decision came from the fact that I knew all these guys, and to a large extent that was their life, that's what they lived, that's what they saw and that's what they wanted to project, and that wasn't my life, that wasn't necessarily what I wanted to project, and even furthermore, if I wanted to project it, dudes would have been like, "Why you frontin?" because they knew me.

Literally I would get dropped off at the college campus, so I'm gonna talk about livin on the streets of LA when I'm livin on campus in a dorm? It didn't make sense, and on top of it I felt that there was a niche for me because there were not a lot of kids in my situation that actually had college degrees that could spit like me, or were coming from that intellectual side of upbringing and could rhyme like me, I felt like that was a great niche. These hardcore artists were appreciative of me in the way that it expanded the medium, I never went around and said that the way I went about things was the perfect way, I said it was my way. There may have been some guys that did the more hardcore gangsta stuff that would say that their way was the perfect way, but you would not find a lot of LA guys that would say that. You'd find a lot of New York guys that would say that. And me growin up in New York, **if I stayed in New York you never would have heard of me.** If you can put that in bold print you should, because if I'd stayed in New York and did the exact same rhymes, trying to make the same records, I never would have gotten a deal and you never would have heard of me, it's just that simple. I was too young, my music was too different, I had a different approach, I was too low in the pecking order, I wasn't out at the clubs enough, I wasn't politicking enough, what I did in LA would be construed as cutting the line if I'd stayed in New York. It may be different now, but back then? Trust me, that's how it was.

Mind you, this was a genre in its infancy. So it wasn't a question of there being a lot of opportunities. That's why I say you never woulda heard of me, it's not like there was a conspiracy, it's just that there was not enough room to get me out at the same time as everybody else that wanted to come, or guys that needed to put out two, three, or four albums and get enough hype, or be on Mr. Magic 15 times, or get a whole bunch of Friday night premiers on Red Alert's show, I didn't have time for that. Not only did I not have time for that but me gettin my degree, I wouldn't have just been able to continue on until somebody felt it was my turn. Put it like this, I sent lyrics that ended up on my first album, double platinum, *Stone Cold Rhymin*, that I won a Grammy for - now mind you, true, the production wasn't that good but the lyrics were exactly the same - I sent them to Sutra, Tommy Boy, Profile, Jive, and got rejected by all of them. These same exact rhymes ended up on "I Let em Know," "My Name is Young," and "Got More Rhymes" on my album. Maybe it is just the A & R would be like, "Alright fine we need to hear better beats." That's fine, hey I'm literally a 15 year-old kid and I don't have access to the stuff but lyrically, exactly the same. There are lyrics on *Stone Cold Rhymin* that came out in my 20s that I wrote when I was 12 years old. The irony of it was I made my first records and I realized that my 16 bar verses, usually you spit the 16 and then you bounce, well, on a record you have three 16s, so literally I had 9 verses on those records pretty much saying how great I was. You could almost interchange them because I would finish the verse, I'd be like "I let em know!" or "My name is Young!" or "I got more rhymes!" whatever, I could just put the verse in, throw the hook in afterwards. There would be no chorus or anything except adding more music. But me I would just let the hook go and that would be how I made my records; that was the New York in me. "Bust a Move," "Principal's Office" to a certain extent, those were really the first records where I'm like, "OK this is actually a song, this is actually a chorus, I'm gonna build a story." That started me on the path of really being the artist that I would become known to be; a storytelling rapper where you build in the first verse, expound in the second verse, then twist in the third verse and be done. Or "Bust a Move" with four verses, you tell the four stories but it all kind of comes back to the same theme and the like. There were records on that first album where the verses are basically saying how great I am, not much thematic except I'm a good rapper because that's what New York taught you to be. Say how great you are and show it. So coming from that place to expand to "your best friend Harry" and all that, I just could not initially see that happening.

The positive aspect of my influence on other artists was that there were people lookin around for more different types of rappers because I, for lack of a better term, was seen as non-threatening and more relatable. "Oh, he went to college," or "Oh he's more like this or more like that." I had a bunch of people come up to me and tell me that when they were kids their parents wouldn't let them listen to rap, but they would actually buy them my record because they would read a story, see that I didn't curse, see that I went to college and say, "OK, you can listen to this kid." So that was the positive in terms of the people's idea of rap being more open and that allowing a lot more different types of rappers to be able to get in. Plus the fact

that I wrote and did behind the scenes stuff, too, kinda showed
that the rap artist and the business mind were not mutually
exclusive phenomenon, at least in terms of the music business.
Obviously now you have guys that are moguls, but at that time,
other than label heads, when you're looking at artists being able
to write for someone else, being known for that and then turning
around and doing it for yourself in the groundbreaking aspect of
a genre, that was pretty new.

The negative was that I knew of a couple of cases where
guys would have albums either completed, nearly completed, or
pretty much sketched out on what they wanted to do, then "Bust
a Move" comes out and hits and now they get dragged into the A
& R's office saying they gotta have an uptempo joint with a girl
singin on it. Even if that's not the rapper's style or intent, hey this
record just sold a bunch. Or "Wild Thing" sells a bunch, now we
gotta get an uptempo record with some rock guitars in it. Or we
gotta talk about sex a little bit more, or talk about gettin girls a
little bit more, make it more story oriented or whatever. Those
things were what I found to be negative because I came up
rapping about 2-3 years before "Rapper's Delight," so I'm
rhymin at my friend's house over beats and it's all underground.

Someone asked me the other day if I considered my early music underground and I said I guess you could call it underground because there really was no overground.

Before "Rapper's Delight" I didn't even know what rap sounded like on FM. What did a high hat sound like on the radio? Because I don't know. So WBLS starts playin it, and as soon as it would play I would call up and request it again cause I'm like, "Wow, a rap record on FM." So I went basically trying to put my music out, trying to put everything together, trying to get it known, and the idea was to make a record that could be played anywhere. So you didn't curse in it, you'll remember there's certain records on Sugar Hill where they wouldn't say "go to bed," they would say "go to uhh" because they were so concerned about being censored. So the thought of cursing was not even in the picture. They wanted to make sure it could be played anywhere; that someone could just pick it up and put it on the radio, so that's how I approached my rhymes. I didn't curse in them because I came from a time where you didn't know how long rap was gonna be around, or you didn't know how many people rap could reach. So the whole idea of selling out didn't exist because we weren't selling.

It's interesting because I could say rappers today, but really rappers for the last 15-20 years, know that rap is gonna be around. Rap is on the same level as country, probably a bigger level than jazz and gospel and other genres, so they know it's gonna be there. When I was doin my thing with *Stone Cold Rhymin* not only was I concerned about West Coast hip-hop, all the guys that I came up with for two years before "Bust a Move" came out, but I was concerned about hip-hop in general [lasting]. You know because if a rapper did anything it was all stereotypical and there was no idea of a major rap label and it just seemed like the entire industry could be taken away. Getting back to the positive and the negative, I liked the variety of it. So when I'm coming out in the same 3-5 year window as Tone-Loc, NWA, Boogie Down Productions, Poor Righteous Teachers, X Clan, Public Enemy, De La Soul, Digital Underground, we're all comin out at the same time, we're all able to go gold and platinum and sound totally different, no problem, that's a thriving industry. There's too many targets to hit to knock out the whole industry, so I'm lovin that. When it got to the point where you had the major labels taking over and they were controlling the distribution and the money behind A & R, they would say "OK this is the hot record on the radio right now, let's get that producer to make something that sounds exactly like it." That's a 12-18 month process, but that's the sound they want to go with, all of sudden things start becoming more homogenized. When you have a single target, it's a lot easier to either dismiss or destroy. That was the way I looked at it when I would hear about people trying to make "Bust a Move" clones, I didn't care if they made something that sounded like mine, but I didn't want the industry to sound like me.

In all fairness, when "Wild Thing" [which Young MC co-wrote] came out me and Tone [Loc] talked and we were hoping that it would sell 30-50 thousand records so he could get a car and I could pay off my college loans. That's literally the level we were thinking on; that record sold over 4 million singles. His album, [*Loc-ed After Dark*] was triple platinum plus, and he had the single "Funky Cold Medina," which was double platinum plus, and I'm just sittin there! I'm seeing this happen and I'm like, "Oh my goodness!" So I'm puttin "Bust A Move" out, which sounds totally different, and I'm hoping, "At least let me go gold, let somebody hear me," because I sound totally different. Each of those records were groundbreaking so there's no way to know, there's no rubric, there's no guideline to go by.

You can't tell people what to like and not like. In essence, we put out the equivalent of someone's first girlfriend two or three times in a row. This goes for every artist, directors, this goes for all kinds of people [who have initial success]; you just have that assumption like, "Oh, I've got the touch of gold." No, you're new, you're different, they have no expectations of you so you're great on that one.

Yeah, it's exciting if you if don't attach your entire identity to it, it's exciting if you're not attaching your potential future and your earnings and your social standing to it. If you just look at it in a vacuum it's totally exciting. But if you're attaching all these other aspects of your life and your future and existence to it, of course it's stressful! Here, what we're gonna do right now is take something that's never been done before and you're whole life and future is gonna be based on it. You cool with that? By the way, all this at 21 or 22 years old. This is me after going through essentially four years of college, and loans and dealing with my parents across the country and all that other stuff, there's a lot more to it. It looks great from the outside, but for every me there's a bunch of people that tried and didn't [make it], or a bunch of people that had a little bit of a hit and then you didn't hear from them again. I was extremely lucky, and that's great and my life has been wonderful because of it. I wouldn't change, a thing but I can't sit here and say that it was always a pleasant exercise.

Rap was seen as angry and rebellious, somewhat counter-culture to those outside the culture. So being able to come from a place that wasn't as angry or counter-culture, but still was true to making sure I was a good MC, my lyrics really flowed and that kind of thing, I know for a fact because people have come up to me and told me that the first rap record they listened to was either mine or one that I wrote. And that started them on their journey in terms of liking, enjoying, and understanding hip-hop. That's what makes me most proud because not saying that they wouldn't have listened to it without me, but it may have taken them longer, or they may not have been as enthusiastic. So all those people that I helped lead into hip-hop I'm grateful to and grateful for and it makes me feel like what I did had a lot more meaning than just, "Oh, he had a record that girls liked." At least at that time New York could be very insular in terms of how they felt what their influence was on the rest of the country. I say 'they' because I didn't put out a record in New York. You go places and whether it be coastal, flyover, or whatever, they all knew about the New York rappers. But then California really started a regional thing that was able to embrace their own on top of having respect for what was going on in New York. I think seeing what it was like to support your own, to support someone who talked about the things you knew, mentioned streets or stores that you went to or local people that you idolized, there's a certain enthusiasm that comes with that. I think that not only helped expand the West Coast but helped expand the rap industry as a whole. It made it more diverse by showing other regions that, hey, if you've got a sound that's different than what you hear coming out of New York, go ahead and put it together, have your people support it and something could happen.

Also in New York, which has a large population, there was massive buying power so you would assume that a lot of people there buy records. But at least during those times, New York only accounted for like four percent of the record sales because a lot of people in New York City had industry connections, or they were taping music off the radio. They weren't buying as many units in New York; if you were to spread that same number of people out over a whole bunch of cities across the country you would get a bigger sales number. But because they were squeezed together in New York, and there was such an industry influence on people there, you wouldn't get as many sales per capita. That plays in LA as well to a certain extent, but there's a hell of a lot more cities in California than LA. I heard it said one time, I don't know if it's true, but I heard that you could go platinum in California. Definitely go platinum if you include the West Coast and throw in Arizona, New Mexico, basically two states from the left [of the West Coast states], you can go platinum just in that region easily during that time without selling a single record in New York, Chicago, Philly, Miami, Dallas, or Atlanta. Don't have to sell in any of those places, just work on the left; Mountain and Pacific [time zones] and you could go platinum during those times. That was big, because you couldn't go platinum with a record just in New York. That was an eye opener. That's where Def Jam says, "Okay, we need to open an office in LA." Then the Aristas and these other labels say, "Oh maybe we should have a rap label out here." This wasn't a shift in the record industry because these were new records. This was an addition; it's not like they weren't selling records out of New York, but they weren't the only records selling. Mind you, this coincides with a time when record sales are reaching a peak. Imagine creating a new Nashville, that's essentially what you did.

To the issue of what the legacy of this time and place is, you know what, I've got a lot of words in my vocabulary but the answer to that question is too big to articulate. Its musical, its cultural, its racial, its regional, its political, in fact the better question would be the opposite: What didn't it affect? Here's the thing, my concept of what someone construes as a minority is one size fits all, the actions of one reflect on many and the whole bit, you put that to a rap artist versus other genres. You could have your hardcore death metal and all that other stuff, but you know that's different than the Gin Blossoms. But in rap music, you couldn't necessarily say that you knew a rapper that wasn't talking about bitches and hos and guns and all that other stuff. As soon as you got to the point where you could distinguish not only from subject matter but from region, and thus by artist, and we became individuals like that, that had so much of an influence on not only how people construed rappers but I would say how a lot of people would view Brown and Black people in this country.

If everybody's iPod shuffles were public you'd be

fascinated by what a lot of these folks listen to. I'm watching "Morning Joe" [on MSNBC] and I see Peggy Noonan, she's basically right wing, wrote speeches for Reagan, and Kanye West comes up and she says "Jesus Walks" is one of her favorite songs. My thing, before 9-11 George W. Bush used to take a lot of vacations down at the ranch in Crawford, Texas, and I believe this was down there, he has the whole staff with him and Ari Fleischer, who was his press secretary, does "Bust A Move" on the karaoke for the press corps. It makes *U.S. News and World Report* and my stock guy sends me the story because I don't think there's any footage of it, but they said that Ari Fleischer did a good job, and I'm like, "Oh my God!" I mean, what it does in terms of the culture, I don't how many New York rap songs Ari Fleischer knew. He might know "It's Like That," there may be some Run-DMC stuff he knows, or whatever, but the fact that he would pick mine and go and do it, that's pretty interesting. And my politics lean left!

In terms of rap records beginning to sell in the millions, using Run-DMC as the model, you can go back to before *Raising Hell*. *Raising Hell* could only go platinum in 5-6 weeks because of what their first album did. It was called *Run-DMC*, and "Sucker MCs" comes out with "It's Like That." Two singles

that people were playin into the ground. Then "Rock Box"
comes out, another single, and people are playin that, and only
then does the album come out. And that album takes a long time
but there's bunch of singles off that record. Pretty much every
track on that record; plus they had "Here We Go" and the
equivalent of mixtape stuff, it's like "Oh you gotta get that!" It
created such a buzz around the group that literally, you talk
about strong arming a crossover, that's what Run-DMC did.

The impact that they had and how saturated the listeners
were with their music, there were so many records that are
classics that basically kind of took the brunt of, "Oh yeah, that's a
rap record we'll put it in this category," to the point of, "Oh
these guys are gonna be around, this isn't just a fad, maybe we
should listen to them." So *Raising Hell* comes out, and obviously
the Aerosmith connection [on the single "Walk This Way"]
helps with that, but the legitimacy of that album and that group
and that whole vibe was really brought by their first album. If
you have time to go look back on the history of that first
Run-DMC record, there's a lot that went on with that record
that never went on with anything else. It seemed like it was such
an underground record and then you see a whole album and

you're like, "Oh my God, it's a whole album," and it's relevant. Not like, "Oh it's a whole album and here's a couple of songs that no one will hear just so they can make it an album," that whole thing was relevant.

That is the one album that I would think motivated more people to get into rhyming than anything else because I had been doing it already for a while, but there's a difference in saying you can re-make Jimmy Spicer's "Super Rhymes" and another thing when you say, "OK I'm gonna re-make Run-DMC's first album. I'm gonna do a track like this and different from that." Before, when it was single driven, you're like "OK I'ma put out this single and they gonna know me like this, and then I gotta follow up with something better, but it's gotta be kinda the same so they know it's me." When you saw that Run-DMC record, your songs didn't have to be the same anymore. Well, my first two can be over here, and I can do uptempo and then talk about girls over here, I can talk about rhyming over there, I can talk about money over here, and have it all be on the same record with my name on it. Obviously you would know that as an artist that this was possible, but you didn't see it in action until you saw that first Run-DMC record. If you want to bring it back to the West Coast, I would dare to say that that record had a ton of influence on not only West Coast rappers, but rappers outside of New York that said, "I want to make a diverse record."

Putting my name and 'legacy' in the same sentence is a little uncomfortable. What I will say is I think people remember me for being intelligent, people remember me for having good rhyme skill, people remember me for being positive/party, that kind of thing, and a good influence on their kids to a certain extent. And people remember me for "Bust A Move." A lot of people, they run from the thought of being a one-hit wonder, "Oh no, I want to be known for more than that." That's a hell of thing to be known for. So, if someone says, "Oh, well all I know you for is 'Bust A Move,'" I'm like, okay. I'm good with that, because if I say there's 300 million people in the country, I can guarantee you over 200 million people heard of my song or heard of me. If that's all I'm known for, I'll take two-thirds of the country knowin me; they've got a lot of things in their heads and there's a lot of different people.

If I can be one little shuffle on the iPod, if I can hold a memory, cause that's really what it was. I was lucky enough to come from the end of the time of artist development. So there were articles about me and I got to be honest and I got to be real, and I got to be relatable in interviews and all those things where people cared not only about the song or what the track was or who guested on it or who produced it or any of those things, they cared about the artist. That's why they wanted to buy the albums, that's why they wanted to see the liner notes, that's why they wanted to see the thank yous and see the pictures, to have something tangible in their hands that they didn't have before they went to the record store. I'm lucky to come from the end of that era, so if "Bust A Move" is all they know me for, I'll take that. But I think there's more to it for people that were in the music industry, I definitely know there was more to it for people that were in LA.

That whole time, 1987-1992, I know when I came out in 1987, I would go into these places where I had to worry about what color I wore. And these guys were lookin at me tough and then they're like, "Damn he's from here and he's spittin!" I'd have rough guys come up to me and tell me that they like the way I rhyme. I would have guys tellin me how they were in jail and they played some of my stuff like "Got More Rhymes" and "I Let Em Know," in the cellblock. That's not the demographic I'm even thinkin of or goin for but just the fact that I could appeal to them, and a lot of it was because, "Yo, that nigga's from LA."

And I say it like that! There was something to that coming back at me. At the same time, I could go to Nebraska and literally drive past cornfields and go to a club with dust on the floor and people in cowboy boots and they'll sing the hook, cause I've never had to bring a woman on the road with me to sing the hook. I've done fraternities with mostly male crowds. Sing it! Some may sing it an octave low, but they sing it.

I feel that the East Coast blew up, got fat and lazy, and then fell off a little bit. And then the West Coast blew up, got fat and lazy, and fell off a little bit. And then you see what the South does and what other regions do, but what it says is it's really not meant to be a regional genre. But the whole idea of a certain part of the country dominating an industry is pretty much dead. The mistake was that the concept of a regional record was; if it comes from a certain region you're gonna get equal love from all over the country, and that's gonna dominate every other region. That's not the case: If it starts in a region you will get the most love from your region and you'll get some love from the rest of the country, and then we'll see what that amalgamated love adds up to. It got to, "Yo, West Coast is hot, we can put out whatever." It got to the point after Westside Connection, before

Game, and if Snoop and Dre had a little bit of a lull, where dudes was puttin out anything. Like, "Oh I'ma go through Macola, I'ma do this, I'ma do that, I'ma get this little deal over here and I'ma put it that I'm West Coast," and then you kept hearin these huge numbers. This one went gold, this one went platinum, and then all of a sudden you stopped hearin them numbers. You didn't hear those numbers anymore. You start to feel like you kinda heard that before, or everybody wants this person on it, or that person on it. So it really just got to a point where it stops being new, and when it stops being new it has trouble holding on to unique. Because at that point there's nothing preventing someone from another region saying, "This little facet is what I like about LA hip-hop, I'ma take that. And then I'ma add on some local seasoning and I'ma call it my own local music." That local seasoning will be the title, or the singing, or the slang, or the beat or something like that. But it's definitely going to include some things that people like about West Coast hip-hop, but it's gonna be in the Midwest or in the Northwest or wherever. All of a sudden a lot of the people that were listenin to the West Coast hip-hop that weren't from the West Coast will say, "This Midwest thing sounds kinda cool, I think I'ma get on that." That would never be explicitly said, but trust me, there were a lot of people that were influenced by what they heard on the West Coast. Other than a lot of the southern stuff with the drum machines and the 808s, a lot of the other music was musical. It didn't go back to break beats, it didn't really go back to drum machines, if it had drum machines it would have synthesizers and stuff on top of it, some live playing or other elements that would make it for the region, but it was musical. So they had a choice at that point to say, "I'm gonna go the drum route, the break beat route, the drum machine route, or I'ma go the more music synthesized route," and a lot of them took the music synthesized route. Plus the slang, plus the references, a lot of them will make reference to West Coast artists and all that, so there's something to it.

Don't hang yourself with a celibate rope

As a label mate of Tone-Loc on Delicious Vinyl Records, Young MC had contributed to Tone-Loc's success by co-writing the smash hit "Wild Thing." Young MC's debut album was supposed to be the label's first release. However, the sudden and explosive success of *Loc-ed After Dark* caused Delicious Vinyl to push the Young MC project back and allowed Tone-Loc's popularity to run its course. Young MC's album, *Stone Cold Rhymin*, cleared out its own space once it was released. The signature single from this album, "Bust a Move," followed Tone-Loc's blueprint of lighthearted, non-threatening rhymes over danceable, radio-friendly tracks. "Bust a Move" added a rhythm and blues sounding chorus and a video full of dancing bodies:

> *Your best friend Harry has a brother Larry*
> *In five days from now he's gonna marry*

He's hopin you can make it there if you can

Cause in the ceremony you'll be the best man

You say neat-o check your libido

And roll to the church in your new tuxedo

Young MC had attended the University of Southern California where he earned a Bachelor's degree in Economics. His background and rhyme style offered a safe alternative to not only the language of NWA, but the sexual subject matter of Tone-Loc as well. The media coverage Young MC garnered made him one of the first West Coast hip-hop media darlings. Discussing his younger years, an article in *The Los Angeles Times* stated:

At the age when many rappers were busy acquiring the colorful police records they would later disavow in interviews, Young was an honors student (he is still clean cut in an age of gangster chic, his rhymes too clever by half).

This clear shot at the likes of NWA appeared to link Young MC's cleverness, as opposed to 'gangsta' rappers, to his honor student background. The mainstream's love for Young MC spilled over in the description of his rhyme style:

Young raps in a clear, smooth tenor; he

enunciates complex rhymes cleanly as a scat singer where many rappers these days are content to hunch forward and let their dancers put on the show. Young's swinging performance is closer to Smokey Robinson's than Kool Moe Dee's – he knows he is an entertainer, not a guy at a poetry reading.

The attempt to distance Young MC from an old school hip-hop legend like Kool Moe Dee, yet liken him to an old school rhythm and blues performer like Smokey Robinson, seemed to imply that hip-hop to that point had been lacking artists who knew how to move a crowd. Whatever the case, radio and video outlets carried Young MC and "Bust a Move" to mass popularity. The single reached the Top 10, and *Stone Cold Rhymin* entered the Top 20. The follow up single to "Bust a Move" was a song called "Principal's Office," another humor laced tale, this time about high school life.

It is apparent, by looking at the 1990 Grammy Awards, how West Coast hip-hop music during this period was shifting mainstream cultural perceptions. "Bust A Move" won a Grammy Award for Best Rap Performance, while Tone-Loc's

"Funky Cold Medina" was also nominated. The fact that two West Coast artists were nominated for the Grammy in the rap category, and one of them won, sent a signal to both the hip-hop nation as well as the mainstream that the West Coast was poised to lead the way artistically and financially in the 1990s. At the same time, the mainstream was put on notice that, far from being a fad, hip-hop was here to stay for the foreseeable future, and it was the children of the mainstream who were helping to propel hip-hop into the national consciousness.

And All Bitches Ain't Women

With the release of *Short Dog's In The House* in 1990, Too $hort established himself as one of the busiest artists in the rap game. Visually, the album reflected the West Coast rappers' trend of using illustrations as cover art. The regional practice of men using the word 'dog' as a term of endearment was illustrated not only in the title of the album, but with a picture of a big dog, presumably representing Too $hort, in an Oakland Starter jacket with gold chains, holding up the two-fingered 'peace' sign. Below the $hort 'dog' is a side show scene with Mercedes Benzes, lots of other male and female dogs dressed in outfits, wearing Nikes, and talking on cell phones.

As he had on *Life Is... Too $hort*, $hort included something that would ensure him play within the mainstream. "The Ghetto" sampled the Donnie Hathaway song of the same name and was a cautionary tale of contemporary urban life:

The story I tell is so incomplete

5 kids in the house no food to eat

Don't look at me and don't ask me why

Mamas' next door gettin high

Even though she's got 5 mouths to feed

She'd rather spend her money on a H-I-T

I always tell the truth about things like this

I wonder if the mayor overlooked that list

Instead of addin to the task force sendin some help

Waitin on him I better help myself

Housing Authority and the OPD

All these guns just to handle me

In the ghetto

Too $hort had gained a well-earned reputation for misogynistic content and lyrics. But he also demonstrated an awareness of the need for Black self-empowerment:

So much game in a Too $hort rap

Can't be White and Whites can't be Black

Why you wanna act like someone else

When all you gotta do is just be yourself

We're all the same color underneath
$hort Dog is in the house you'd better listen to me
Never be ashamed of what you are
Proud to be Black stand tall and hard
Even though some people give you no respect
Be intelligent when you put em in check
Cause when you're ignorant you get treated that way
And when they throw you in jail you got nothing to say
So if you don't listen it's not my fault
I'll be getting paid and you'll be payin the cost
Sittin in the jailhouse runnin your mouth
While me and my people try to get out

Too $hort then says, "For all you brothers runnin around here usin that 'N' word, lets let the original rappers kick the last verse." The song ends with a voice exclaiming: "Die nigger die! So us black folk can take over!"

Certainly *Short Dog's In The House* contained the trademark toasting that had come to characterize the Too $hort style. As he attempted to explain on "Short But Funky,"

I'm not your average every day fake rapper on the mic
though
I might say somethin that your mama don't like so

Don't play it loud if she's around to see

But you can play this cause its rated PG

When I'm rated X I'm just havin my fun

I bring a smile to each and every one

But there's a serious side to everything that I say

Life is too short for you to wait till the next day

Critics of Too $hort and rappers like him, would argue that there was little to smile about when it came to a song such as "Ain't Nothin But A Word To Me," featuring Ice Cube:

Too $hort:

Now take my bitch she won't complain about shit

Cause she's my ho she don't belong to a trick

So when you fuck her and give her all you cash

I get paid or put my foot in her ass

Ice Cube:

Cause I'm the B the I the T the C the H

The K the I the L the L the A

Ice Cube a nigga that's bigger than a nut

Cause a bitch is a bitch is a ho is a slut

The contrast of ideas between "The Ghetto" and "Ain't Nothin But A Word To Me" was an example of the contradictions that have continued to be a part of hip-hop. Songs with titles such as "Punk Bitch," "Paula & Janet" (perhaps a vague reference to Paula Abdul and Janet Jackson), and "Pimpology," were other misogynist examples that caused the mainstream to question whether such controversial content discredited the messages on songs like "The Ghetto."

Pro Black and it Ain't No Joke

While West Coast hip-hop music in the early 1990s had its DJ
Jazzy Jeff and Fresh Prince style 'pop' rap and Schoolly D
inspired hardcore material, it also had a Black Nationalist side.
Paris mixed political awareness, a militant attitude, and straight
up rage with an intellectual approach, calling himself 'The Black
Panther of Rap.' Such a nickname seemed particularly
appropriate given that Paris and his record label Scarface: a) was
out of the Bay Area, where the Black Panther Party for
Self-Defense was born, and b) he brought a style that was
reminiscent of Public Enemy, who was clearly influenced by the
Panthers. Paris' debut album, *The Devil Made Me Do It*, echoed
the fury that characterized the more militant fringes, as well as,
the Nation of Islam during the Civil Rights movement of the
1960s and mixed it with contemporary issues. The title track of
the album argued:

They spit on your flag and government

Cause help the Black was a concept never meant

Nigger please food stamps and free cheese

Can't be the cure for a sick disease

Just the way the devil had planned it

Rape then pillage everyone on the planet

Then give 'em fake gods at odds with Allah

Love thy enemy and all that hooplah

Hear close to the words I wrote

Crack cocaine are genocide on Black folks

Cool when I write mine never coulda missed this

Damn right when you think seditious

And I move swiftly you can't get with me

The triple-six moved quick but missed me

When I came off involved in conscience

So don't ask why next time I start this

Paris' juxtaposed Christianity and Islam and used them to question the true intentions of entitlement programs such as welfare and food stamps, which were already hotly debated issues within the Black Nationalist movement. However, it was another song by Paris that offered possibly his most powerful commentary.

On the evening of August 23, 1989, Yusuf Hawkins and
three friends traveled to the Bensonhurst area of New York City
to look at a used car for sale. These four African-Americans stood
out in the predominantly White neighborhood and word spread
quickly among its residents. Very soon a group of roughly 30
White teenagers carrying bats, sticks, and a gun approached
Hawkins and his friends. The White kids were allegedly already
upset because one of their ex-girlfriends had supposedly invited
other youths of color to her 18th birthday party. Thinking the
four African-Americans were there for the party, the White teens
attacked them, fatally shooting Hawkins. Paris' single verse song
"The Hate That Hate Made" was loosely based on these events:

> *June 6th in the time of six o'clock*
> *Hot summer night in the city of hard knocks*
> *Two Black brothers took a walk in the Southside*
> *Could've been any brother lookin for a dope ride*
> *Seein a White girl wasn't in the plan*
> *But the plan had plans of its own for a brother man*
> *A bad case of the right place at the right time*
> *Makes you just ask why*
> *I guess you suppose you know what a nigga do*

To a female that was meant for you

Jealous cause your girlfriend screwin a Black man

So you bust caps on an innocent bystand

But I guess we all look the same

A Goddamn shame you don't know my name

Musta just been two Blacks so the payback

Fit the ID for someone like me

But you see I don't think like you do

I come much sicker with the retribut'

Rollin twenty-five deep troop down in a parking lot

Ready movin steady when I bust your spot

Huh you dumb motherfuckers

Just don't know me you don't control me so leave me lonely

Step and be prone to a cap to the dome

I don't quit {*BLAM*} I'll start tearin up shit

This is a Scarface set and no snakes allowed

Keep the pace ready set brothers rollin out

Packin a Mac-10 strapped and capped in

Now who's to blame for the hate that hate made?

The one stanza track won't let the listener escape as it emphasizes the heavy lyrical content and message. Paris's stylistic approach was largely unique on the West Coast during this period, but it still found play in the mainstream. "The Hate That Hate Made" received some critical praise, though the video for "The Devil Made Me Do It" was banned by MTV. Although the ban did not necessarily boost Paris's career in the way it did NWA's, it still helped solidify his reputation as a powerful 'pro-Black' MC from the increasingly 'gangsta' dominated West Coast.

Apparently the Police Have Been Beating Up Negroes Like Hotcakes

The comedian Dave Chappelle observed that when you see something reported in *Newsweek* magazine, you can tell it has truly entered the mainstream consciousness of the United States. The March 19, 1990 issue was perhaps the coming out party for the fact that hip-hop music had established another foothold as it invaded mainstream culture. On the cover was a picture of Tone-Loc, with the headline "Rap Rage: Yo! Street rhyme has gone big time. But are those sounds out of bounds?" The first story, entitled "The Rap Attitude," by Jerry Adler, offered an establishment-toned review of hip-hop's cultural rise:

> Let's talk about 'attitude.' And I don't mean a
> good attitude, either. I mean 'attitude' by itself,
> which is always bad, as in you'd better not be
> bringing any attitude around here, boy, and,

when that bitch gave me some attitude, I cut her
good.

One clear marker of negative mainstream reaction to something
considered 'ethnic' is the awkward attempt to appropriate
language, in this case Ebonics and/or urban vernacular and slang.
The article worked to qualify attitude as something that must be
earned:

> Attitude primarily is a working-class and
> underclass phenomenon, a response to the
> diminishing expectations of the millions of
> American youths who forgot to go to business
> school in the 1980s. *If* they had ever listened to
> anything except homeboys talking trash, *if* they
> had ever studied anything but the strings of a
> guitar, they might have some more interesting
> justifications to offer.

From the beginning of United States history, the word 'they' has
been used as code to identify a group of people, often male and
of color, who have somehow supposedly not done enough to

ensure themselves a life of prosperity and happiness. The author was clearly suggesting that simply listening to 'homeboys talking trash' (an overtly prejudiced term) was a reasonable way to understand and morally judge the origins of hip-hop and urban decay without mentioning the devastating effects Reaganomics and crack had on the inner cities of the U.S. in the 1980s.

Newsweek's approach attempted to bring balance to the discussion at certain points, for example, citing some 'offensive' lyrics by the rock group Guns-N-Roses, but the article continued down a path of rigid perspective and limited vision. It described NWA's home base as "the sorry Los Angeles slum of Compton." Whether or not Compton was a 'sorry Los Angeles slum' in 1990, there is a difference between a resident and a stranger from the outside describing it this way. Residents of Compton would surely characterize their community differently than a White, male magazine writer who lives in New York.

The artists themselves were given a chance to speak, but bias of a national publication ensured that the writer always got the last word. Eazy-E noted:

> 'Fuck the Police' was something people been
> wanting to say for years but they were too scared

to say it. The next album might be 'Fuck tha
FBI.'

Adler responded:

> Yes, having an attitude means it's always
> someone else's fault. The viler the message, the
> more fervent the assertion that honesty underlies
> it.

NWA had long positioned themselves as simply reflecting what
was really going on in the streets. Eazy-E was further quoted:

> We're like underground reporters. We just telling
> it like it is, we don't hold back.

Adler's follow-up:

> The fact is, rap grows out of a violent culture in
> which getting shot by a cop is a real fear. But
> music isn't reportage, and the way to deal with
> police brutality is not to glorify 'taking out a cop
> or two.'

Why was getting shot by a cop a real fear? The author failed to address the relationship between places like Compton and the police, and in the process missed the opportunity to connect police violence against young Black males to the creation of hip-hop. The opinion that music 'isn't reportage' may have been a previous generation's reality, but many hip-hop followers from around the world would argue that the exact opposite is true.

The article insisted on classifying hip-hop as an 'attitude' instead of a culture and a way of life. As he continued to define and discuss 'attitude' within a negative context, the author's personal disdain for hip-hop was obvious. His 'attitude'/hip-hop connection limited his view of the culture's ability to find intelligent solutions to their problems:

> But of course attitude resists any such attempts at
> intellectualizing. To call it visceral is to give it the
> benefit of the doubt. It has its origins in parts of
> the body even less mentionable.

You might not expect to necessarily see an article in a mainstream publication like *Newsweek* just come out and sing hip-hop's praises, but the magazine seemed determined to play hip-hop

music into a dead end, similar to what had happened with rock
and roll:

> The end of attitude is nihilism, which by
> definition leads nowhere. The culture of attitude
> is repulsive, but it's mostly empty of political
> content. As Gitlin puts it, 'There's always a
> population of kids looking to be bad. As soon as
> the establishment tells them what's bad this
> season, some of them are going to go off and do
> it.' And that's not good, but it's probably not a
> case for the FBI, either. If we learned one thing
> from the '60s, it's how *little* power rock and roll
> has to change the world.

In making the comparison to rock and roll, the author was right
on one level but wrong on another. Like rock and roll, hip-hop
was eventually co-opted by the corporate mainstream and in the
process lost much of the anti-establishment blood that made the
culture so popular to begin with. However, what separated
hip-hop from rock and roll is that hip-hop culture grew from
social conditions and turmoil involving race, gender, and class

that have yet to be resolved. These issues speak to people across ethnic and geographic boundaries, which accounts for hip-hop's global presence and influence today.

The follow up piece in *Newsweek*, written by David Gates, brought a somewhat different tone to the magazine's discussion of rap and hip-hop. Gates initially linked the development of hip-hop to the legacy of African-American musical influence on United States culture:

> You know that American popular music is unimaginable without such Black contributions as blues, jazz, and rock and roll. Maybe you even agree that rap is the next evolutionary step. And you recognize its social significance as a communiqué from the 'underclass' – or, less euphemistically, poor Blacks.

The fact that these different types of initially African-American musical genres had become absorbed by the mainstream was only part of the story. Another piece of the equation was that both the mainstream and hip-hop were beginning to engage in a flirtation that threatened to lead to something much more serious, with West Coast MC's leading the way in getting their

mack on, so to speak:

> For over a decade, the music [hip-hop] had
>
> remained largely unassimilated; crossover hits
>
> like 'Wild Thing' now seem to threaten its
>
> integrity.

While Tone-Loc and other rappers found success on the pop

charts, the level of skepticism in the hip-hop community toward

the mainstream and its motives rose alongside "Wild Thing's"

popularity. The question of hip-hop's integrity and how it was

potentially 'threatened' by increasing mainstream attention

began a passionate debate within the hip-hop community

around the notion of the MC as a 'sellout.' Tone –Loc's response

to the charge that he was shortchanging the essence of hip-hop in

order to appeal to the masses would become a familiar one as this

issue expanded. "I'm glad as hell," he argued back. "Anybody

saying something would love to be played on the pop charts."

Whether that is true or not is almost beside the point. As a

culture that was still essentially on the margins, many of

hip-hop's kids were naturally protective of the music and culture from 'outsiders' who all of a sudden wanted to be down. This is a point Gates seemed to understand:

> Rap's coded language, mystic monikers and Martian-sounding background noises *keep* outsiders outside – and create a sense of community among those in the know.

Also included in this article was a clear refute of Adler's statement that music isn't 'reportage.' Chuck D discussed what he knew about Too $hort from listening to his records:

> I know what kind of car he drives, I know the police give him a hard time, I know that there's *trees* in the area, you know what I'm sayin? It's like a CNN that Black kids never had.

Gates also offered a few insightful thoughts regarding some of the subtle social points being made by groups such as NWA, and even started to sound like an advocate:

> As their name (Niggas With Attitude) suggests, NWA caricatures ghetto misbehavior partly to rub White America's nose in its own racism...

rapping about smoking people is still *rapping*,

not smoking people. Whether such theatrics vent

your rage or aggravate it, they keep you on the

mic and off the streets. (One of rap's oft-repeated

themes is that rap itself is the safe and legal road

to riches.)

More than a few people got rich legally as hip-hop music continued to grow. However, the high profile murders of Tupac Shakur and the Notorious B.I.G. in the coming decade would raise doubts about the 'safe' part. But Gates displayed some awareness that gave his article a different flavor as he argued NWA's "Dopeman" "may be the strongest anti-drug rap ever recorded." He also noted that "Fuck tha Police" was a sentiment that "is hardly novel in the Black community," and that while songs like this are "nothing the kiddies should hear, they're not the end of civilization, either. That comes when the rhyming dictionaries and microphones are gone."

The mainstream splash created by the *Newsweek* cover stories brought a range of responses. Within a week, *The Los Angeles Times* ran a story that examined the fallout and included the *Newsweek* writers, David Gates and Jerry Adler, defending their work. Adler: "I really have no particular interest in rap. This was just an assignment. Our stories reflect opinions other than the writers themselves." Gates: "It was a long term project. We first contemplated doing it as long ago as last summer. I'd be very surprised if anyone sat down and said, 'OK. Let's trash rap.' That's not the way we work around here."

Whether anyone said "let's trash rap" was not the point. The so-called debate between Adler and Gates only reinforced how, as older, middle to upper class White men, far apart their lives and perspectives were from the musical lives and reality authored and directed by young, urban Black males. *Newsweek's* moral authoritarian and elitist tone was entirely predictable.

Speaking to *The Los Angeles Times*, Ice-T gave perhaps the most telling insight as to what was really behind the mainstream's simultaneous fascination and fear of hip-hop culture:

> The story is really a reflection of White parents
> who are freaked out that their kids are all into
> rap. More than half my fans are White kids now.
> That's what's scary about rap to the people

who're in power – it breaks down barriers

between the races.

Even before *Newsweek* jumped on the bandwagon, hip-hop had

been making inroads to the mainstream. And while some may

not have appreciated the tone of the articles, there is no doubt

that it raised the public profile of rap music and hip-hop culture.

The implication of the *Newsweek* story was that hip-hop was a

new, cool thing that started in the inner city and was now

beginning to conquer the suburbs. The fact that large numbers

of kids with money to spend were becoming infatuated with

hip-hop culture meant corporations would soon be there to

profit in any way they could.

Yeah I Got Some Last Words: Fuck All Y'all!

The end of the 1980s marked the beginning of the general public's struggle with the meanings and implications of hip-hop's growing emergence into mainstream culture. Meanwhile, the start of the 1990s brought an internal conflict within what had become known as 'the world's most dangerous group' that would raise hip-hop's profile even more. Following the recording of the D.O.C.'s *No One Can Do It Better*, Ice Cube left NWA to pursue a solo career amid accusations of financial mismanagement on the part of Eazy-E and the group's manager, Jerry Heller. The subsequent beef between Ice Cube and NWA would capture the attention of the hip-hop nation like none before.

Ice Cube was clearly the lyrical conscience of NWA, and his departure signaled the beginning of the end for the group whose album *Newsweek* rated "X" and commented that content wise it was equivalent to "' *The Godfather'* in gutter language." While some questioned his ability to carry an album on his own without the magic touch of Dr. Dre, there was a high profile production team that believed Ice Cube had what it took to be a successful solo artist. The Bomb Squad, consisting of Hank Shocklee, Keith Shocklee, Eric 'Vietnam' Sadler, and Chuck D, had achieved elite status in hip-hop as the architects of the Public Enemy sound. Instead of remaining in Los Angeles, Ice Cube traveled to Greene Street Studios in New York City to collaborate with an East Coast powerhouse and record his solo debut.

For those who had followed him closely since the "Dopeman" days, Ice Cube's first post-NWA album was among the most highly anticipated hip-hop records ever. *AmeriKKKa's Most Wanted,* brought a lot of aural muscle and attitude. The album's title, with its substitution of 'KKK' for 'c' in the spelling of America, claimed that the U.S. government's White supremacist ideology led to a shameful history of racial inequality, which was mirrored by the philosophy of the Ku Klux Klan. On the album itself, Ice Cube's sledgehammer delivery, both in content and style, took the rawness and politically flavored 'street knowledge' that was present in his earlier work and clarified it as an overt political and personal stance. After an intro track called "Better Off Dead," which bears audio witness to Ice Cube's execution in an electric chair, he was resurrected on the next song as "The Nigga Ya Love to Hate." Featuring a chorus of people screaming "Fuck you, Ice Cube!" he clearly relished his role as the 'villain.' However, the things that made people hate him were related to his aggressive questioning of social reality and issues that spoke to and affected young Black males and others, continuing to this day:

> *Kickin shit called street knowledge*
> *Why more niggas in the pen than in college?*
> *Because of that line I might be your cellmate*
> *That's from the nigga ya love to hate!*

Ice Cube seemed anxious to stretch himself out lyrically, stylistically, and thematically on his initial solo project and the hectic, funk based sounds provided by the Bomb Squad laid the perfect foundation. The subject matters addressed included sociopolitical commentary on the ghetto, the radio, the media, promiscuity, and women, that was sometimes serious and other times comical. "Once Upon a Time in the Projects" followed Ice

Cube along as he traveled to the home of a young lady he was

going to take out on a date. After witnessing drug use and sales,

teenage pregnancy, gang activity, and some badass Be-Be's kids,

Ice Cube's moral to the story was "Don't fuck with a bitch from

the projects." "Turn Off The Radio" was yet another example of

a West Coast MC criticizing radio for not playing hip-hop music:

> *Turn on the radio take a listen*
> *What you're missin personally I'm sick of the ass kissin*
> *What I'm kickin to you won't get in rotation*
> *Nowhere in the nation*
> *Program directors and DJs annoy me*
> *Cause I simply say fuck top 40*
> *And top 30 top 20 and top 10*
> *Until you put more hip-hop in*

"Endangered Species (Tales From The Darkside)" featured

Chuck D as guest rhymer about Black people as a group on the

verge of extinction. This jam coincided with a 1990 report

published in the *New England Journal of Medicine* that

suggested a Black man living in Harlem had less chance of

reaching his 65th birthday than a man living in Bangladesh. *Rap*

Attack author David Toop quoted then Secretary for Health and Human Services Louis Sullivan, who stated, "I do not think it is an exaggeration to suggest that the young Black American male is a species in danger."

One track that built on the previously discussed pimp legacy employed by Ice-T and Too $hort posed the question, "Who's the Mack?" It began with a description of a man named Sonny who gets girls as he rolls in a "fucked up Lincoln" with a leopard interior. The song then moved to an example of "that fool who wants to pump your gas, gives you a sad story and you give him cash." Ice Cube noted "He claims he wants to get something to eat," then suggested that the person's real motivation for asking for money was to buy crack. The next verse described a club scene with a man trying to convince a woman that they should leave together as he brags to her:

> *He could go buck wild*
> *For a girl like you and make it feel good*
> *You know it's drama but it sounds real good*
> Despite the woman's misgivings, she does in fact leave
>   with him, prompting Ice Cube to comment:
> *You grab his hand you leave and its over*
> *Cause the nigga ain't nothin but a rover*

You knew the game and you still ended up on your back
Now ask yourself who's the mack?

However, in this song the concept of macking extends well beyond the ghetto, women, and money, and into everyday life, as Ice Cube explained:

Mackin is a game that everybody's playin
And as long as you believe what they sayin
Consider them a M-A-C-K
And with no delay they are gonna get all of the play

The video for the song further pushed the idea of who qualified as a 'mack' into the mainstream by showing a picture of President George H.W. Bush and labeling him a "Presidential Mack."

Two interludes also contributed a critical flavor to the messages contained within *AmeriKKKa's Most Wanted*. One featured Ice Cube sending "a message to the Oreo cookie" (Blacks trying to fit in with Whites). "No matter how much you wanna switch," he warned, "here's what they think about you." What followed was the racist rant performed by actor John

Turturro in the Spike Lee joint, *Do the Right Thing*. Ice Cube closed the segment by muttering in disgust, "Think about it, fuckin sellout."

A second piece demonstrated the duality of existence within the crack era. The drug epidemic and the conflict that accompanied attempts by street level dealers to secure the corners with the highest traffic for sales gave rise to the phenomenon of the drive-by shooting. The skit entitled "The Drive-By" gave no real reason for what was about to happen other than one of the characters did not like the people they were about to target. Someone starts a car, and strangely, Young MC's "Bust a Move" was playing on the stereo. As the shooting, started one of the car's occupants yelled a warning that there were children in the area, while another replies, "Fuck that! Smoke them muthafuckas!"

A humorous element was added to *AmeriKKKa's Most Wanted* in the form of songs like "A Gangsta's Fairytale." Here, Ice Cube took several well-known fairytales and added a street twist:

> *So Jack and Jill ran up the hill to catch a little nap*
> *Dumb bitch gave him the clap*

Then he had to go see Dr. Bombay

Got a shot in the ass and he was on his way

To make some money why not

Down on Sesame Street the dope spot

There he saw the lady who lived in a shoe

Sold dope out the front by the back marijuana grew

For the man who was really important

Who lived down the street in an Air Jordan

In addition to all of the social commentary, Ice Cube certainly pushed misogynistic images on this record. Aside from his heavy use of the word 'bitch,' there was a song like "You Can't Fade Me," which tells the story of Ice Cube possibly being the one who impregnated a woman known on the block as "the neighborhood hussy:"

Cause all I saw was Ice Cube in court

Payin a gang of child support

Then I thought deep about givin up the money

What I need to do is kick the bitch in the tummy

Nah cause then I'll really get faded

That's murder one cause it was premeditated

However, misogyny did not go completely unchallenged on *AmeriKKKa's Most Wanted*. The song "It's A Man's World" introduced Yo-Yo, a woman who went toe to toe with Ice Cube and challenged him on his own album much in the way of Roxanne vs. UTFO and Too $hort's "Don't Fight the Feelin." Ice Cube began with his customary position:

> *Women they good for nothing nah maybe one thing*
> *To serve needs to my ding-a-ling*
> *I'm a man who loves the one night stand*
> *Cause after I do ya I never knew ya*

The line of thought that had been stated time and time again without a response was suddenly put in check by a woman who seemed ready for whatever Ice Cube could throw her way.

> *Yo-Yo's not a ho or a whore*
> *And if that's what you're here for*
> *Exit through the door there's more*
> *To see of me but you're blind so*
> *Women like me'll fade brothas in the 9-0*

The concept of this being 'a man's world' plays both ways, from hip-hop culture to society in general. There was plenty of back and forth with Yo-Yo's point of view being, "I'm trying to say all women are superior over men." As Yo-Yo deftly rhymes her counterpoints to Ice Cube's male chauvinistic, ego-driven verses, she eventually earns MC props.

> **Yo-Yo:** *Yeah, I can see you got it good*
> **Ice Cube:** *Oh that I know*
> **Yo-Yo:** *But you see you're not better than Yo-Yo*
> *the brand new intelligent Black lady*
> **Ice Cube:** *You're kinda dope but you still can't fade me*
> **Yo-Yo:** *So what up then?*
> **Ice Cube:** *Girl what you tryin to do?*
> **Yo-Yo:** *To prove a Black woman like me can bring the*
> *funk through*
> **Ice Cube:** *This is a man's world thank you very much*
> **Yo-Yo:** *But it wouldn't be a damn thing without a*
> *woman's touch*

In the end, perhaps the most surprising thing about *AmeriKKKa's Most Wanted* was what was not present on the album. Given the perceived animosity resulting from Ice Cube's departure from NWA, as well as the natural tendencies for people to have hard feelings over issues involving money, the natural assumption was that Ice Cube would use *AmeriKKKa's Most Wanted* as a platform to publicly address the members of his former group. This was not the case. Try as you might, you will not find a single reference to NWA, Eazy-E, Dr. Dre, MC Ren, DJ Yella, or even Jerry Heller, on the entire album. This, combined with his decision to go to New York to record *AmeriKKKa's Most Wanted*, appeared to be an attempt by Ice Cube to make a clean break from his former group and leave the drama associated with his decision to go solo, as well as the reasons behind that choice, in the past. If Ice Cube was the one trying to be mature about the situation and just let it be, he would quickly find out that the remaining members of NWA had no intention of returning the favor.

I Pack a Real Small Gat in My Purse

Yo-Yo's association with Ice Cube positioned her to be a pioneer as the first big name, solo female MC from the West Coast. On her debut album, *Make Way For The Motherlode*, Yo-Yo continued to project the strong, independent voice she displayed on "It's A Man's World." Similar to Ice Cube, Yo-Yo also had an organization behind her as she embarked on her solo career. The Intelligent Black Women's Conference, or I.B.W.C., was Yo-Yo's equivalent to Ice Cube's Lench Mob.

The male dominated landscape of rap music in general, and the West Coast in particular, was always in need of the other half of humanity's perspective, one that could only be provided by a female MC. "Girl Don't Be No Fool" challenged women who do not hold their men to any kind of standards. The intro asked:

*Due to the fact you spend sleepless nights in the
  company of no one*

Holding on to a pillow waiting for a phone call

From your man saying he'll be late again

*The question is: Is he out there working to make himself
  a better brother?*

After dedicating the song to Ice Cube and calling him a dog,

Yo-Yo proceeded:

Girl you're gettin played like a sucker

I know it's none of my business

But what the hell is this

Lettin a guy get the best of you

But here we go Yo-Yo is to the rescue

Cause you see I'm more than a softie

I'm here to open your eyes so you can smell the coffee

Guys ain't nothin but dirt and they'll flirt with anything

Dressed in a mini-skirt you know your man's cheatin

While you're sleepin he's leavin your side to start creepin

But you pretend like you don't see the man

I heard love is blind but damn

*You can read it in Braille and still tell without a bright
  light*

That somethin ain't right you know that he's sleepin

with

This girl and that girl

I even saw your man with a fat girl

But you know two can play at that game

He's got another on the side do the same

Bein in love is cool (true) but I'ma tell you like this

Girl don't be no fool

While it is not possible to always completely control the behavior of any individual, people do have the ability to set limits and boundaries with regard to what they will tolerate from another person. Yo-Yo's overall theme of women empowering themselves by refusing to buy into the emerging male hip-hop image of the 'player' was reminiscent of an East Coast female rapper like MC Lyte. Meanwhile, the message in "Girl Don't Be No Fool" was similar to the one found in the song "Tramp" by Salt-N-Pepa.

The most recognizable song from *Make Way For The Mother Lode* was "You Can't Play With My Yo-Yo," a semi-duet with Ice Cube that harmonized the track with Yo-Yo's varied subject matters and styles of delivery:

My name is Yo-Yo I'm not a ho no

I like to flow so swift it's got to be a gift so yo
Let the beat lift as I rip and rhyme
And rap and slap all the girls who can't adapt
To the fact I get the 8-ball often
The earrings I wear are called dolphins
Check the booty yo its kinda soft and
If you touch it you livin in a coffin
I'm in the 90s your still in the 80s right
I rock the mic they say I'm not lady like
But I'm a lady who will pull a stunt though

Yo-Yo went from this self-definition that simultaneously established her womanhood and skill as an MC to the 'other' woman who contributed to the misery of women like those in "Girl Don't Be No Fool:"

I'll steal yo man that's if he is an hunk and
He'll call me baby yo or even pumpkin
Or maybe buttercup or even Ms. Yo
We had dinner and now we drinkin Cisco
Hit the slow jams its gettin cozy
You're home alone so now you gettin nosy
You're kinda young so of course you had to call my place
Hang up in my face it's a sad case

Of who ya man's givin the dollars

What yup I'm puttin lipstick on his collar

At home he's gotta listen to ya holla

But he'll slap ya and sock ya

So why bother?

After Ice Cube exclaimed, "Yo-Yo, the brand new intelligent Black lady, stompin to the 90s!" between verses, Yo-Yo concluded:

Similar to a metaphor make someone to yell encore

Keep it at a limit to where they're yelling more more

I am very versatile changin my ways to different styles

Knowledge is the key experience formed my background

Label me as a woman and sometimes I feel inferior

Fallin back over the sands of time makes no man
  superior

Should we dare to take a stand and dis back all the

Men who know no more but slut slang

And thinks with his ding-a-ling

I think its time that we defeat

By standin on our on two feet

If we wanna live with justice and harmony

How many more rounds must I go

In order to let my people know
Times were hard things have changed

Yo-Yo's willingness to take it and ability to dish it out with the likes of Ice Cube was significant. Ice Cube's support and respect certainly helped Yo-Yo get her big break, but her unmistakably feminist stance and skillful flow solidified her status as a strong, independent voice in West Coast hip-hop.

If We Die We Still Gonna be Some Dead Niggaz

The departure of Ice Cube from NWA left a lyrical void that the group would have to fill. Given the quality of MC that Ice Cube had developed into, many thought that NWA would take a step back lyrically. However between MC Ren, Dr. Dre, Eazy-E, the D.O.C., who now functioned as a full time ghostwriter, and Dr. Dre's increasingly complex yet subtle production techniques, the formula was still in place for the 'world's most dangerous group' to conquer the mainstream.

NWA's first post-Ice Cube release was *100 Miles And Runnin,* and it reflected a couple of trends that occurred within this period of West Coast hip-hop music. One was that *100 Miles And Runnin* was an EP release: Five tracks, four new songs. The other was the illustrated cover. Album covers by Too $hort (*Short Dog's in the House*), 415 (*4-1-Fivin*), Snoop Doggy Dogg

(*Doggystyle*), the Pharcyde (*Bizarre Ride II The Pharcyde*) and Del Tha Funkee Homosapien (*I Wish My Brother George Was Here*), among others, were all examples of the West Coast's visual artistic representation of hip-hop.

The cover and concept of *100 Miles And Runnin* was the young urban Black male always on the move while attempting to navigate the pitfalls of his existence. Dressed in blue shirts, pants, and beanie caps, Eazy-E, Dr. Dre, Yella, and MC Ren were shown running through an alley away from a massive fireball. Above the fire and the outline of skyscrapers in the background was a helicopter in hot pursuit.

NWA's stance on *100 Miles And Runnin*, at least to a certain extent, continued the challenge to the social status quo that had been so firmly established on *Straight Outta Compton*. As a song, "100 Miles And Runnin" reiterated racist law enforcement tactics. MC Ren:

> *Chances are usually not good*
> *Cause I'm frisked with my hands on a hot hood*
> *And getting jacked by the you know who*
> *When in a black and white the capacity is two*
> *I didn't stutter when I said 'Fuck Tha Police'*

> *Cause it's hard for a nigga to get peace*
> *Now it's broken and can't be fixed*
> *Cause police and little Black niggaz don't mix*

Dr. Dre, in a high-pitched, yell-like delivery, took time to defend his position against critics suggesting he was a negative influence on the youth:

> *Confused yo but Dre's a nigga with nothing to lose*
> *One of the few that's been abused and accused*
> *Of the crime of poisoning young minds*
> *But you don't know shit till you been in my shoes*

Here again is a group arguing back and forth on the issue of content and the level of influence it carries with youth within the music itself, signifying self-awareness of their cultural influence and admitting they were thinking things through along with the listener. There were also several references to the FBI, the group still milking the fact that they had gotten the attention of the federal government.

In light of Ice Cube's decision not to mention his old group a single time on his entire debut solo album, there were public questions about what NWA would do. On *100 Miles And Runnin* the only attention given to Ice Cube was a brief reference by Dr. Dre:

> *Started with five but yo one couldn't take it*
> *So now there's four cause the fifth couldn't make it*

The kid glove treatment was somewhat puzzling. It appeared from the outside that Ice Cube's departure from the group should have generated more animosity than this. However, the early whimper that marked the beginning of the Ice Cube-NWA beef would be made up for by the roar toward the end.

The raunchier side of West Coast hip-hop tradition established by the likes of Ice-T and Too $hort was carried on by NWA with the song "Just Don't Bite It." The title was a reference to a woman who uses her teeth while performing oral sex, and the beginning of the track consisted of discussion and sounds of Eazy-E receiving a blowjob. After an unfortunate biting episode, a very White sounding voice came in and said, "Well, I had that same problem, until my bitch went out and bought NWA's new book entitled 'The Art of Sucking Dick.'" Cartoon-like representations such as this would eventually strip

NWA of its socially conscious credibility. It also fed into the growing voice of protest against the misogynistic element of West Coast hip-hop music. Still, as was becoming the case with Dr. Dre every single time, the music was simply undeniable. The beat to "Just Don't Bite It" had a hypnotic, flute sounding sample over a banging drum and snaking bassline that made it impossible to keep your head still.

NWA's willingness to push the buttons of the mainstream's conservative side continued with the song "Sa Prize (Part 2)." This was essentially a remake of "Fuck Tha Police" which had gotten the FBI's attention in the first place. It began with a phone call taken in a police station by a 'Sgt. Kickass,' in which an informant advised Kickass about a deal that was going down. After Kickass got off the phone, there was the following exchange with his partner:

> "Hey I don't feel good about this one, man"
> "Hey we've been doin this for fuckin ten years, and we haven't been caught yet."
> "Yeah I just don't know about this one."
> "Hey just shut the fuck up and pass me a doughnut!"

The informant then called Dr. Dre and told him what time the police would be showing up. Cut to the two officers outside about to start their raid, and one said to another:

"Sarge said this was gonna be pretty easy."
"Yeah, but never underestimate those fuckin niggers!"

After a count of 3, the officers burst into a room and are massacred by NWA in a hail of gunfire sound effects.

The song also questioned the role that some Black police officers played in oppressing Black neighborhoods after the massive flow of drugs were dumped into the community:

And yo the Black police the house niggas
They gave you a muthafuckin gun so I guess ya figure
Ya made out good to go but ya didn't know
They would stick your Black ass in the ghetto yo
To kill another nigga catch him with crack in fact
Freebase they put in the neighborhood in the first place

This perspective was reinforced by testimonials in between verses. Dr. Dre: "Muthafuckas that come from high crime areas view the police as a threat, and that's some shit you better not

forget." Eazy-E: "See, I got this problem. A big problem. Cops
don't like me, so I don't like muthafuckin cops!" Another
unidentified man stated, "Police brutality is common in my
neighborhood. That's why I hate them muthafuckas."

The most controversial piece of this song may have been a
skit placed in between Eazy-E and MC Ren's verses:

> *Officer: Get outta the fuckin car!*
>
> *Woman: Wait goddam a minute, what the hell did I do?*
>
> *Officer: Hey! Just shut the fuck up Black bitch and get
> outta the fuckin car!*
>
> *Woman: Wait a minute you ain't gotta be me pullin by
> my muthafuckin hair!*
>
> *Bystander: Hey yo why you gotta treat a sista so damn
> bad?*
>
> *Woman: Let go of my muthafuckin hair!*
>
> *Officer: Hey just step the fuck back! Shut up!*
>
> *Woman: Get your muthafuckin hands offa me!*
>
> *Officer: Calm down, clam down. Now listen, we're
> gonna go around this corner and you're gonna suck
> me and my partner's dicks, or you're gonna be one
> Black, dead, nigger bitch!*

Depending on your life experience, this was either a completely believable scenario, or a gross exaggeration that was unfair to the police.

The track "Kamurshol" was basically an advertisement for NWA's upcoming album as MC Ren repeatedly stated "The name of the new album is..." On vinyl, you could move the record backwards to hear the name of what would be NWA's final album of new music.

I'm Spunky I Like My Oatmeal Lumpy

As the 1990s began, West Coast hip-hop music continued to gain

widespread notoriety. Much of this attention was rooted in the

content of hardcore artists such as NWA, Ice-T, Too $hort, and

others. However, as the hip-hop music scene in the region

expanded, diverse MCs with various styles began to assert

themselves. Digital Underground was a prime example. Far from

the hardcore style expressed by more controversial rappers,

Digital Underground offered a sort of hip-hop comic relief that

provided an escape from the more serious matters addressed in

what had become known as 'gangsta' rap. After releasing a

couple of 12-inch singles on Macola Records, the group put out

their first album, *Sex Packets*. The primary microphone

personalities that appeared on *Sex Packets* were Money B, Shock

G, and Humpty Hump. Humpty Hump was actually the

clownish alter ego of Shock G, with Humpty wearing those

glasses with the big plastic nose and some sort of hat. The first single, "Doowutchyalike," was a definite feel good party-type jam that freely sampled New York rapper Doug E. Fresh's line "I see guys and girls dancing" from his song "Keep Risin To The Top:"

> Now just act a fool its okay if you drool
> Cuz everybody's gonna strip and jump in the pool
> And do what we like

Complete with a piano solo, "Doowutchyalike" was a unique among the sounds and subject matter that had come to dominate the West Coast hip-hop scene. Digital Underground worked to position themselves as odd, fun-loving, good timing cats, part of a continuum with the eclectic reputation of their home, the Bay Area.

The concept behind the name *Sex Packets* was this: Fictional, packaged, oral hallucinogenics purchased on the street that enabled you to engage in imaginary sex acts with various women of your choice. The song "Sex Packets" offered an explanation:

> It's like a pill you can either chew it up
> Or like an Alka-Seltzer dissolve it in a cup

And get this see the girl on the cover?

You black out and she becomes your lover

Shock G, Money B, and Humpty Hump were not shy about discussing their sex life in a non-explicit manner. This method offered a safer alternative to the rawness of other hip-hop artists while still providing a level of naughtiness that ever-increasing mainstream audiences could dance to. The skit "Gutfest '89" and the song "Freaks of the Industry" combined with the concept of "Sex Packets" to inform the Digital Underground brand of hip-hop.

The tracks produced by Digital Underground were firmly grounded in the emerging funk influence that had begun to work its way into the evolving hip-hop production sounds of the period. "Rhymin On The Funk," "The Danger Zone," and "Packet Man," all displayed elements of the legacy that funk masters such as George Clinton, Bootsy Collins, and Parliament Funkadelic left for hip-hop to discover. Digital Underground's greatest hip-hop impact was the song that essentially stood as Humpty Hump's theme, "The Humpty Dance."

"The Humpty Dance" was Humpty Hump's solo debut,

and even though the character had made an appearance on the song and video "Doowutchyalike," "The Humpty Dance" took hip-hop by storm for a couple of reasons. First and foremost was the song's bassline. It had an incredibly saucy, roller coaster-like sound that was nearly impossible to forget. Nothing quite like it had been heard before, the unique bassline sample in "The Humpty Dance" has yet to be replicated. Funky and original, it set a standard not only for hip-hop production on the West Coast, but worldwide as well. Lyrically, Humpty Hump used the song as a platform to introduce himself. He was silly, crazy, self-deprecating, at times non-rhyming, and always down for the kick:

> *Alright stop what you're doin cause I'm about to ruin*
> *The image and the style that you're used to*
> *I look funny but yo I'm makin money see*
> *So yo world I hope you're ready for me*
> *Now gather round I'm the new fool in town*
> *And my sound is laid down by the Underground*
> *I'll drink a bottle of Hennessey you got on your shelf*
> *So just let me introduce myself*

Calling himself a fool and making fun of his own appearance

brought a level of comic humility that was fresh, yet still allowed Humpty Hump to cast himself as the life of the party and a lover of fly girls:

> *Oh yes ladies I'm really bein sincere*
> *Cause in a 69 my Humpty nose'll tickle you rear*
> *My nose is big uh-uh I'm not ashamed*
> *Big like a pickle I'm still getting paid*
> *I get laid by the ladies you know I'm in charge*
> *Both how I'm livin and my nose is large*

The second piece of "The Humpty Dance's" popularity lay in the fact that it was a new dance. Hip-hop has always produced songs that have popularized new dance steps. Humpty Hump went so far as to give instructions for his dance, including a perceived shot at a fellow Bay Area MC:

> *First I limp to the side like my legs was broken*
> *Shakin and twitchin kinda like I was smokin*
> *Crazy wack funky*
> *People say you look like MC Hammer on crack Humpty*
> *That's alright cause my body's in motion*
> *It's supposed to look like a fit or a convulsion*

Anyone can play this game

This is my dance y'all Humpty Hump's my name

The reference to MC Hammer was viewed by many as a dis, most likely because dissing Hammer was becoming a fashionable thing to do within hip-hop. Besides that, the dance itself was relatively easy to do and the video even featured, among others, a young Tupac Shakur in the background.

Have You Ever Seen a Vogue Tire Smoke?

While the Bay Area was producing mainstream friendly hip-hop like Digital Underground and MC Hammer, it was also the source of significant underground material. Chunk, the Funk Lab All-Stars, Conscious Daughters, and Dangerous Dame were among those active in the Bay Area underground scene. RBL Posse's song "Don't Give Me No Bammer" introduced a new term for weak marijuana that could be used to describe just about anything that was corny. Totally Insane's album cover for *Direct From The Backstreet* was a photo of the group literally standing on a backstreet in East Palo Alto. The music had a backstreet feel as well, and this was part of the appeal. The opportunity for kids like these to tell their story and represent their community from their perspective was one thing that always made hip-hop unique.

Spice 1's song "187 Proof" used the names of different

liquors to tell a clever story. The introduction ensured everyone
knew where Spice-1 was from:

> *Coolin on the corner with the cellular phone*
> *You can tell that the East Bay was his home*
> *More mail than the rest of the pushers*
> *Cuz he's got a tech-nine in the bushes*
> *And that's how the shit was handled*
> *First name Jack last name Daniels*
> *Had two boys named E and J*
> *E had the nine and J the AK*
> *Clocked on a street called Hennessey*
> *Robs with a motherfucker named Old E*
> *E had a bitch and her name was Gin*
> *Had a nigga named Juice doin time in the pen*
> *You could tell that Gin was a bitch though*
> *Cuz she was fuckin some nigga named Cisco*
> *E and J knew tonight they'd come*
> *With two fat niggas named Bacardi and Rum*

415 in particular pushed underground hip-hop's growth. Up
until the early 1990s, 415 was the area code that Oakland shared
with San Francisco. The area code for the East Bay has since been
changed to 510, but at the time it was not uncommon for

hip-hop kids to identify themselves by these geographically based digits. For example, Snoop Doggy Dogg, Warren G, and Nate Dogg would note that in their early days they were collectively known as the group 213, the area code for downtown Los Angeles and Long Beach.

415 displayed a rougher edge to their brand of hip-hop that fell more along the lines of the 'gangsta' rap movement that was coming from Los Angeles. *4-1-Fivin* told the increasingly familiar stories that surrounded life in urban communities affected by unemployment, drug use and sales, and poverty. With songs like "Snitches & Bitches," "Ruthless is Reality," and "Court in the Street," the violence and misery that was coming through on evening newscasts was captured on wax from a grassroots point of view.

While the darker side of inner-city life was certainly represented on *4-1-Fivin*, a more celebratory aspect was also present. In the song "415," Richie Rich asked, "Have you ever seen a Vogue tire smoke?" Unpacking this question provides perspective about West Coast hip-hop culture's relationship to what was commonly known as the 'side show.'

Vogues are high-end tires that were consistently

referenced in rhyme and photos by West Coast MCs in particular. They are another aspect of the pimp culture that found its way into hip-hop, this time regarding automobiles, as Vogues were frequently found on Cadillacs. The previously discussed Too $hort album cover for *Born to Mack* is an illustration of this connection.

Many listeners might want to ask Rich: Why would the Vogue tire be smoking? Perhaps anticipating this, the answer can be found in 415's song "Side Show." California's famous abundance of sunshine allows for year round outdoor gatherings, and in this case, young people socialize for a few hours around miniature car shows and street racing. Richie Rich laid out the guidelines for the event:

> *Now listen this is the code to the show*
> *For the people out there who just don't know*
> *If your shit is hella clean then bring it*
> *If it's high performance then swing it*
> *If it's a motorcycle then you better serve it*
> *And if you get a ticket you better deserve it*
> *As long as you can say man I let em know*
> *Then peace you did it at the side show*

Side shows, sometimes planned, sometimes spontaneous, could occur at parks, on city streets, or in parking lots, among other places. They are constantly subject to police interference given that cars are being driven at high speeds, there may be alcohol present, and there are lots of young people.

One of the most symbolic images that indicated the transition West Coast hip-hop music was making in the early 1990s was the *4-1-Fivin* album cover. The illustrated picture was of four individuals dressed in black, three of whom were carrying automatic weapons. The three men with the guns are identified by lettering on their clothes as the primary members of the group, D-Loc, RR (Richie Rich), and DJ D (DJ Daryl). All four are wearing Oakland A's baseball caps and have bandanas over their faces. The fourth person is unloading a briefcase filled with money, all of which gives the clear impression that these people just finished carrying out a robbery. This scene would appear to fit nicely the reputation that underground West Coast hip-hop had gained in the mainstream of glorifying violence, guns, and materialism. However, the left side of this picture requires further examination and interpretation.

Nearly one quarter of the *4-1-Fivin* album cover is

devoted to a vertical bar with the colors red, black, and green. These colors were significant during this period because they tied into the Black power/nationalist movement that was being pushed by 'conscious' and political MCs, mostly on the East Coast. Groups such as X Clan, Public Enemy, and Brand Nubian were all known for making references to these colors while discussing economic issues and political, grassroots community empowerment. The fact that a group like 415 tied themselves to this larger, 'conscious' movement while employing illegal survival methods illustrated the continuing contradictions that are present in the lives of many disenfranchised people even today. The album cover implied a righteousness as justifiable action toward whatever went down as an antidote to a racist, capitalist society. The contrast of ideals represented by the red, the black, and the green versus the 'robbery' mindset shown in the rest of the picture speaks to the daily hardships that engulf many residents of impoverished communities, and is crucial to understanding the social, political, and economic dynamics at work in the United States then and now.

All Hail to Those Who Believe in Rhyme

While *No One Can Do It Better* certainly displayed the skills of
the NWA production team, it also provided a foundation on
which to build. The LA hip-hop scene cultivated a seemingly
endless stream of local MC talent, elevating artists both
associated with and independent of NWA. One project attached
to NWA was the album *Livin Like Hustlers* by the group Above
The Law. Cold 187um and KM.G, the group's vocalists, reflected
some of the topical influence of their mentors. Casting
themselves as supreme hustlers, the track "Murder Rap" featured
the high-pitched synthesized sound that was swiftly becoming a
trademark production sound of Dr. Dre. Other song titles like
"Livin Like Hustlers," "Ballin'," "Another Execution," and
"Menace to Society," correctly suggested a good amount of
violence, drugs and sex.

While there were no direct lyrical shots taken at Cube on

Livin Like Hustlers, it was impossible not to notice his absence on the "The Last Song," where NWA's new trademark, guest MCing on the final track of an artist they were producing, was heard. Listening to MC Ren, Dr. Dre, and Eazy-E rhyme without Ice Cube's piercing vocals coming in somewhere was a strange void of sound.

Other groups emerging from Compton included the group Compton's Most Wanted, who while not having any direct ties to NWA technically, their name made clear the influence NWA had making Compton a major locale on the hip-hop map. Thematically, CMW's album, *It's a Compton Thang*, touched on many of the scenarios and themes that would eventually become cliché in discussions of 'gangsta' rap with songs like "One Time Gaffled Em Up," "Duck Sick," and "It's A Compton Thang." With jheri curls and ball caps, they fit the image of the West Coast 'gangsta' rapper. The presence of a standout lyrical talent in MC Eiht enabled CMW to further define and refine the sound of West Coast, and more specifically, Los Angeles hip-hop.

Although labeled with a Parental Advisory sticker, the King Tee album, *At Your Own Risk*, displayed a commercial sensibility alongside the emerging Compton 'hardcore' aesthetic. By the time this album dropped, King Tee was a recognized veteran of the Los Angeles hip-hop scene and one of the pioneers of this new and exciting style of music. In 1989 his hit singles, "Act A Fool," which was reminiscent of "6 'N Tha Morning" both in its sound and stories of life in the streets, and "Bass," helped establish and extend his influence within the rap mainstream both on the West Coast and nationally. *At Your Own Risk* contained the radio friendly "Diss You" and "Ruff Rhyme (Back Again)," which was also a music video. "Played Like a Piano" featured Ice Cube, who boasted:

> *So bust a cap or swing and die*
> *Fuck Yul Brenner it's still the King and I*

WC was another consistent presence throughout LA hip-hop history, originally as part of the '80s group Low Profile, which included DJ Alladin, and later resurfacing as WC and the Maad Circle. The latter's album, *Ain't A Damn Thing Changed* featured the hit single "Ghetto Serenade."

Meanwhile, Delicious Vinyl's expanding list of artists included Def Jef. Def Jef was regarded by some as an 'alternative' rapper because of his overtly sociopolitical content minus the 'gangsta-ism.' His style was most often compared to the De La Soul/Jungle Brothers/Native Tongue vibe. Def Jef's first album, *Just A Poet With Soul*, was a diverse record with songs like "Droppin Rhymes On Drums," with Etta James, "Black To The Future," and the radio and video friendly "Give It Here."

Yo We're Not Here to Preach Because We're Not Ministers

As a result of the national attention that West Coast hip-hop was receiving, the conditions of life in places like Compton also received media scrutiny, generating discussion and argument over the relationship between hip-hop music and economic and/or political realities. Compton became a metaphor for all those left behind by the American dream, the music stood up to the urban decay, unemployment, drugs, and said, We can recreate ourselves and in the process change our world. The furor surrounding West Coast hip-hop often reflected the Compton music initiative. These socio-political-artistic circumstances combined with the involvement of community activists helped create the West Coast All-Stars.

The West Coast All-Stars was similar to a project undertaken by KRS-One of Boogie Down Productions the year before. BDP, from the South Bronx, was one of the first high profile hip-hop artists to confront the connection between violence in their music and real life. The cover of their 1986 debut album, *Criminal Minded*, showed a heavily armed KRS-One and DJ Scott La Rock. The next year Scott La Rock was shot and killed on a street in New York City. Partially in response to these events, KRS-One first released the song "Stop The Violence," which appeared on the 1988 BDP album, *By All Means Necessary*, and later formed the Stop the Violence Movement. In 1989 the Stop The Violence Movement released "Self-Destruction," a "We Are the World" conscious raising collaboration that featured many of the biggest names in East Coast hip-hop: KRS- One, Kool Moe Dee, MC Lyte, Stetsasonic, D-Nice, Doug E. Fresh, Just Ice, Heavy D, and Public Enemy's Chuck D and Flavor Flav.

Mike Conception, a former Los Angeles gang member turned community activist, organized the West Coast All-Stars. Essentially the California equivalent to the Stop the Violence Movement, the All-Stars included just about every big name hip-hop artist from the Bay Area and Southern California, from the mainstream friendly to the hardcore. The result was the song "We're All in the Same Gang." Among the participants were

King Tee, Def Jef, Tone-Loc, Above the Law, Ice-T, N.W.A, JJ Fad, Young MC, Digital Underground, MC Hammer, and Eazy-E.

Inevitably, given the reputation of some of the MCs who rapped on "We're All in the Same Gang," questions arose regarding the credibility of the project. Take Eazy-E's verse:

> *I'm not tryin to tell you what to do*
> *You have your own freedom of choice who to listen to*
> *You know good from bad fair from foul right from*
>   *wrong*
> *Now your mother's singin that sad song*
> *My baby ain't never hurt nobody*
> *But he still got smoked at Be-Be's party*
> *But you're not the first or the last*
> *You're nothing but a short story from the past*
> *You're dead now not number one but a zero*
> *Take notes from Eazy-E the violent hero*

For critics of Eazy-E and NWA, spitting this verse on a song like "We're All in the Same Gang," then return to producing the violent content that made him and NWA famous, was the height of hypocrisy. Many critics of "We're All in the Same Gang" applied a strict either/or standard to artists and their messages, in effect asking, "How can this person who has said these 'negative' things have any credibility when trying to say something 'positive?'" This ultimately led to the question of whether a project like the West Coast All-Stars was of any redeeming value. Yet given the inner city conditions, flavored by the intersection of poverty, crime, and crack, faced by young African-American males of the time, it would be hard to argue against the importance of any and all efforts to find solutions.

Bust It!

As MC Hammer approached the release of his second major label album, he was poised to become the premier performer in hip-hop. Hammer possibly benefited more than any hip-hop artist from the rising popularity of music videos. Whereas music had been primarily an audio experience in the past, there was now a heavy visual element. An artist that may or may not have been able to stand solely on the quality of his or her music alone could now compensate by putting on a great performance in a video.

Please Hammer, Don't Hurt 'Em was the strongest effort yet to marry hip-hop and the mainstream. Building on the success of the MC as mega-performer, MC Hammer moved well beyond the traditional b-boy approach he had embraced on *Let's Get It Started.* Musically the album was loaded with radio and mainstream friendly material, and image-wise Hammer had apparently decided to leave the Troop sweat suits in the closet.

The biggest single from *Please Hammer, Don't Hurt 'Em,* without question, was "U Can't Touch This." It took the formula of sampling a well-known song and pairing it with an eye catching video propelling hip-hop culture into homes where it had never been seen before. The song sampled Rick James' 1981 hit "Superfreak" so extensively that James was given credit as a co-author. MC Hammer laced this familiar beat with his trademark, relatively simple delivery:

> *My my my my music hits me so hard*
> *Makes me say oh my Lord*
> *Thank you for blessin me*
> *With a mind to rhyme and too hype beat*
> *It feels good when you know you're down*
> *A super dope home boy from the Oak-town*
> *And I'm known as such*
> *And this is the beat you can't touch*

While 'being down' and 'super dope homeboy' were still markers of hip-hop language, the overall sense within hip-hop seemed to be that MC Hammer was most interested in appealing to a mainstream that still looked at the culture with somewhat of a crooked eye. Instead of viewing rappers such as Hammer and Young MC as necessary bridges between hip-hop and the mainstream that would enable future hip-hop artists everywhere to reap the financial benefits, they were widely characterized as 'sellouts,' often for nothing more than their lack of controversial material. A 1990 article in *Time* magazine noted:

> Critics have savaged rap for everything from violence to racism to sexism, but all these elements have been blended out of Hammer's material. Hardcore rappers who fall for the Hammer are hard to find. Public Enemy's Chuck D is strongly in his corner, but Hammer has been called out by the rap press ("cheesy, pop-oriented production") and torched by fellow rappers from Digital Underground to MC Serch and 3rd Bass, who kept the heat high in the pointedly titled "Gas Face." Hammer handles such criticism with equanimity. 'Rather than cross over [into the pop market], let's just say that I expanded,' he suggests. 'My music caught on because the people are ready for it.'

Hammer's critics said he lacked creativity and originality, citing his replication of commercial, non-threatening samples numerous times on *Please Hammer Don't Hurt 'Em*. In addition to "U Can't Touch This" there was "Have You Seen Her," based on a remake of the Chi-Lites hit, the self-explanatory "Pray," which sampled Prince's "When Doves Cry," "Help the Children," its chorus rooted in Marvin Gaye's "Mercy Mercy Me (The Ecology)," and to a lesser extent "Yo!! Sweetness," which appeared conceptually similar to Barry White's "Your Sweetness is My Weakness."

Stylistically, MC Hammer exited what most considered the standard dress code within hip-hop culture. But the short, sparkly jackets with no shirt underneath and the oversized 'diaper' pants actually recalled an earlier time in hip-hop when artists dressed up to go on stage. Groups like Grand Master Flash and the Furious Five would routinely perform in leather jackets, tight pants with tassels, shirts with fur collars, gloves, studded belts, and boots. The beginning of the end for this early hip-hop fashion aesthetic was the mid-1980s when Run-DMC went on stage in the Adidas shoes and Lee jeans they had worn coming to the show. Street became stage.

Regardless of the criticism, "U Can't Touch This" would win 1991 Grammy awards for Best R & B Song and Best Solo Rap Performance. The award for Best R & B Song was apparent validation for those who argued that what Hammer was doing was not hip-hop at all, but pop with an R & B twist. In any case, Hammer was on a roll. He told *Time* magazine:

> Currently we're on a 60-city tour, selling out everywhere, including Salt Lake City in Mormon country. *Please Hammer Don't Hurt Em* is one of the few albums since *Thriller* to hold the No. 1 in Billboard – No. 1 pop, No. 1 Black album at the same time. It's the biggest selling album of this year, bar any – rock n' roll, pop, blues, toe tappin, whatever it is. We went out and sold 5 million albums in four months. Twelve weeks at No. 1 on the R & B charts, nine weeks at No. 1 on the pop side – ahead of New Kids on the Block and Madonna.

With 32 performers on stage for Hammer's live show, the same article pointed out that, "he has dumped the more or less standard rap choreography (strut, turn, grab crotch, strut) in favor of a stops-out, Paula Abdul kind of abandon."

Please Hammer Don't Hurt 'Em eventually became the biggest selling rap album ever, seventeen million-plus copies sold. This meant that more and more new faces from new places were being exposed to rap music. Although there was debate within hip-hop culture as to whether MC Hammer was still hip-hop or not, there could be no debating that he had become an entry point for millions of people as they made their way into hip-hop culture. Proving the mainstream's recognition of this was Pepsi's sponsorship deal with Hammer, as reported in the newsletter *Beverage World*:

> To kick off the partnership, Pepsi broadcast a commercial that featured clips from the "U Can't Touch This" video during September's MTV Video Music Awards. Hammer was apparently so pleased with the agreement that he brought a can of the sponsor's product to the podium when he accepted a statue for Best Dance Video.

Cause I'm Sittin in History Learnin Bout a Sucka Who Didn't Give a Fuck About Me

Even though Ice Cube didn't discuss his rupture with NWA on *AmeriKKKa's Most Wanted,* the shots against him that came from *100 Miles and Runnin* weren't surprising. As hard as NWA was supposed to be, how could they have a member leave over money, one of rap music's greatest subject matters, and not dis him? What would be Ice Cube's response? Given his recognized lyrical superiority, many expected Ice Cube to go after his former group something fierce. However, on Ice Cube's own EP, *Kill at Will,* the continued pursuit of 'street knowledge' seemed to take precedence over any notions of all out lyrical warfare with NWA.

Symbolically, the *Kill at Will* cover shows a still jheri curled Ice Cube handing a gun, butt first, over to the viewer/listener. The EP contained a total of seven tracks; three new songs, two remixes, one skit, and a shout out track. The skit,

"JD's Gafflin (part 2)" featured JD, a member of Ice Cube's crew The Lench Mob. On "I Gotta Say What Up!!!" Cube spends 3 minutes shouting out the names of folks from LL Cool J to Ice-T.

Two songs that were initially released on *AmeriKKKa's Most Wanted* appeared as remixes on *Kill at Will*, "Endangered Species," featuring Chuck D, and "Get Off My Dick and Tell Yo Bitch to Come Here." "Endangered Species" opened with a sample of longtime NBC News anchor Tom Brokaw in which he proclaimed Los Angeles "the gang capital of the nation" and pointedly noted that there were 452 gang related murders in the greater Los Angeles area the previous year. In "Get Off My Dick and Tell Yo Bitch to Come Here," Ice Cube continued the discussion regarding what Dr. Todd Boyd in the book *Young, Black, Rich and Famous* called, "the often unspoken though well-known code between Black men, 'never ride another man's jock.' That was the quickest way to lose respect." Boyd referenced Ice Cube's song as an example, noting that while this concept "might not inspire a feminist embrace, it is at the root of most communication between Black men."

The three new songs Ice Cube dropped on *Kill at Will*

solidified his status as one of the premier figures in the world of hip-hop music. "Jackin for Beats" was a brilliant play on Ice Cube's image as hip-hop gangster/hoodlum who, in the process of taking whatever from whomever, would go as far as 'jackin' beats to make a song. In order, Ice Cube sampled the beats from "Call Me D-Nice" by D-Nice, "So Whatcha Sayin" by EPMD, "Welcome to the Terrordome" by Public Enemy, "I Know You Got Soul" by Eric B. and Rakim, "The Humpty Dance" by Digital Underground," "Big Ol Butt" by LL Cool J, and "Heed the Word of the Brotha" by X Clan. "Jackin for Beats" was a surefire mainstream hit that further cemented Ice Cube's place in the rotations of shows like "Yo! MTV Raps" and BET's "Rap City."

While "Jackin For Beats" was something for the mainstream, two other new songs on *Kill at Will* made it clear that Ice Cube was still focused on the life and times of the young Black, urban American male. In "The Product," with its hectic, post-Bomb Squad influenced production sound, Ice Cube literally started from the beginning:

I was told cause I didn't witness the whole act

In and out was the movement of the bozack
It was hot and sweaty with lots of pushin
Then the nut came gushin
And it was hell tryin to bail to the ovary
With nothing but the Lord looking over me
I was white with a tail
But when I reached the finish line young Black male
One cell made two and two cells made fo
And so on so now I'm an embryo

As "The Product," Ice Cube traced marginal economic existence and unstable home environments as contributors to failure in school:

They try to shape us
But I know Uncle Sam is a muthafuckin rapist
So I stopped payin attention
Ice Cube headed straight for detention
Which led to a life of crime:
Now bein on my own is a factor
So I become the neighborhood jacker
Gimme your car run your jewels
Makin a livin robbin fools
Which led to time in prison:

Sent to a concrete ho house

Where all the products go no doubt

Yo Momma I gotta do eleven

Livin in a five-by-seven

Which led to another young man without a father
  present:

And it's drivin me batty

Cause my little boy is missin daddy

Which led to the cycle starting all over again. "The Product" was also laced with messages outside of Ice Cube's lyrics that provided context for the situations he rhymed about. Between the first and second verses a voice said, "Ghetto ass nigga, you ain't shit and you ain't gonna never be shit!" Between the second and third verses, a woman said, "Uh uh, muthafucka you gots to get a job if you wanna stay in my muthafuckin house!" This was followed by the line "See momma didn't love me!," then a newscaster sounding voice saying, "Many young men reject the traditional values that are important to their parents. Church, school, and family have been replaced by street, turf, and gang."

Ice Cube's "The Product" was and still is viewed generally in one of two ways: It either represents an insightful window into the social hows and whys that impact the lives of young Black men in the United States, or a series of poor decisions that show a lack of morality and reluctance to take accountability for your actions.

Given that the beginning of *Kill at Will* noted that there were 452 murders in Los Angeles within the span of one year, the inclusion of the song "Dead Homiez" seemed an appropriate anthem for the period. Over a low key, piano laced track, Ice Cube delivered a monotone tribute to all the young men who were the true faces of the incredible homicide statistics in the late 1980s and early 1990s.

Ice Cube harnessed and expressed the rage of seeing family and friends dying due to lack of economic opportunity:

> *Still hear the screams from his mother*
> *While my nigga lay dead in the gutter*
> *And it's gettin to my temple*
> *Why is that the only time Black folks get to ride in a limo*
> *It makes me so mad I wanna get my sawed off*
> *And have some bodies hauled off*

However, he also dissected failings of the Black family, which for some within the Black community was the equivalent of airing

dirty laundry in public:

> *But somethin ain't right*
> *When it's a tragedy that's the only time the family's tight*
> *Loving each other in a caring mood*
> *There's lots of people and lots of food*

Sadly this song became a theme for many rides to and from

funeral services all over the country in the early 1990s. "Dead

Homiez" also offered a therapeutic release for the tremendous

sense of loss felt by so many people in so many communities,

those mourning could be assured that there were others who

could relate and empathize.

In LA Heroes Don't Fly thru the Sky or Stars They Live Behind Bars

In the early 1990s music and the music video were the primary modes of connection between West Coast hip-hop and the mainstream. However, the music and culture had cross-over appeal in other commercial formats as evidenced in 1991, with the release of two movies. *New Jack City*, starring Ice-T, and *Boyz N The Hood* with Ice Cube. Both films represented a hip-hop perspective on the issues faced by the youth of the culture. *New Jack City*, a gangstafied tale of rags to riches, was set in New York and incorporated the crack epidemic as a major part of its storyline.

New Jack City was hip-hop's version of *Scarface*. In *Scarface*, Al Pacino as Antonio Montana was one of some 125,000 refugees from Cuba who came to Miami during the Mariel Boat Lift between April and October of 1980. These refugees allegedly included a number of people Fidel Castro

released from Cuban prisons and mental health facilities. In *New

Jack City* Wesley Snipes as Nino Brown began as a small time

hustler in 'The City.' Starting from basically nothing both

characters became powerful players in the drug game, Tony

Montana with cocaine and Nino Brown with crack. Their

organizational skills and brutality were so efficient that their

former White bosses/partners tried to kill them both, and each

took deadly revenge on those that were responsible for the

attempts on their lives. Tony and Nino eventually got so caught

up in the game that they shot and killed their best friends, and

both characters fell in a dramatic way after being shot themselves

at the end of each movie. The connection between these two

movies was brought home when *New Jack City* featured several

scenes with Nino Brown actually watching *Scarface* on television

and quoting lines from Tony Montana.

Ice-T's performance as a police officer in *New Jack City*

was significant, but by 1991 he was far from the first rapper to try

acting. Busy Bee played himself in *WildStyle* (1982), the first

hip-hop movie. The Fat Boys starred in *Disorderlies* (1987), Kid

and Play made *House Party* (1990), and Run-DMC was featured in two films, *Krush Groove* (1985) and *Tougher Than Leather* (1988). However, there were two things that distinguished Ice-T's role in *New Jack City*. One was that he was the first West Coast hip-hop artist to successfully make a high profile multimedia crossover move. Secondly, his dramatic role as veteran policeman, Scotty Appleton, was a departure from what rappers had normally done in movies, which was basically play themselves.

Ice-T also appeared on the film's soundtrack with the song "New Jack Hustler." As was the case in "Colors," he made use of the song to lay out background info for the type of character the movie focused on:

> *Hustler word I pull the trigger long*
> *Grit my teeth spray till every niggas gone*
> *Got my block sewn armored dope spots*
> *Last thing I sweat is a sucka punk cop*
> *Move like a king when I roll hops*
> *You try to flex bang! Another nigga drops*
> *You gotta deal with this cause there's no way out*
> *Why? Cash money ain't never gonna play out*
> *I got nothin to lose much to gain in my brain*
> *I got a capitalist migraine*

I gotta get paid tonight

You muthafuckin right

The 'capitalist migraine' mentality was very much a thematic
undercurrent not only throughout the fictional story of *New
Jack City*, but the real life narratives of people who would like to
be the next Nino Brown. The individualist nature of United
States mainstream culture has always placed a premium on
financial gain by any means necessary. In a society of haves and
have nots, the fact that a new generation of urban entrepreneurs
appeared when drugs became big business was a natural function
of supply and demand economics.

In contrast to the location of *New Jack City*, *Boyz N The
Hood* was all Los Angeles. Ice Cube was cast as Dough Boy, a
character that was basically an acting version of his music to that
point. Although crack was an underlying piece of the storyline,
Boyz N The Hood also addressed numerous other issues facing
urban communities like South Central. One of the more
powerful moments in the movie was Furious Styles', played by
Larry Fishburne, lecture on poverty, the availability of cheap,
potent alcohol and illegal drugs, gangs and Black on Black crime,
and gentrification in the community.

The essence of *Boyz N The Hood* was the often told tale of the struggles and obstacles faced by a group of friends growing up, similar to movies like *Cooley High* and even *Stand By Me.* What made *Boyz N The Hood* different was the use of the still developing West Coast hip-hop culture to frame the story, and Ice Cube's performance solidified the expanding multimedia bridge to the mainstream. The growing demand for hip-hop was evident by the simple fact that a movie like *Boyz N The Hood* was made. Its cultural impact was reinforced and elevated by the recognition it received on the award circuit. First time director John Singleton won an MTV Movie Award for Best New Filmmaker, a New York Film Critics Circle Award for Best New Director, a LAFCA New Generation Award, and a ShoWest Award for Screenwriter of the Year. If all that were not enough, Singleton made history as the first African-American and youngest filmmaker ever to simultaneously earn Academy Award nominations for Best Original Screenplay and Best Director.

As West Coast rappers began to appear as actors in films, they continued to appear on the soundtracks as well. Ice Cube's contribution to the *Boys N The Hood* soundtrack was "How to Survive in South Central." The song was actually an articulation of the show and tell approach Ice Cube took in bringing his

stories to the masses, complete with a helpful tour guide named

Elaine in between verses. According to Ice Cube, there are three

basic rules of survival in South Central:

> *Rule number one get yourself a gun*
> *A nine and your ass'll be fine...*
> *Rule number two don't trust nobody*
> *Especially a bitch with a hooker's body...*
> *Rule number three don't get caught up*
> *Cause niggaz aren't doin anything that's thought up...*

The rules summarized the complexities of a character like Dough

Boy, who continued with growing misogyny, yet questioned the

long term wisdom in some of the choices being made by Ice

Cube's peers. Other West Coast contributors to the *Boyz N The

Hood* soundtrack included Yo-Yo, Compton's Most Wanted,

Kam, and Too $hort.

The commercial packaging of movies like *New Jack City*

and *Boyz N The Hood* with their accompanying soundtracks

gave hip-hop in general significant inroads to the mainstream.

However, the critical acclaim received by *Boyz N The Hood*

meant that it was delivering specifically West Coast hip-hop flavor to the general public on an unprecedented level. That public profile would continue to gain cultural relevance and attract increasing amounts of investment.

Everybody Killin Tryin to Make a Killin

The album cover for *EFIL4ZAGGIN* showed all four members of NWA gunned down on the little strip of grass that separated the street from the sidewalk. Yellow tape, bloody white sheets, police investigation, chalk outlines, and the souls of Eazy-E, Dr. Dre, MC Ren, and DJ Yella were shown floating away.

The group was very much alive and looking to answer the question, "How angry can we make Tipper Gore and the PMRC?" Their answer was provocative lyrics and Dr. Dre's profound production throwing gasoline on the controversial witch's brew of profanity, misogyny, and the use of the word 'nigga' with Dr. Dre's production skills behind it all.

EFIL4ZAGGIN seemed motivated by the group defining themselves as 'real niggaz' compared to the parade of pretenders in the game. The intro, "Prelude" featured several voices, including Above the Law, praising the return of the 'real niggaz,' and MC Ren began:

> *The real niggaz is back*
> *Cuz its too many bullshit records out*

To make sure NWA got the point across there were also songs such as "Real Niggaz Don't Die," "Niggaz 4 Life," and "Real Niggaz," which originally appeared on *100 Miles And Runnin*. According to the playlist, other characteristics of 'real niggaz' were that they had an "Appetite For Destruction" and were "Alwayz Into Somethin." It was clear that NWA was catering to the segment of the mainstream obsessively fascinated with the negative stereotyping of young Black males. How convincingly can you continuously portray yourself as a foul-mouthed, criminal minded, violent, promiscuous, woman hater? Dr. Dre acknowledged the question and argued back in "Niggaz 4 Life:"

> *Why do I call myself a nigga you ask me?*
> *Because my mouth is so motherfuckin nasty*
> *Bitch this bitch that nigga this nigga that*
> *In the mean while my pockets are gettin fat*
> *Gettin paid to say this shit here*
> *Makin more in a week than a doctor makes in a year*

So why not call myself a nigga?

It's better than pullin the trigger and goin up the river

And then I get called a nigga anyway

Broke as a motherfucker and locked away

So cut out all that bullshit

Yo! I guess I'll be a nigga for life

His point that if he is going to be called a 'nigga' either way, doing it on terms that produce financial benefit made good business sense to him and actually fits the capitalist narrative. Dr. Dre also argued that a life of crime and extended jail time was the alternative to being a "Nigga 4 Life" with NWA, and the incarceration rates for young Black males in the United States did somewhat validate his alternative stance. But this represents a strictly capitalist approach to these issues. Capitalism only worries about the bottom line. A more socially conscious approach to this artistic dilemma would question whether doing and saying literally anything on a record for financial gain takes precedence over any negative messages it might send.

NWA did challenge the status quo in places. MC Ren in "Niggaz 4 Life:"

Why do I call myself a nigga you ask me?
Well it's because motherfuckers wanna blast me
And run me outta my neighborhood
And label me as a dope dealer yo
And say that I'm no good
But I can't find jobs so niggaz wouldn't have to go out
Save up some dope on the corner so they could show out
When the cops came they gave a fake name
Because the life in the streets is just a head game
So therefore to make more
A 15 year-old Black kid'll go and rob a liquor store
And get shot in the process
He ate up a nine bullet and now he's put to rest

Dr. Dre in the same song:

Why do I call myself a nigga you ask me?
I guess it's just the way shit has to be
Back when I was young gettin a job was murder
Fuck flippin burgers cause I deserve a
Nine-to-five I can be proud of
That I can speak loud of
And to help a nigga get out of
Yo! The concrete playground

But most motherfuckers only want you to stay down

Both verses speak to the notion of economic injustice and the lack of opportunity within communities like Compton. However, this social justice angle was lost in the sea of sensationalism NWA chose to make the focus of *EFIL4ZAGGIN.* Even so, Dr. Dre brought major heat to the record's production. The raw funk of tracks like "Alwayz Into Somethin," "Real Niggaz," (where, interestingly, Dr. Dre referred to NWA as "the generals in this fuckin hip-hop army") and "The Dayz Of Wayback," was undeniable.

The song titles toward the back end of the album flirted with snuff films and pornographic misogyny. These included "One Less Bitch," "Findum, Fuckum & Flee," and "I'd Rather Fuck You." There were shocking lyrical extremes, like MC Ren on the track "She Swallowed It:"

> *And for the shit that she does give her a jumbo*
> *Because the dumb bitch licks out the asshole*
> *And she'll let you videotape her*
> *And if you got a gang of niggaz the bitch'll let you rape her*

342

She like suckin on dicks and lickin up nut
And they even take the broomstick up the butt

But even that was relatively mild compared with the skit "To Kill A Hooker," which qualified as some of the most over the top material ever put on wax. It began with the group in a car talking about how they "need some pussy." After they "bust a left on Sunset," they saw some women and called one of them over. There was some back and forth negotiation when suddenly NWA had had enough as they grabbed the woman and forced her into the car. Above the woman's screams was the sound of blows being landed and men yelling, "Fuck that bitch!" Seconds later, three gunshots are heard and MC Ren yells, "Man, what the fuck is wrong with you man, shootin this bitch in my shit [car]?" The shooter, Eazy-E, blamed the others for bringing the woman in the car in the first place, MC Ren went on to complain about the stains on his seats, and Dr. Dre concluded, "Ay man fuck that bitch man, throw her muthafuckin ass out. Yo there go some more bitches over there, blow the muthafuckin horn!"

A natural question, both for the Black community and the mainstream, coming out of *EFIL4ZAGGIN* was what exactly a 'real nigga' was. According to NWA, the answer was not a pretty picture. Their version took two of the most telling signs of male insecurity, violence against women and constant self-promotion, and ran with them. The old proverb, "If you have to keep saying you are something, then you're really not" can be applied here. If NWA had to keep saying how 'real' they were, a thinking person may be led to ask; how 'real' were they?

Was a 'real nigga' actually an insecure mess? The answer was important to the Black community, who were constantly media interrogated, and argued internally, about potential negative effects rap music had on Black youth. For the mainstream, obviously less vested in the outcome of the discussion, *EFIL4ZAGGIN* offered a tourist-like thrill similar to the roller coaster that balances fear and fun. This factor cannot be discounted in the sensationalist marketing that has continued to play into the representation of young Black males to this day.

Adding to the publicity frenzy around the group was Dr. Dre's 1991 assault of Dee Barnes, host of a hip-hop television show on Fox called "Pump It Up." NWA was allegedly upset after Barnes interviewed Ice Cube at the height of their beef, and confronted her at a record release party in Hollywood. Dre pleaded no contest to the assault and was fined, given probation and required to perform community service. Barnes subsequently filed a multi-million dollar lawsuit, which was settled out of court.

As influential as NWA was during this era, it is easy to forget they produced only three original albums. *EFIL4ZAGGIN* was so extreme that it eventually made the group a caricature of itself. The phenomenon was perhaps most famously captured in the 1993 film *CB4*. In this comedy loosely based on NWA, Chris Rock played a middle-class wannabe who turns into a gangsta rap star by starting a group, CB4 (short for Cell Block 4) and going hardcore. In the movie, CB4 even had an NWA-like theme song about their hometown called "Straight Outta Locash."

NWA recognized that if they kept pushing the envelope, more critics would become upset, yet more publicity would be generated, and more people would be exposed to the record. The plan worked to perfection as *EFIL4ZAGGIN* reached number one on the *Billboard* 200. Part of this chart success can be attributed to the introduction of SoundScan into the music business. SoundScan accurately tracked the sale of music across the United States and Canada. Informed observers felt rappers

sales figures were historically underreported, but SoundScan
provided a more accurate count.

Any discussion of *EFIL4ZAGGIN* would not be
complete without mentioning where this album took the
relationship between NWA and Ice Cube. Ice Cube completely
ignored NWA on his first solo album, *AmeriKKKa's Most
Wanted*. NWA had then started a public beef by taking a
relatively mild shot at Ice Cube on the *100 Miles and Runnin* EP.
Cube returned the favor on *Kill At Will*. But *EFIL4ZAGGIN*
changed things with an interlude entitled "Message to B.A."
NWA had started referring to Ice Cube as Benedict Arnold,
perhaps the most famous traitor in United States history. A
decorated member of the Continental Army, Arnold switched
sides and joined the British during America's war for
independence in 1779.

In a take off of an Ice Cube piece from *AmeriKKKa's
Most Wanted*, Dr. Dre announced: "A message to Benedict
Arnold: No matter how hard you try to be, here's what they
think about you." What followed was a series of apparent phone
messages insulting Ice Cube and suggesting he and his crew had
been getting beat down in various cities around the country. One

woman asked: "All I wanna know is why y'all let his punk ass in the group in the first place, when you knew what kinda bitch he was!" Where the exchanges between NWA and Ice Cube had been fairly light and generalized, it was now highly personal:

> **MC Ren:** *Yeah nigga, when we see yo ass we gonna cut your hair off and fuck you with a broomstick!*
> **Dr. Dre:** *Think about it, punk muthafucka!*

This was the beginning of the public redefinition of what it was for one MC to 'beef' with another MC. Within the history of hip-hop to this point, battles between artists had remained relatively non-threatening and on wax for the most part. In New York, during the mid to late 1980s, there were several high profile conflicts between rappers such as Busy Bee vs. Kool Moe Dee, Roxanne vs. UTFO, and MC Shan vs. Boogie Down Productions. Generally, these differences were resolved and fell back on hip-hop's spirit of forgiveness and unity. The NWA approach on *EFIL4ZAGGIN* elevated the stakes and set the stage not only for an Ice Cube response, but also a new direction for future beefs within hip-hop.

Rather Be Judged by 12 Than Carried by 6

Hip-hop's past has seen numerous rappers challenging the status quo by presenting radical protest music that both confronts society and beats heavily on speakers. Thematically and conceptually, Ice Cube's second full album, *Death Certificate*, was one of the most audacious combinations of social discourse and musical heat the genre had ever produced. His ambition was apparent before one even heard a lick of music. On the cover Ice Cube stood in a morgue over a body covered by an American flag with a tag on a toe that read 'Uncle Sam.' In addition, a quick glance at the song list revealed that the album was split into two parts: The Death Side and The Life Side.

The cover inset provided several insights to the mentality of the project. One was a picture of Ice Cube reading a copy of the Nation of Islam newspaper *The Final Call* with the headlines "Unite or Perish!" on the front page and "Domestic Violence" on the back page. Over Ice Cube's left shoulder were nine Nation of Islam members in bowties and dark glasses standing at attention. Meanwhile, over Ice Cube's right shoulder are ten young Black males dressed in black, some sitting on the ground, others standing and looking over at the Muslims across from them.

Ice Cube's manifesto was printed on the left margin. One item addressed the reason behind the two sides of the album:

> *Niggas are in the state of emergency:*
> *The death side a mirrored image of where we are today*
> *The life side a vision of where we need to go*
> *So sign your death certificate*

He also explained his use of the word nigga:

> The reason I say nigga is because we are mentally dead even in 1991. We have limited knowledge of self, so it leads to a nigga mentality. The best place for a young Black male or female is the Nation of Islam. Soon as we as a people use our knowledge of self to our advantage we will then be able to become and be called Blacks.

Ice Cube's vision was large, describing Black history and yet offering to overcome its fatal effects. In the midst of the madness engulfing the lives of many young African-Americans, here was a rapper with the utmost 'street' credibility involved in hardcore social agitation and offering solutions. While his former group mates in NWA had gone cartoonishly overboard with their representations of life for a young urban, Black male, Ice Cube seemed intent on pushing the other way. His direction reflected the lasting influence of his work and time spent with Chuck D and Public Enemy during the making of *AmeriKKKa's Most Wanted*. In the early 1990s, Public Enemy was the epitome of socially and politically relevant hip-hop. Sharing a common belief with Minister Louis Farrakhan and the Nation of Islam in community empowerment, Ice Cube added a West Coast sensibility to the message while assuming the role of both executive producer and co-producer of *Death Certificate*.

Mainstream media was now not only aware of artists like Ice Cube, they were becoming familiar with and even respectful of the depth of styles and content. *The Seattle Times* stated:

Cube's word play formed a more-than-frank

depiction of the stucco suburban jungle, the
drive-by shootings, the welfare trap, cheap drugs
and the even cheaper value put on life. Death was
shrugged off on the tar-veined asphalt of the
South Side; rage rose like the heat vapors off
those same streets. Cube captured that.

Death Certificate is a two-sided coin: death on
one side, life on the other. Cube says the
recording is about more than the life cycle of one
person, but the cycle of his race. He sees the
death side as an image of where his people are
today – in a state of emergency – and the life side
as an image of where he feels they need to go.
The argument over what Ice Cube does or
doesn't mean has been going on since his first hit
was released. It continues today. The only thing
that seems certain is that this powerful young rap
star means to stir things up with his music.

Appropriate to the theme of the album, a skit called "The
Funeral" opened The Death Side. The first voice heard is Ice

Cube reciting the written message from the liner notes. Then
sounds of what are presumably pallbearers, crying, screaming,
church music, and a preacher's voice who ends his eulogy by
saying Cube was "The Wrong Nigga to Fuck Wit!" That
happened to be the name of the next song, and Ice Cube came
out swinging:

> *It ain't no pop cause that sucks*
> *And you can new jack swing on my nuts*
> *Fuck R & B and the runnin man*
> *I'm the one to stand with a gun in hand...*
> *Don't let me catch Daryl Gates in traffic*
> *I got a habit to peel his cap backward*
> *I hope he wear a vest too in his best blue*
> *goin up against the Zulu*
> *Stop givin juice to the Raiders*
> *Cause Al Davis never paid us*

New Jack Swing was the name of the sound created by super
producer/artist Teddy Riley in the late 1980s. It incorporated
catchy rhythm and blues hooks into the sampling and electronic
techniques of hip-hop, yet was looked at with suspicion by many
within the hip-hop community because of its close association

with R & B, club music, and perceived lack of social meaning. The reference to Los Angeles Police Department Chief Daryl Gates was hardly surprising, but there was heavy irony in Ice Cube's call to stop rockin Raiders gear because of his direct involvement in making it so popular in the first place.

The remaining portion of the Death Side was a no holds barred narrative that sliced the discourse on urban socio-political issues wide open. It was a mixture of heavy story telling, radio friendly music, comedic interludes, gratuitous toasting, a forum on safe sex and sexually transmitted diseases, a debate on the issue of guns, the death of a young Black man, and finally a message of resurrection.

"My Summer Vacation" made a direct connection between the rise of street gangs and the spread of crack across the United States. After complaining about how "everybody and they mama sell dope" and police interference in Los Angeles, Ice Cube found an answer:

> *They tryin to stop it*
> *So what the fuck can I do to make a profit*
> *Catch a flight to St. Louis*
> *That's cool cause nobody knew us*

We stepped off the plane

Four gang bangers

Professional crack slangers

Rented a car at wholesale

Drove to the ghetto and checked in a motel

It didn't take long for these professionals to get to work:

Unpacked and I grabbed my .380

Cause where we stayin niggaz look shady

But they can't fade South Central

Cause bustin a cap is fundamental

Peepin out every block close

Seein which one will clock the most

Yeah this is the one no doubt

Bust a U Bone and let's clear these niggaz out

The American heartland was unprepared for the violence that crack brought with it:

Now clearin em out meant casualties

Still had the LA mentality

Bust a cap and outta there in a hurry

Wouldn't you know a drive-by in Missouri?

Them fools got popped

Took they corner next day set up shop

And it's better than slangin in the Valley
Triple the profit makin more than I did in Cali

Meanwhile, it was taking local law enforcement some time to realize what was happening:

And we ain't on edge when we do work
Police don't recognize the khakis and the sweatshirt
Getting bitches and they can't stand a 1991 Tony
  Montana
Now the shit's like a war
Of gang violence where it was never seen before

Then there were the local followers and gangsta wannabes that seemed to mystify Ice Cube as much as everyone else:

Punks run when the gat bust
Four jheri curled niggaz kickin up dust
And some of them are even looking up to us
Wearin our colors and talking that gang fuss
Givin up much love
Dyin for a street that they never heard of

As would happen in nearly every city, local residents are only going to take so much from aggressive out of towners:

BOOM! My homie got shot he's a goner black

St. Louis niggaz want they corner back

Shootin in snowy weather

Its illegal business niggaz still can't stick together

Plus the police got the 411

That LA ain't all surf and sun

The song articulated how the crack economy imploded so many communities in the late 1980s. "Steady Mobbin'" on the other hand was a light-hearted, radio friendly story of a day in the life of Ice Cube that used a sample of the song "Reach Out" by The Average White Band. Next was a skit entitled "Robin Lench," a parody of the popular television show "Lifestyles of the Rich and Famous" hosted by Robin Leach, which aired from 1984-1995. In this case, 'Robin Lench' hosted "Lifestyles of the Poor and Unfortunate."

The remainder of the Death Side was a blazing sequence that addressed circumstances and consequences associated with sexual activity and living the life of the streets. "Givin' Up the Nappy Dugout," nappy dugout being slang for sex, plays upon a fear of every father who has a daughter: That the fast, nasty female in the neighborhood was daddy's little girl. The track begins with Ice Cube knocking on the door and the father answering. After the father went off about "raising his daughter right" and sending her to private school, Ice Cube revealed:

> *Your daughter was a nice girl now she is a slut*
> *A queen treatin niggaz just like King Tut*
> *Gobblin up nuts sorta like a humming bird*
> *Suckin up the Lench Mob crew and I'm comin third*
> *Used to get straight As now she just skippin class*
> *Oh my do I like to grip the hips and ass*
> *Only seventeen but with a lot of practice*
> *On Black boys jimmys and White boy's cactus*

This is certainly not anything out of the ordinary in terms of the conversations that happen between men on a daily basis. However as stated previously, when in-group discussions are made available for public consumption, there will inevitably be static. This does not excuse misogynistic lyrics or images that objectify, it only acknowledges the reality of in-group/out-group communication dynamics.

While there certainly was an appearance of reckless sexual

behavior in "Givin Up the Nappy Dugout," the next song "Look Who's Burnin'" addressed sexually transmitted diseases. The fact that free condoms could be found at public health clinics was mentioned twice, along with a lecture to women about the poor decisions that left them 'burnin.' Overall, the message refrained from judgment regarding pre-marital sex and focused on the practice of safe sex through consistent use of condoms. "Look Who's Burnin" was similar to the 1988 Boogie Down Productions song "Jimmy."

While the finality associated with the spread of HIV was acknowledged by Ice Cube in "Look Who's Burnin," a much more immediate question of survival was brought up in "A Bird in the Hand." The beginning of the track contained a sample from the children's television show "Sesame Street" with Big Bird saying, "Say, look at this! I've been cleaning out my nest, and I found an old book of my poetry!" What followed was some of the most powerful social commentary to emerge from the hip-hop scene to that point:

> *Fresh outta school cause I was a high school grad*
> *Gots to get a job cause I was a high school dad*
> *Wish I got paid by rappin to the nation*

But that's not likely so here's my application...

Always knew that I would clock Gs

But welcome to McDonald's may I take your order
*   please*

Gotta serve you food that might give you cancer

Cause my son doesn't take no for an answer

Now I pay taxes that you never gimme back

What about diapers bottles and Similac

Do I have to sell me a whole lotta crack

For decent shelter and clothes on my back

Or should I just wait for help from Bush

Or Jesse Jackson and Operation PUSH?

Facing these questions the song's main character "got me a bird, better known as a kilo" of cocaine. Ice Cube noted the hypocrisy of the government's response:

So now you put the Feds against me

Cause I couldn't follow the plan of the presidency

I'm never getting love again

But Blacks are too fuckin broke to be Republican

Now I remember I used to be cool

Till I stopped fillin out my W-2

Now senators are gettin high

And you plan against the ghetto backfired

Ice Cube's reference to a 'plan' associated with the destruction of
inner city neighborhoods was generally viewed by the
mainstream as conspiracy theory hype. However, it made sense
to many mixed income urban communities where, beginning in
the 1970s large numbers of manufacturing jobs were lost,
funding for social programs was slashed, and drugs and firearms
became readily available.

Following the decision of whether to take the 'bad' path
instead of the 'good' was a song highlighting the tools necessary
for this line of work. "Man's Best Friend" argued that a gun
should replace man's traditional number one companion:

> *Here is the reason why Ice Cube pack*
> *Just in case a little punk tries to jack*
> *I can't put a muthafuckin pitbull*
> *Under a coat in the small of my back*
> *So I gotta take my Beretta and I'll betcha*
> *It'll probably work a hundred percent better*
> *Cause it'll keep me outta danger*
> *With sixteen in the clip and one in the chamber*

So this goes to all y'all intruders
Beware of the owner cause the owner is a shooter
I don't just wanna give ya ass rabies
I'd rather have ya ass pushin up daisies
And I can't do that with Benji
Rin-Tin-Tin or Spuds McKenzie
Forget about a dog fool he'll shit in the den
Nowadays a gat is man's best friend

The decision to carry a gun and engage in the lifestyle that came with it represented the basis of the last song of the Death Side. Coming off of his discussion of firearms, and taking into account mass media representations on who the people are with guns, Ice Cube took time to sample the words of longtime ABC News anchor Peter Jennings: "The profile of a typical American gun owner is this: Over 30, White, male, middle class." Out of this arrives the beginning of "Alive on Arrival," a hanging out with friends, wrong place at the wrong time scenario, and a critique of a healthcare system that fails the underclasses:

But why a muthafucka like me have to fall down
Not knowin why I dropped out
Fuck it still can't afford to get popped out

So now I gotta jet

Only ran one block but my shirt is soakin wet

Tryin to see if we got em

Looked down and my sweatshirt's red at the bottom

Didn't panic but I still looked cracked out

Yelled to the homies then I blacked out

If being shot weren't bad enough, the message became clear that a hospital did not automatically mean safety:

Woke up in the back of a Trey

On my way to MLK

That's the county hospital jack

Where niggaz die over a little scratch

Sittin in the trauma center

In my back is where the bullet entered

Yo nurse, I'm getting kinda warm

Bitch still made me fill out the fuckin form

Coughin up blood on my hands and knees

Then I heard "Freeze nigger don't move!" yo

I didn't do a thing

Don't wanna go out like my man Rodney King

After being interrogated about the shooting:

Since we po the hospital moves slow
Now I'm laid out
People stepping over me
To get closer to the TV
Just like a piece of dog shit
Now will I die on this nappy-ass carpet?
One hour done passed
Done watched two episodes of MASH
And when I'm almost through
They call my name and put me in ICU

At this point in the song, a heart monitor beat is heard. Still being questioned by the police, the end finally comes:

Why o why can't I get help?
Cause I'm Black I gots to go for self
Too many Black bodies the hospital housin
So at 10 pm I was Audi 5000
[heart monitor sounds flat-line]

The finale is controversial Nation of Islam minister Dr. Khallid Muhammad's eulogy to the conditions that created the Death Side while planting a seed of hope for the "rebirth, resurrection, and rise" of the Life Side.

In a scene that would be echoed at the beginning of The Notorious B.I.G.'s 1994 debut album, *Ready to Die*, the Life Side of *Death Certificate* started with the sounds of a baby being born. After the doctor pronounced, "It's a boy," Dr. Muhammad spoke again, this time framing the way forward for Black men and women and concluding, "Before we can make a way for the peace-maker, we must kill and get rid of the peace-breaker."

The Life Side is activist, militantly confronting the mainstream's patriotic image of "Uncle Sam," and expanding on sexual harassment of Black women in the workplace, tensions between Korean store owners and African-American customers, loyalty to the community, and gang activity.

In "I Wanna Kill Sam," Ice Cube described his desire to grab his AK-47 and pull off "the ultimate drive-by." The song begins with a U.S. Army 'recruiter' saying, "The Army is the only way out for young Black teenagers!" The end of the song offered a visual of the fury Ice Cube directed at the United States society Uncle Sam represented:

So if you see a man in red white and blue

Getting chased by the Lench Mob crew
It's a man who deserves to buckle
I wanna kill Sam cause he ain't my muthafuckin uncle!

Ice Cube remained on the offensive in "Horny Lil' Devil," which sprayed verbal shrapnel in numerous directions. Beginning as a stand against sexual harassment of Black women by White men in the workplace, Ice Cube insulted the "devil" and threatened to put "his dick on the woodblock: Swing, swing, swing, and chop, chop, chop!" While there was indeed debatable controversial and homophobic material here, racial flak was generated by the song "Black Korea." The tension between Korean storeowners and African-American communities was reflected in the 1989 Spike Lee joint *Do The Right Thing*, where Black perception of Korean neighborhood market owners was that they were penny pinching, suspicious, and hard to deal with because of their limited English.

While Ice Cube's threats in a song like "Horny Lil' Devil" went relatively unnoticed, the ones in "Black Korea" did not:

Thinkin every brotha in the worlds out to take
So they watch every damn move that I make

They hope I don't pull out a gat and try to rob

Their funky little store but bitch I got a job

So don't follow me up and down your market

Or your little chop suey ass'll be a target

Of the nationwide boycott

Juice with the people that's what the boy got

So pay respect to the black fist

Or we'll burn your store right down to a crisp

And then we'll see ya

Cause you can't turn the ghetto into Black Korea

The threat of arson was seized upon by mainstream critics as proof that hip-hop was really just a bunch of reactionary thugs with loose morals. Ice Cube's self-acknowledged 'juice' with the people demonstrated his recognition of the sway he held as a leader in hip-hop's rapidly expanding sphere of influence and implied a communal threat to seize social power and use it as a tool in the fight for social and economic justice.

In recent years, the phrase 'keep it real' has been reduced to cliché status by its overuse. But even though the term had not yet become famous, Ice Cube was already hammering away at the concept. "True to the Game" criticized individuals who make some money and then flee the community:

> *Cause soon as y'all get some dough*
> *You wanna put a White bitch on your elbow*
> *Movin out your neighborhood*
> *But I walk through the ghetto and the flavor's good*

Ice Cube's assertion that those who follow this path could "fuck around and get your ghetto pass revoked" implied a good riddance attitude. If you don't want to live here, don't come around here. This struck many in the mainstream as confusing to say the least. If South Central was really as bad as Ice Cube had always described, why wouldn't you want to move if you could?

With the mainstream's increasing commercial interest in hip-hop, there were now rappers being criticized for openly courting crossover appeal:

> *You was hardcore hip-hop*
> *Now look at yourself boy you done flip-flopped*
> *Givin our music away to the mainstream*
> *Don't you know they ain't down with the team*
> *They just sent they boss over*
> *Put a bug in your ear and now you crossed over*

On MTV but they don't care

They'll have a new nigga next year

Last but not least was a "message to the Oreo cookie" who wishes to distance himself from his Blackness:

You put on your suit and tie and your big clothes

You don't associate with the Negroes

You wanna be just like Jack

But Jack is callin you a nigga behind your back

So back off genius

I don't need you to correct my broken English

You know that's right you ain't White

So stop holdin your ass tight

At the conclusion of the song, Ice Cube made certain that his listeners knew that he was one of these people being true to the game. A female sounding like a reporter announced: "And Ice Cube practices what he preaches, he continues to live in South Central Los Angeles and he puts his money into projects that improve the neighborhood."

Given the rise in popularity of gangs, the song "Color Blind" was along the lines of "We're All In the Same Gang," which Ice Cube did not participate in. Also collaborating on the song were King Tee, Kam, and J-Dee from the Lench Mob. The message was exclusively anti-gang and progressive.

When Ice Cube left NWA, most expected his first solo album would be a dis-fest against his former group. Somewhat surprisingly, Ice Cube did not even mention NWA on *AmeriKKKa's Most Wanted*. However, beef eventually surfaced between the two camps, culminating with the previously discussed remarks contained on NWA's *EFIL4ZAGGIN*. The final track on *Death Certificate* began with Ice Cube muttering, "Damn, I forgot somethin!" After thinking for a few seconds, he said "Oh yeah, it ain't over muthafuckas!" What followed was a montage of old NWA songs and pieces of audio, with Ice Cube and Dr. Dre both heard repeating "Here's what they think about you!"

The conflict between NWA and Ice Cube was at the time the highest profile drama in hip-hop history. All eyes were now on Ice Cube to see how he would respond in the wake of NWA's no-holds barred comments about him on *EFIL4ZAGGIN*. The personal attacks potentially moved the threat of bodily injury from wax to the streets.

The title "No Vaseline," referring to the idea of not using any lubricant in the performance of anal sex, was only the beginning of Ice Cube's answer. The song erupted in a systematic deconstruction of NWA to which, even if the group had not essentially been through anyway, there could be no reply. Sampling LL Cool J's "Now you getting done without Vaseline" from his song "To Tha Breaka Dawn" as the hook, Ice Cube connected the dots from "True to the Game" by claiming NWA members had moved straight outta Compton. Then he went after the group as individuals:

> *Yella Boy is on your team so you're losin*
> *Ay yo Dre stick to producin*
> *Callin me Arnold but you been a dick*
> *Eazy-E saw your ass and ran in it quick*
> *You got jealous when I got my own company*
> *But I'm the man and ain't nobody humpin me*
> *Tryin to sound like AmeriKKKa's Most*
> *You can yell all day but you don't come close*

Dr. Dre got off relatively easy in relation to the other members of NWA. MC Ren, who would essentially disappear after the demise of the group, got his next:

So don't believe what Ren say

Cause he's goin out like Kunta Kinte

But I got a whip for ya Toby

Used to be my homie now you act like you don't know
me

It's a case of divide and conquer

Cause you let a Jew break up my crew

House nigga gotta run and hide

Yellin Compton but you moved to Riverside

So don't front MC Ren

Cause I remember when you drove a B-210

Broke as a muthafuckin joke

Let you on the scene to back up the first team

The mention of Kunta Kinte and Toby, the character from the epic 1970s television mini-series "Roots," was vintage Ice Cube. The 'Jew' who Ice Cube blamed for the disintegration of NWA was manager Jerry Heller, and later Dr. Dre would publicly agree. The final insult for MC Ren was Ice Cube painting him as some sort of rhyme scrub who simply got a chance as a substitute.

However, even MC Ren got off pretty lightly in comparison when Ice Cube let loose on Eazy-E. Referring to the

luncheon Eazy-E had attended with President George H.W.
Bush in the White House, Ice Cube started:

> *I'll never have dinner with the President*
> *And when I see your ass again I'll be hesitant*
> *Now I think you a snitch*
> *Throw a house nigga in the ditch half-pint bitch*
> *With your manager fella*
> *Fuckin MC Ren Dr. Dre and Yella*
> *But if they was smart as me*
> *Eazy E'll be hangin from a tree*
> *With no Vaseline*
> *Just a match and a little bit of gasoline*
> *Light em up burn em up flame on*
> *Till that jheri curl is gone...*
> *Cause you can't be the Nigga 4 Life crew*
> *With a White dude tellin you what to do*
> *Pullin wools with the scams*
> *Now I gotta play the Silence of the Lambs*
> *With a midget who's a punk too*
> *Tryin to fuck me but I'd rather fuck you*
> *Eric Wright punk always into somthin*
> *Gettin fucked at night by Mr. Shit Packer*

Bend over for the goddam cracker

No Vaseline!

Ice Cube's dark homophobic imagery left little doubt regarding his feelings toward his former group. As a unit, NWA would never release another new record. But in the aftermath of the group's breakup, new beef would spout between Dr. Dre and Eazy-E that while comical (see Dr. Dre's characterization of Eazy-E in the video "Dre Day" & Eazy-E's circulation of an old picture of Dr. Dre as a member of the World Class Wrecking Cru), didn't duplicate the original energy and escalation of this conflict.

You and Your Heroes

The street knowledge that was both the name of Ice Cube's production company and the bread and butter of his lyrical content also brought forth a debut album by Da Lench Mob. Introduced on Ice Cube's *AmeriKKKa's Most Wanted* album, Da Lench Mob had evolved to three members: J-Dee, T-Bone and Shorty. Ice Cube was both producer and executive producer on Da Lench Mob's initial offering, *Guerillas In The Mist*, an artistic and strategic move by Ice Cube to extend his musical brand similar to the way Eazy-E had done with NWA. The album began with a track entitled "Capital Punishment in America." This insert sampled a description of different ways people have been executed throughout history, the methods currently in use, and also discussed the last public execution in the United States. The date was August 14, 1936, when 20,000 people gathered to watch the hanging of a Black man accused of raping a White woman. The voice of a very southern sounding White man followed:

> Well they sold lemonade on the grounds, and of course the saloons get a bump of business and all of that, and everybody had a good time and the mob was just totally unruly...

"...mob was just totally unruly" repeated three times and transitioned to the second track, "Buck Tha Devil," which began with J-Dee saying, "Damn, I'm sweatin like a nigga at a White woman's funeral!"

Ice Cube, who essentially functioned as a fourth Lench Mob member, heavily influenced *Guerillas In Tha Mist*, a Nation of Islam flavored, Black Nationalist challenge to mainstream norms backed up with unapologetic militancy, similar to *Death Certificate*:

> *See the fuckin cop with the flat-top*
> *Standin over niggaz face down on the blacktop?*
> *That shit's gotta stop so I kick the hip-hop*

Pop that devil in his ass and make him flip-flop

"Buck tha Devil," using the term 'devil' to refer to White people, made reference to personal changes that were occurring within members of the group:

> *Shootin thru yellow pages*
> *That's why Whitey wanna catch us in cages*
> *But no no no I don't think so*
> *Shorty joined The Nation and he don't drink no mo*
> *Show em How To Eat To Live*
> *And how to beat the shit*

The reference to former Nation of Islam leader Elijah Muhammad's dietary manifesto, *How To Eat To Live*, illustrated ways in which the Nation of Islam could positively impact lifestyle choices that were widely viewed as detracting from the overall health of young Black males. But the challenges found in "Buck Tha Devil" were not simply for White people:

> *Never caught the Holy Ghost sorta like you do*
> *Just like X Clan relyin on my Voodoo*
> *Who you one flew over the Cuckoo's nest*

Now I guess that you think you're blessed
Get that fuckin cross off your chest
Can I kick it like A Tribe Called Quest? Yes!

The remarks about the Holy Ghost and Christianity were a specific challenge to the mainstream Black community. There are African-Americans, particularly those associated with the Nation of Islam, that question why other African-Americans would subscribe to a religion perceived by some to have been introduced to their ancestors by slave owners essentially as a control mechanism. Also of significance were the shout outs to East Coast groups A Tribe Called Quest and ultra-Black Nationalists X Clan.

While a track like "Lost In The System" explained how the failure to pay a simple traffic ticket eventually led to an extended incarceration, "You and Your Heroes" attacked a series of traditionally mainstream White American icons. These included Abraham Lincoln, Rocky Marciano, Madonna, the Beatles, the Fonz, Bryant Gumble (who is Black but viewed by some as 'White acting'), Babe Ruth, Marilyn Monroe, Uncle Sam, George Washington, Rock Hudson, Liberace, Larry Bird, Arsenio Hall (see Bryant Gumble), and Elvis Pressley.

One song that stood out conceptually was "All On My Nut Sac." Although the title might suggest another shocking misogynistic 'gangsta' rap single, this track actually offered a complex discussion on problems and possible solutions for the economic dysfunction of urban communities. In an exchange at the beginning, J-Dee played a fed up neighborhood resident while Ice Cube was the hustler on the corner:

> *J-Dee: Ay home boy!*
>
> *Ice Cube: Whatsup man, what you need nigga?*
>
> *J-Dee: What you mean what I need? Man y'all niggas got to get the fuck up off the block!*
>
> *Ice Cube: What you talking about man?*
>
> *J-Dee: Just what I said, y'all been on this muthafucka three or four years sellin this bullshit, and ain't put no money on nothing! Y'all niggas got to get the fuck up off the block!*

The concept of reinvesting proceeds from drug sales into the community, and the moral questions that come with it, has been in play since the first transaction took place. Further dialogue came during the song:

> *Ice Cube: Now do you wanna join my crew?*

J-Dee: Man fuck you nigga I thought you knew
Now I gotta lay you out play you out
For sellin' that shit all about
Ice Cube: Nigga I got clout
throughout the projects
J-Dee: Yeah for robbin' Black folks for their checks
Now we gotta break necks
Ice Cube: Black man don't flex on a brother
Unless you a plain clothes undercover
J-Dee: Man fuck you you can't get your slang on
Cause you got Black folks singin that same song
Ice Cube: I used to get my bang on
Now I got money anythang's on
J-Dee: Man fuck you because you're dead wrong
Use your mind Black man I can tell that your head
    strong
Ice Cube: So what should I do?
Work for $3.22? 'Welcome to McDonald's may I please
    help you?'
I don't think so homey don't play that
J-Dee: But here's a gun can homey say gat?

Limited opportunities for young urban males to earn legal wages
that covered the cost of living led directly to the explosion of

illegal entrepreneurship that took place in the midst of the drug

epidemic of the late 1980s and early 90s across the United States.

McDonald's had become a punch line of sorts in this discussion

as an example of a job that was there to be had, but whose pay

was at or around minimum wage level. Since money has always

been equated with respect in Western culture, the implication

was that minimum wage jobs are at the bottom of the respect

ladder. The decision between maintaining one's self-respect and

breaking the law is completely subjective. Da Lench Mob's

description of the problem spoke directly to African-American

youth, but it was also heard by other kids of many colors and

backgrounds who recognized this discussion was as much about

class as it was about race.

The title track, "Guerrillas in the Mist," was a play on the

book and movie *Gorillas in the Mist*, which was the story of

Dian Fossey, a native of San Francisco who began studying

gorillas in Zaire and Rwanda in 1967. She remained among the

gorillas for 18 years, interacting with them, even playing with

their children. When poachers killed one of Fossey's favorite

gorillas, she began to campaign against the practice of poaching.

On December 26, 1985, Fossey was found murdered in her cabin in Rwanda. The movie *Gorillas In The Mist* was nominated for several Academy Awards, including Best Actress (Sigourney Weaver), best editing, best music and original score, best writing, and best screenplay.

Da Lench Mob's twist was to use 'guerilla,' defined in Webster's Dictionary as "any member of a small defensive force or irregular soldiers, usually volunteers, making surprise raids, especially behind the lines of an invading enemy army," in the title. After stating "never thought you'd see South Central niggas in the forest," the Mob goes after perhaps the two best known mainstream jungle inhabitants of all time:

> *Comin real hard man bumpin in your car man*
> *Finally caught up with a devil named Tarzan*
> *Swingin on a vine suckin on a piece of swine*
> *Jigaboo come up from behind*
> *Hit him with a coconut stab him in his gut*
> *Push him out the tree he falls right on his nuts*
> *And just like EPMD I don't like a bitch*
> *Named J to the A to the N-E*
> *Can't wait to meet her I'm gonna kill her*
> *Cause that little muthafuckin Cheetah can't hang with a guerilla!*

The attack on Tarzan and his woman Jane were the result of the absurd idea that a White man would be the king of the African jungle. Da Lench Mob's philosophical and political message, including the rejection of White entertainment like Tarzan, revealed the intellectual and ideological 'guerilla' tactics that informed their expressive ideology.

Ay is That Nigga Del Your Cousin?

In the latter half of the 1980s, several groups and individuals from New York presented an alternative vibe to the 'hardcore' image portrayed by many rappers of the day. The group De La Soul, in particular, introduced a low key, funk lite style with the song and video "Me, Myself & I" from the album *3 Feet High And Rising*. The song featured an understated, monotone delivery that was a far cry from the intense vocals of some of their peers such as fellow New York rhymer and rap icon LL Cool J. The video sent a direct message as to what De La Soul was about. The scene was a school classroom and the members of the group were dressed in loose jeans, collared shirts, dreadlocks and beads around their necks. It was very much a 1960s/hippie type of feel. De La Soul stood out and was mocked by the rest of the students who were all dressed in sweat suits, chunky gold chains and red Kangol hats, looking suspiciously like LL Cool J wannabes.

The teacher of this class, Professor Defbeat, was dressed the same way as the students, and the video ended with De La Soul being kicked out of class and sent to the principal's office. The message that hip-hop and rap was more than simply hardcore was reflected in the language of the group. De La Soul's members were the DJ named Mase and two MCs, Posdnuos and Trugoy the Dove. A rapper identifying himself as a peaceful bird whose name was yogurt spelled backward was definitely something different. In addition, the De La Soul style was something that they termed "D.A.I.S.Y.," or "DA Inner Sound Y'all." This led to the inevitable identification of De La Soul and their counterparts A Tribe Called Quest, the Jungle Brothers, and Queen Latifah, collectively known as the Native Tongues, as peace-loving, sandal and bead wearing, granola eating, flower children. The success of this trend indicated that hip-hop had a broad base with room for more than the increasingly popular hardcore sound that was coming to dominate the rap music landscape. As David Toop put it in *Rap Attack*, "On the one side, rap is a spoken newspaper, a fax from the wax; on the other side, rap fits into the storytelling tradition of oral history and symbolic teaching."

This 'peacenik' style had ripple effects that went all the way to the West Coast, which had an equally vibrant scene at the time. Since his departure from NWA, Ice Cube had not only raised his own musical profile as an artist, but was also introducing and mentoring new artists with his production company, Street Knowledge. One of these artists was Ice Cube's cousin, a rapper from the Bay Area known as Del Tha Funkee Homosapien. Del's quirkiness and nearly opposite approach from Ice Cube was evident from the beginning; his debut album was called *I Wish My Brother George Was Here*. The title was lifted from an old Bugs Bunny cartoon in which, just as he is about to play the piano, Bugs delivers this line. The album cover is a semi-illustrated picture of Del hunched forward sitting with his elbows on his knees and his chin in his hands. Musically, the album was reflective of the West Coast's continued fixation with funk-laced tracks and samples from the likes of the P-Funk All Stars and Parliament Funkadelic.

> *Del covered an eclectic variety of topics. Take "The Wacky World of Rapid Transit:"*
> *I waited at the bus stop feelin kinda high*
> *From a spliff that I smoked*
> *I riffed and provoked a little scene when the bus arrived*

late

Like a joke with a corny punch line

And it was only lunch time

There is an age old debate about skin tone in the
African-American community that started about nine months
after the first slave master raped his first female slave. Del and Ice
Cube went back and forth in "Dark Skin Girls," Ice Cube
claiming that light skinned girls look better and Del advocating
for his "Black Nubian sisters." Their dialogue in between Del's
verses sounded surprisingly real with Ice Cube provoking Del by
calling dark skinned girls "ashy, black, jigaboo" and Del sounding
genuinely frustrated with Ice Cube's intolerance.

"Money For Sex," as the title implies, is a statement
against women using sex for financial gain:

You say crack sellers are swell fellas

Takin you to school in his 5.0 [Ford Mustang]

Like I don't know that your boyfriend's paid

You must've told me 18 times the other day

Del even talked about friends who overstay their
welcome in "Sleepin On My Couch:"

Maybe this was just my upbringing perhaps

386

> *But I was taught that I shouldn't take seven day naps*
> *At other brothers cribs like I don't have a home*
> *Brothers on my couch so much there's like foam*
> *Comin out the seams and a pair of jeans*
> *Is missin from my closet*

While Del certainly presented a different West Coast sensibility from his cousin Ice Cube, he also took steps to ensure that he was not simply lumped into the De La Soul category. Aside from being a practicing marijuana smoker (the beginning of the song "Sunny Meadows" is the sound of someone taking a massive bong hit), Del was unafraid to employ the occasional curse word to emphasize a point. In addition, he took several direct shots at other artists in the song "Pissin On Your Steps." About MC Hammer:

> *Now what you gonna do with the boy with no talent*
> *Usin step 1 and step 2 to keep his show valid*
> *Let's have a vote and try to register a ballot*
> *And realize a hammer is just a mallet*
> *Toss him like a salad because he ain't truly gifted*

On White pop-rapper Vanilla Ice:

Ice is cool but I can't stand Vanilla

Because he takes our style and tries to mock it

Ain't nothing personal G but I'm kinda into chocolate

Even De La Soul:

See I'm kinda mellow some call it lazy

Me and myself and I ain't with the Daisys

Cause I'm no goddam flower

And every single dancer in circumference receives a
golden shower

Del, thanks in part to Ice Cube's presence, was able to present his laid back style yet retain a touch of street credibility. This spoke to the level of diversity in the material that was being produced on the West Coast at this time. While 'gangsta rap' was getting much of the mainstream media play, a variety of styles were flourishing at the same time. This meant that there was something for virtually all musical tastes tuned into early '90s West Coast rap and hip-hop.

By this time, the general public's growing appetite for West Coast hip-hop meant that up and coming artists like Del would receive mainstream media exposure. A piece by Michael

Small in *People* magazine praised *I Wish My Brother George Was Here,* and noted the collaborative dynamic at work between Ice Cube and Del:

> It's interesting to see how well the cousins understand the differences in their images and shift so easily between attitudes, depending on whose face is on the cover. Cube and Del clearly enjoy each other. At the album's start, Del kids Cube about not knowing what a homosapien is. Later, Cube jokes about Del: "Don't pay no attention to him, man. He's kinda weird." Hmmm. Maybe there is a sitcom in this after all.

People magazine is a weekly publication that focuses primarily on celebrity news. Although there is a section that discusses new music, it is not necessarily considered a music magazine. Del's penetration of celebrity media was further indication of how much the mainstream had hip-hop on its mind.

The Grey One With the Burgundy Trim

As Compton emerged as a musical center of hip-hop on the West Coast, it continued to produce artists that built upon the hardcore flavor of life in Los Angeles. The addition of DJ Quik to this soundtrack brought both an artist and a producer who personified the visual image of the time. On the cover of his debut album he was dressed in a black t-shirt, khakis, and black baseball cap with a jheri curl and a gold chain. Aside from the curl, this had become a standard uniform of the rap scene outside the northeastern United States.

The NWA formula of combining the toast element of rhyming with consistent representation of Compton was a proven one. By the early 1990s, for a rapper to have Compton listed as his hometown on his hip-hop resume was the equivalent of an aspiring Wall Street banker who had a graduate degree from the Harvard Business School. The credibility that was associated with being from Compton was golden. DJ Quik added unique personality, creativity, and wit to this blueprint to produce his debut *Quik is the Name*. Quik made sure everyone knew where he was from by making his initial single "Born and Raised in Compton."

Quik's mindset was immediately apparent in the album's first song, "Sweet Black Pussy." He discussed his approach in an article in *The Los Angeles Times*:

> Quik characterizes his album as almost gangsta-rap. "It's not as violent or preachy as what Ice Cube and Eazy-E and those guys do," he said. "It's like a day in the life in the hood."

As the album's producer, Quik produced and performed, he knew how to move a crowd. "Tonite," was the detailed account of:

> *A day in the life of a playa named Quik*
> *I'm just a stubborn kinda fella with a head like a brick*
> *It began on Friday morning and ends 24 hours later after*
>   *doing way too much. Quik pleads:*
> *To the man up above to whom thanks I give*

I'll never drink again if you just let me live

The speaker vibrating bassline made it a song of praise for the decadent possibilities of the evening.

At the very end of "Tonite" there was an interesting exchange that in many ways can be viewed as a marker in the shifting priorities of 'mainstream' hip-hop. The relative 'consciousness' of East Coast rap music had often included a shout-out of "Peace!" at the end of songs, presumably to encourage it as well as signal the MC's departure. East Coast heavyweight DJ Eric B. asked his MC Rakim, the question, "Yo, what happened to peace?" at the end of the 1986 song "Paid in Full," and Rakim answered with a resounding "Peace!" that echoed for several seconds. The final seconds of "Tonite" asked: "What about Peace?" "Fuck peace nigga, gimme another brew." DJ Quik's version was clearly an answer to Eric B. and Rakim and reflected differing sensibilities between New York and the West Coast lifestyle. Saying "peace" in an environment that was coping with record setting homicide rates did not fit with the in-group norms of the Compton rap scene. Thus going out of his way to disregard peace in favor of another beer was a DJ Quik mini-rebellion, against that East Coast vibe.

Hip-hop's affinity for smoking marijuana continued with songs like "The Bombudd." Here, Quik broke out his Jamaican accent over a reggae inspired beat to produce what became a sleeper hit on the album. "Quik is the Name" interestingly referenced and sampled Nintendo's Tecmo Bowl football video game. Also in the midst of this track, Quik appears to lose his place in the rhyme and has to stop in the middle of the song, a la the D.O.C.

The reality of the streets couldn't be ignored, "Dedication" took a moment to shout out those who "didn't make it to see the album." The public suspicion that many West Coast artists had gang connections hovered over DJ Quik due to the initials 'TTP' that appeared on the back of the album. It was rumored that it signified 'Tree Top Piru,' an affiliate of the Bloods. While Quik maintained that it simply stood for Total Trak Productions, this instance marked the first time a major rapper claimed a particular gang set. Aside from the TTP reference, those familiar with the cultural nuances of Los Angeles gangs recognized a telltale cue in the way Quik was spelled. Gang historians and researchers have documented codes of communication in which members of the Bloods do not write or speak the letter 'c' because of that letter's association with the word Crip, while the Crips did the same with the letter 'b.' Other artists such as Snoop Doggy Dogg, who claimed Crip, would continue this practice later on.

DJ Quik captured a party spirit and sound within hip-hop that expanded the West Coast musical palate. *Quik Is The Name* was immediately followed by a succession of similar, up-tempo party-type albums by Second II None, AMG, and Hi-C, all members of Quik's crew. Second II None released a self-titled debut that featured everything from the radio friendly "Be True to Yourself," to more raw elements, to singing in R & B style harmony on "If You Want It" and "Let the Rhythm Take You." Hardly the stereotypical musical norm expected from Compton.

At first glance Hi-C appeared to use his album *Skanless* to stick to the script that had become the trend in West Coast 'gangsta' rap, but there were small homages paid hip-hop fundamentals that still lingered within this shifting musical landscape. Hi-C's logo featured a microphone as the 'I,' and the album opened with a scratch intro by DJ Tony A. Meanwhile jheri curls, having been mocked by movies such as the Eddie Murphy film *Coming to America*, were under attack to the point that Hi-C defended his hair on the track "Leave My Curl Alone." Further songs on the album like "Punk Shit," "Compton Hoochies," "Jack Move," "Yo Dick," "2 Drunk Ta F—k," and "Ding-a-ling" all covered aspects of life in South Central Los Angeles that seemed increasingly appealing to the mainstream.

AMG's 21-track album, *Bitch Betta Have My Money,* revitalized the debate over misogyny's large presence in rap music at the beginning of the 1990s. His offering to the mainstream was a song called "Jiggable Pie." Deeper in the album were tracks such as "I Wanna Be Yo Ho," "Mai Sista Izza Bitch," "Lick 'Em Low Lover," "Bitch Betta Have My Money," "Nu Exasize," "Backseat Queenz," "Givva Dogga Bone," "Tha Booty Up," and a skit called "My Ho, My Kids." AMG was so serious about his approach that "304," the name of the posse he claimed, supposedly spelled "hoe" if you wrote the four correctly and looked at it upside down. The X-rated, anti-woman mindset, titles, and hip-hop inspired spelling are representative of the extreme, exaggerated hype by which mainstream rap music is characterized, marketed, and promoted.

DJ Quik was another West Coast hip-hop artist able to produce subsequent records with other artists. The ability of artists to scaffold within the record industry, which involves making the transition from rappers to producers and executive producers on other artist's records, was becoming commonplace.

In terms of image, style, and content, DJ Quik, Second II None, Hi-C, and AMG pushed West Coast rap music image and sound toward good times and debauchery. Ball caps, sometimes with a curl, t-shirt with khakis or jeans, superior production, and subject matter/lyrics to carry a party. There was little pretense on the part of some of these artists about advocating for social change, as any serious socio-political commentary was more or less absent within their strain of music. Hip-hop began as party music, and as such there will always be room for music that can simply move the crowd. The only thing was that in the past it hadn't taken this many guns, niggaz, bitches and hos to get the party started.

Today You Tell Me Somethin y Mañana Otra Cosa

From its beginnings, one of hip-hop's greatest strengths has been its diversity. The Latin presence in the evolution of West Coast hip-hop during this time was not only heard but also seen. The signature fashion statement of the period revolved around sagging pants, a look originally associated with Latino prisoners whose oversized trousers hung low because belts were not allowed in jail. By the time the general public began to pay attention, this style had been adopted by Los Angeles' gang and hip-hop communities. Thus the mainstream came to associate saggy pants with primarily African-American 'gangsta' rappers. However, the West Coast's sizable Latino population was an active piece of the developing hip-hop scene from the start. LA Cubano and Skatemaster Tate forged an early connection between skateboarding and hip-hop cultures, expanding the ethnic and musical boundaries of young Latinos and Whites who used hip-hop as the soundtrack to their lives.

In a sense, hip-hop has always been bilingual, with lyrics delivered in language that can shift between standard and Black English. A variation of this bilingual approach to West Coast rap was employed by Mellow Man Ace, who combined a Spanish-English flow with radio friendly production. "Mentirosa" (Liar) sampled Carlos Santana's songs "Evil Ways" and "No One to Depend On," while Mellow Man Ace told the story of his lying lady friend:

> *Check this out baby tenemos tremendo lio*
> *Last night you didn't go a la casa de tu tio*
> *Resultase hey you were at a party*
> *Higher than the sky emborrachada de Bacardi*
> *I bet you didn't know que conoci al cantinero*
> *He told me that you were drinking and wasting my*
>   *dinero*
> *Talking about come and enjoy what a woman gives a*
>   *hombre*
> *But first of all see I have to know your nombre*
> *Now I really wanna ask ya que si es verdad*
> *And please por favor tell me la verdad*

Because I really need to know yeah necesito entender
If you're gonna be a player or be my mujer
Cause right now you're just a liar
A straight mentirosa
Today you tell me something y mañana otra cosa

Mellow Man Ace embraced that image of his birth place, Havana, Cuba, sporting hats and guayabera shirts with cigars in the pocket. He remained connected to his musical roots as well, incorporating a Cuban style called "guaguanco," which featured vocals chanted over congas.

Mellow Man Ace was not the only Latino MC from Los Angeles who was successful incorporating a bilingual delivery. Kid Frost, a veteran Mexican-American rapper from East Los Angeles whose big label debut album was called *Hispanic Causing Panic*, took it a step further by combining the Spanglish flow with a healthy dose of 'Brown pride.' The signature song on the album was "La Raza" (The Race):

Q-Vo aqui estoy MC Kid Frost
Yo soy jefe maton yes the Big Boss
My cuete's loaded it's full of balas
I put it in your face and you won't say nada

Vatos cholos you call us what you will

You say we are assassins and we are sent to kill

It's in my blood to be an Aztec Warrior

Go to any extreme and hold no barriers

Chicano and I'm Brown and I'm proud

Guantes chingazos simon tu sabes get down

Right now in the dirt

What's the matter you afraid you're gonna get hurt

I'm with my homeboys my camaradas

Kicking back millaje y pa mi no vale nada

Yo soy chingon ese like Al Capone ese

Controlo a todos solo never try to swept me

Some of you don't know what's happening que pasa

It's not for you anyway cuz this is for la Raza

Frost was no rookie to the rap scene in Southern California. In the early 1980s, Ice-T was rapping on the weekends at clubs and house parties. In the book *Rakim Told Me* Brian Coleman noted:

Oftentimes he [Ice-T] was aided by another upstart rapper from LA: Kid Frost. "Once me and Frost started to get known, our names would just start popping up on flyers, whether we said we'd be there or not," Ice says. "So we'd just bumrush parties that had our names on flyers, anywhere we could. When we'd show up, the promoters' eyes would open up 'cause we was actually there, and that meant they'd have to pay us. We were jacking promoters like that. On any given Friday or Saturday night we could run from party to party and make $1,000 or $1,500. That was a lot of money in the rap game back then.

As hip-hop's profile rose, 'hardcore' (East Coast street/political) and 'gangsta' rap (West Coast variant of hardcore) became increasingly synonymous to the mainstream. For rappers from the West Coast, virtually any hardcore content would automatically qualify them for 'gangsta' rap status and societal and political scrutiny. In Kid Frost's case, *The Los Angeles Times* reported, "the violent imagery in "La Raza" met with enough resistance from radio programmers that, at Virgin Records' suggestion, Frost changed some of the lyrics for a "Gringo mix" version." Even though he talked of fighting, guns, and murder, Kid Frost was clearly speaking to deeper racial issues. *The Times* also recognized it: "'La Raza' is the first popular East LA anthem in years, and he [Kid Frost] seems more a spokesman for Chicano solidarity than a merry thug," going as far as to label the song "the first national expression of Latino rap social consciousness."

The group A Lighter Shade of Brown built on this formula with more commercial flair in their song "On a Sunday Afternoon." The track sampled the classic War song "Groovin" as they rhymed about, what else, their Sunday afternoon:

> *I said chill*
> *All the vatos in the park stay ill*
> *Playing horseshoes to win the bill*
> *Carne asada snapping on the grill*
> *So now we eat*
> *The cops cruise by looking for the booze*
> *But what Ruben had was plainly simply apple juice*
> *Coming up short just like a fool*
> *Went back to his car with nothing he could do*
> *All the cars in the parking lot low profiling*
> *Everywhere you look you see somebody styling*

Cars would listen rolling deep with booming sounds
It's a good time to cruise around
In the parking lot where the brownies was stacking
And all the vatos were looking for some action yeah

While this music may have been primarily aimed at the Latino population, the hip-hop community gave these artists props because of the quality mix of the music. This recognition extended beyond hip-hop into multi-cultural demographics, for instance, Mellow Man Ace's album *Escape From Havana*, which charted on Billboard's Black, pop and Latin lists. The single "Mentirosa" charted on the Hot Black and Hot Rap singles chart, peaking at No. 14 on the Hot 100. Kid Frost's "La Raza" cracked the top 50 of the Hot 100 singles list, and *Hispanic Causing Panic* charted on the Top Pop Album and Top Black album lists.

Although not Latino, artists such as the Boo-Yaa T.R.I.B.E. continued this ethnic and musical expansion of West Coast hip-hop. The group was made up of six Samoan brothers from Carson, all weighing in at more than 200 pounds each. Boo —Yaa T.R.I.B.E.'s alleged past gang connections and physical appearance initially intimidated their record label, Island

Records, and the group's name, Boo-Yaa, represented the sound effect of a sawed off shotgun. David Toop depicted their images in *Rap Attack*:

> In Carson, a tranquil south Los Angeles community divided from Compton by the Artesia Freeway, a formidable Samoan extended family and funk/rap group called the Boo-Yaa T.R.I.B.E. lives with a basement full of guns and a daily routine that is close to red alert. Most of them being ex-gangbangers, their raps are written in hardcore prison slang, with joy, pleasure, identity and emergence expressed in metaphors of death, violence, intimidation, fear and imprisonment.

The tough, macho vibe of Boo-Yaa T.R.I.B.E.'s appearance and musical subjects belied a deeper sense of mission. Ted 'The Godfather' Devoux, the eldest brother and group leader, explained his approach to *The Los Angeles Times*:

> We go for what we believe in. We put our music

to our image, and our image is hardcore. We want to get something across to other [Pacific] Islanders out there, that we are opening doors, we're doing something. We want other Samoan kids to wake up and say, 'Hey man, we can do it too... If these big, crazy-looking dudes can stand up on stage and get away from gangs and drugs, so can I.'

Here is Something You Can't Understand

The success of West Coast bilingual rappers deepened the music's mix and cultural complexity and opened the door to new voices. Cypress Hill, from the South Gate area of Los Angeles, near Cypress Street, used a variety of styles to deepen creative sound and content. Cypress Hill, made up of B-Real, Sen Dog and DJ Muggs, incorporated Latino elements into their debut album, *Cypress Hill* with songs such as "Latin Lingo" and "Tres Equis." Other album song titles, displaying two primary aspects of their lyrical content, garnered the most attention.

One theme embedded within Cypress Hill's music common to West Coast's hardcore hip-hop music community. "Hand on the Pump," "Hole in the Head" and "Psycobetabuckdown," displayed the frequently violent environment that was Los Angeles in the early 1990s. But the song that best illustrated the Cypress Hill mindset on this topic was "How I Could Just Kill A Man." The song and video's title alone generated a lot of attention. However, author David Toop in *Rap Attack* viewed it through a critical lens:

> At this point, although much gangsta rap was contrived to shock, the more serious MCs were writing rhymes that seemed a genuine expression of what J-Dee [from the group Da Lench Mob] had described as 'all our sorrows put on wax.' Cypress Hill had released 'How I Could Just Kill A Man' at the beginning of the nineties. A nagging, foggy sound – all crackling squeals, tortured guitar breaks and relentless beats and bass – rolled under lyrics that threw up the challenge: 'Hangin out the window with my Magnum... Here is something you can't understand, how I could just kill a man.' Cut into the brattish vocals was a repeated question – 'What does it all mean?' – sampled from Double D and Steinski's 'Payoff Mix.'

Cypress Hill's chaotic sound, designed by Muggs, was reminiscent of some funked out Public Enemy. And it was a

perfect backdrop to the complex subject matters they were
discussing:

> *Say some punk tried to get you for your auto*
> *Would you call the one-time and play the role model?*
> *No I think you'd play like a thug*
> *Next you hear the shot of a Magnum slug*
> *Hummin cumin atchya*
> *Yeah you know I'm gonna gat ya*
> *How you know where I'm at*
> *When you haven't been where I been*
> *Understand where I'm comin from?*

The challenge to the listener kept the song from simply being a
'glorification' of murder. In addition, given the homicide rate in
Los Angeles at the time, no one could argue that the concept of
the song was not a realistic representation of their living
environment. In the end, the repeated question that played in
the background of the song was perhaps the key to the discussion
that surrounded it: What *does* it all mean?

The second distinguishing piece of Cypress Hill's
emergence was their connection to marijuana. Songs by artists

such as Tone-Loc, DJ Quik, and AMG had already helped make it clear that weed was a big part of West Coast hip-hop culture. Cypress Hill built on this in a major way with tracks like "Light Another," "Ultra Violet Dreams," "Something for the Blunted," and "Stoned is the Way of the Walk:"

> *Well it's the alley cat puffin on a hootie mac*
> *Some think I'm a criminal but yo I ain't all of that*
> *Hit ya with the baseball bat when you wanna ill though*
> *Wanna mess around you get bucked on the Hill bro*
> *Kickin like a steel toe real slow hits from the bong*
> *Make me feel like Cheech and I'm kickin it with Chong*

The group's complete embrace of the marijuana culture combined with its hip-hop roots to expose not only Cypress Hill, but rap music in general to new audiences. The March 1992 issue of *High Times* magazine featured a cover story that noted, "Cypress Hill's self-titled debut contains more marijuana references than a classic Peter Tosh or Bob Marley album."

The shadow of the crack epidemic was still looming over early 1990s society, and it was only a couple of years since Ronald Reagan's 'War on Drugs' and Nancy Reagan's 'Just Say No' campaign had left the White House. The government did not distinguish between 'hard' and 'soft' drugs, so the mainstream popularity of Cypress Hill forced the group to defend and explain their position on marijuana in interviews. They expounded on drug use in *High Times*.

> Many view Cypress Hill's stance as irresponsible, but B-Real insists that the music isn't designed to encourage kids to smoke pot. "It's an individual decision," he says. "What's right for us isn't right for everyone. Smoking weed opens our minds and sparks creativity. It may make other people get drugged-out and crazy."

> There is one line, however, that B-Real draws when it comes to the group's marijuana stance: "I don't want people to think we're drugged-out, common street hoodlums. We like weed, but not all drugs. Crack kills – we're against that and hard drugs."

Cypress Hill would go on to become a voice in the effort to legalize marijuana and became known for blazing up on stage, most famously as musical guests on the television show "Saturday Night Live." The group pioneered the establishment of multiple fan bases with their sound and sensibility. Cypress Hill simultaneously courted the Latino population, the African-American hip-hop community, the stoner/hippie culture, and the general public that watched video shows such as "Yo! MTV Raps." The group's versatility and broad-based appeal did as much to expand West Coast hip-hop's sphere of influence as anyone during this period.

And When They Passed Me They Used to Dis Me Harass Me But Now They Ask Me if They Can Kiss Me

Coming off of the success of *Sex Packets*, Digital Underground followed up in 1991 with *This Is An EP Release*. This 6-track effort reflected a couple of trends present in West Coast hip-hop music during the time. First was the use of illustrated album cover art. The second trend was the EP itself, which was also being used by other big names such as Ice Cube and NWA. An EP could be considered either a maxi-single or a mini-album, depending on how you looked at it. Made up mostly of remixes and scraps from *Sex Packets*, the record was primarily remembered because of one track. "Same Song" brought a head bobbing beat that sampled the Parliament song "Theme From The Black Hole," and featured MCs Shock G, Money B, and Shock's alter ego Humpty Hump, who picked up the silliness right where he left off on *Sex Packets*:

> *It's just a freestyle meanwhile we keep the beat kickin*
> *Sweat drippin girlies in the limo eatin chicken*
> *Oops don't get the grease on your pantyhose*
> *I love you Rover but move over I gotta blow my nose*

In addition to Humpty Hump advocating safe-sex through the use of condoms, there was another significant lyrical aspect to "Same Song:" Tupac Amaru Shakur made his big time hip-hop debut:

> *Now I clown around when I hang around with the*
> *   Underground*
> *Girls used to frown say I'm down when I come around*
> *Gas me and when they pass me they used to dis me*
> *Harass me but now they ask me if they can kiss me*
> *Get some fame people change wanna live they life high*
> *Same song can't go wrong if I play the nice guy*
> *Claimin that they must have changed*
> *Just because we came strong*
> *I remain still the same*
> *Why Tu'? Cause it's the same song*

Tupac Amaru II was a rebel who in 1780 led an indigenous Incan uprising against the colonizing Spaniards in what is now Peru. His rebellion was violently put down, and after his capture Tupac Amaru was sentenced to be tortured and then executed. In 1781, four horses, each tied to an appendage, literally ripped him apart on the city of Cuzco's main plaza. The rapper Tupac also shared his name with the Túpac Amaru Revolutionary Movement or *Movimiento Revolucionario Túpac Amaru* (MRTA). The Marxist MRTA was formed in 1983 with the goal of overthrowing the Peruvian government and instituting socialism. The Peruvian government regarded the MRTA guerillas as a terrorist organization.

Appearing in Afro-centric garb and being carried like royalty in the video, Tupac was clearly both the lyrical and visual star of "Same Song." It was from this position that he would begin down a path that would leave a lasting cultural imprint, both as a hip-hop artist and a citizen of the world.

Just Cause You're in the Ghetto Doesn't Mean You Can't Grow

After Tupac's appearance with Digital Underground on "Same Song," it was time for him to step out on his own. His initial solo effort, *2Pacalypse Now*, helped set the stage for what would become one of the more legendary careers in musical history. Tupac's massive appeal was based on the narrative of his life experience. He was raised by a single mother, Afeni, who went from being a member of the Black Panther Party in the 1960s and 70s to a crackhead in the 1980s. Tupac was also the godson of Elmer 'Geronimo' Pratt, another former Panther who spent 27 years in prison on a murder conviction that was eventually overturned. As a teen at the Baltimore School for the Arts, Tupac trained as an actor in roles ranging from to Shakespeare to *The Nutcracker*. His familial ties to the remnants of the Black Power movement from the Civil Rights era, combined with his first hand experience in the apocalyptic wave of crack that came in its aftermath, gave Tupac unique perspective and artistic credibility.

Indeed, the activist flavor of *2Pacalypse Now* was rooted in the Black Panther's militant approach to urgent social justice issues. "Trapped" delineated life in West Coast urban communities in a flavor similar to Ice Cube:

> *They got me trapped*
> *Can barely walk the city streets*
> *Without a cop harassing me searching me*
> *Then asking my identity*
> *Hands up throw me up against the wall*
> *Didn't do a thing at all*
> *I'm tellin you one day these suckers gotta fall*
> *Cuffed up throw me on the concrete coppers try to kill*
> *me*
> *But they didn't know this was the wrong street*
> *Bang bang down another casualty*
> *But it's a cop who's shot there's brutality*
> *Who do you blame*
> *It's a shame because the man's slain*
> *He got caught in the chains of his own game*

How can I feel guilty after all the things they did to me

Sweated me hunted me trapped in my own community

The chorus featured Tupac repeating, "They got me trapped!" and Shock G answering, "Nah, they can't keep the Black man down!" In the video, this exchange between the two men took place over the phone in a prison visiting room.

Tupac's compassion for the plight of women in dire financial and life circumstances was expressed in "Brenda's Got A Baby." The song was based on the true story of a 12 year-old rape victim who dumped her baby into a garbage can. "Brenda's Got A Baby" was a one-verse song, a la Eric B. and Rakim's classic "Paid In Full":

I hear Brenda's got a baby well Brenda's barely got a
brain

A damn shame the girl can hardly spell her name

(That's not our problem that's up to Brenda's family)

Well let me show you how it affects the whole
community

Now Brenda never really knew her moms and her dad
was a junky

Pushing death into his arms it's sad cause I bet Brenda
doesn't even know

*Just cause you're in the ghetto doesn't mean you can't
grow*

But oh that's a thought my own revelation

Do whatever it takes to resist the temptation

Brenda got herself a boyfriend

*Her boyfriend was her cousin now let's watch the joy
end*

Tried to hide her pregnancy from her family

Who didn't really care to see or give a damn if she

Went out and had a church of kids

As long as when the check came they got first dibs

Now Brenda's belly is gettin bigger

But no one seems to notice any change in her figure

She's 12 years-old and she's having a baby

In love with a molester who's sexin her crazy

And yet she thinks that he'll be with her forever

*And dreams of a world with the two of them are
together whatever*

He left her and she had the baby solo

She had it on the bathroom floor and didn't know so

She didn't know what to throw away and what to keep

*She wrapped the baby up and threw him in the trash
heap*

*I guess she thought she'd get away wouldn't hear the
cries*

She didn't realize how much the little baby had her eyes

Now the baby's in the trash heap bawlin

Momma can't help her but it hurts to hear her callin

Brenda wants to run away momma say you makin' me lose pay

The social workers here every day

Now Brenda's gotta make her own way

Can't go to her family they won't let her stay

No money no babysitter she couldn't keep a job

She tried to sell crack but end up getting robbed

So now what's next there ain't nothin left to sell

So she sees sex as a way of leavin hell

It's payin the rent so she really can't complain

Prostitute found slain and Brenda's her name

She's got a baby...

Challenging, socially critical material like this is what prompted Tupac to describe *2Pacalypse Now* to *Billboard* magazine as a "battle cry," and that the genesis of the album came "from stories from my whole life."

The general hip-hop public was already keenly aware that Tupac was much more warrior than thug. Tupac's social stance was strengthened by fierce and undying loyalty to his friends, fully on display in "If My Homie Calls":

> *It's a shame you chose the dope game*
> *Now you slang cane on the streets with no name*
> *It was plain that your aim was mo' caine*
> *You got game now you run with no shame*
> *I chose rappin tracks to make stacks*
> *In fact I travel the map with raps that spray cats*
> *But now I don't wanna down my homie*
> *No matter how low you go you're not lowly*
> *And I hear that you made a few enemies*
> *But when you need a friend you can depend on me*
> *Call if you need my assistance*
> *There'll be no resistance I'll be there in an instant*
> *Who am I to judge another brother only on his cover*
> *I'd be no different than the other*

Released as a double A side with "Brenda's Got A Baby," "If My Homie Calls" was initially more attractive to the mainstream. Some urban radio programmers were nervous about playing "Brenda" because of the 'controversial' subject matter. Video outlets, however, were more open to the song and found that it was well received.

Interscope, Tupac's record label, devised a ground level promotional strategy to spread the word about Tupac's first album. Interscope's Ed Strickland noted, "We took a real grassroots/underground promotion and marketing approach. We worked college radio and the streets, did specialty shows, and a mini-retail run. We didn't want to come out shooting the big guns. Our main concern was creating awareness." To this end, Tupac took to visiting schools during February, 1992 for Black History Month. Combined with Tupac's unique, musical social consciousness, Interscope's strategic marketing plan for his product pushed Tupac into the public's eye. His philosophy was already carefully thought out for his public arrival, so that, as he stated, "this country would know that I'm not just a gun-totin' hooligan."

In 1992, Tupac's star continued to rise with his appearance in the movie *Juice*. The film told the story of four relatively normal Harlem teenagers involved in a robbery turned murder, and its tragic aftermath. Tupac's chilling portrayal of the unbalanced Bishop fully displayed his considerable acting talent.

And All Them Other Goddam Kings From Africa!

Of all the noteworthy dates in the development and identity of West Coast hip-hop music and the mainstream, none is more significant than March 3, 1991. This was the day that 27 year-old Black motorist Rodney King and his white Hyundai reportedly led police on a high speed chase. When King was caught, he was beaten by Los Angeles Police Department Sgt. Stacy Koon, Officer Laurence M. Powell, Officer Theodore Briseno, and Officer Timothy Winn, all of whom were White. Between four LAPD batons King was struck 56 times in two minutes, suffering numerous injuries including multiple skull fractures and brain and kidney damage.

All of this may have just been another day at the office for the LAPD if it had not been for the view from George Holliday's balcony. Holliday's front row seat allowed him to videotape the entire episode without being seen by the 17 other LAPD and California Highway Patrol officers who were also on the scene. The next day, he gave his tape to television station KTLA and within hours the world was focusing on what Ice-T, NWA, Ice Cube, and many others had been arguing for years; law enforcement's systemic and brutal war waged against African-Americans.

The LAPD was forced to react to the international attention focused on the images of four White police officers beating the shit out of a defenseless Black man lying on the ground. On March 5, Koon, Powell, Briseno and Winn were arraigned on charges of assault with a deadly weapon and use of excessive force. A grand jury refused to indict the other officers on the scene who witnessed the beating. Three weeks later all four pled not guilty, arguing that they were acting in self-defense to restrain King, who allegedly was aggressive and resisting arrest. The trial itself would not start for nearly a year, but during that time defense attorneys succeeded in moving the trial to the suburb of Simi Valley despite concerns that this would significantly influence the makeup of the jury pool.

You Had to Get Rodney to Stop Me

Testimony in the trial of the four Los Angeles Police officers accused of beating Rodney King began on March 5, 1992 in front of an all-White jury. The racial climate in Southern California became more aggravated and even more explosive during the year and two days since the King beating.

On March 16, 1991, a couple of weeks after the King beating, Latasha Harlins, a 15 year-old African-American girl, entered the Empire Liquor Market and Deli in South Central. Minutes later she was shot in the back of the head by a Korean grocer after an altercation over a bottle of orange juice. The killing was recorded by a security camera in the store. It showed Harlins scuffling with the Korean woman, 49 year-old Soon Ja Du, at the counter. Harlins, who was unarmed, turned around and walked away taking only a few steps before Du pulled out a handgun and fired a single shot. Several months later Du was found guilty of voluntary manslaughter, but Judge Joyce Carlin granted the defendant probation.

The sentence aggravated racial tensions that already existed between African-Americans and Asians in places like South Central, which Ice Cube had described in his song "Black Korea." For years, Asian store-owners in African-American neighborhoods have been viewed as economic colonialists by the community. The contending sides' antagonism was defined by African-Americans frustration with language difficulties and poor treatment and storeowner's anger over shoplifting.

In some ways, the framework of the Latasha Harlins incident paralleled the Bernard Goetz case in New York City. On December 22 1984, Goetz, a White man, shot four young Black men in a Manhattan subway car when he thought they were going to rob him. One of the young men was paralyzed as a result of the shooting. Three years later, Goetz was acquitted of attempted murder and assault. Instead, he was convicted of criminal possession of an unlicensed weapon and served 250 days in jail.

To the African-American community it appeared to be open season on Black people: Two high profile cases where gun wielding citizens were sentenced to little or no jail time for

shooting and killing unarmed African-Americans. It seemed that

the general public's fear of African-Americans had caught up to

that of the police. A perceived threat, whether real or not, was

apparently sufficient reason to use deadly force against young

Black men and women. The legal system's sentencing seemed

partial to the police and other perspectives of violence against

African-Americans. Endangered species indeed.

More fuel was added to the fire. In July of 1991, some four

months after the King beating, an independent panel led by

attorney Warren Christopher, who would later become United

States Secretary of State, released a report on the Los Angeles

Police Department designed to provide "a full and fair

examination of the structure and operation of the LAPD,"

including assessment of recruitment and training practices,

internal disciplinary protocols, and the citizen complaint system.

The report reviewed transmissions between squad cars and police

stations, internal use of force reports, and eighty-three civil

damage cases involving alleged use of excessive force that were

settled out of court by the Los Angeles City Attorney's office for

amounts greater than $15,000 over a five year period. In addition, the commission also held public hearings and interviewed numerous officials and residents.

The Christopher Commission, as it was named, presented evidence most Black residents of Los Angeles above the age of five already knew. The LAPD's culture was one of institutionalized racism, which was acted out on a routine basis by the use of excessive force against minorities and the underclass. Among other things, the commission found:

- There is a significant number of officers in the LAPD who repetitively use excessive force against the public and persistently ignore the written guidelines of the department regarding force.

- The failure to control these officers is a management issue that is at the heart of the problem. The documents and data that we have analyzed have all been available to the department; indeed, most of this information came from that source. The LAPD's failure to analyze and act upon these revealing data evidences a significant breakdown in the management and leadership of the Department. The Police Commission, lacking investigators or other resources, failed in its duty to monitor the Department in this sensitive use of force area. The Department not only failed to deal with the problem group of officers but it often rewarded them with positive evaluations and promotions.

- The commission highlighted the problem of "repeat offenders" on the force, finding that of approximately 1,800 officers against whom an allegation of excessive force or improper tactics was made from 1986 to 1990, more than 1,400 had only one or two allegations. But 183 officers had four or more allegations, 44 had six or more, 16 had eight or more, and 1 had sixteen such allegations. Generally, the forty-four officers with six complaints or more had received positive performance evaluations that failed to record "sustained" complaints or to discuss their significance.

The commission confirmed what the King videotape had already visually described and would eventually bring about the resignation of already unpopular LAPD Chief Darryl Gates. In the court of public opinion it all but sealed a guilty verdict for the four officers involved in the King beating.

When testimony began in the trial of Stacy Koon, Laurence Powell, Theodore Briseno, and Timothy Winn in a Simi Valley courtroom on April 5, 1992, a fuse that took twenty-four days to burn was lit. On April 29, a stunned world heard what would eventually become the second most infamous 'not-guilty' verdict in United States judicial history (O.J. being #1). The explosive energy reflected in much of West Coast hip-hop music at this time had been steadily building in South Central Los Angeles since the Watts Rebellion of 1965, in which 34 people died. Back then issues related to Chuck D's 'three Es' for healthy community development, education, economics, and (law) enforcement, were at the root of the unrest. In the aftermath of what took place in Watts, city officials proposed a 25-year plan to help rectify the root problems. This plan never came together, thanks in part to Ronald Reagan's funding cuts for social programs. When you consider the added weight of the crack epidemic, and all of the previously discussed crack-related issues during the 1980s, conditions for young people had arguably gotten worse in communities like South Central, almost exactly 25 years later the same community was on the verge of another uprising.

News of the verdict spread quickly and almost immediately the explosion came. There would be protests in several other cities around the United States in response to the verdict, but Los Angeles is where it really went down. Buildings were stormed and looted, fires were set, and people were beaten and murdered in the streets for four days. Rodney King himself appeared on television to try and encourage calm, offering his now famous plea, "Can we all just get along?"

Television news reports broadcast the action into the homes of shocked Americans and cemented what became the signature image of the uprising. A news helicopter filmed Reginald Denny, a White truck driver in the wrong place at the wrong time, as he was pulled from his vehicle and severely beaten by several Black men. Denny would later testify that the beating left him with over 90 broken bones in his face. More tragic irony, this visual was the flip side of the Rodney King tape that started it all.

In the end, the California National Guard and Federal troops were deployed to help the police restore order in Los Angeles. Best estimates state 60 people were killed, 2,383 injured, and 13,212 arrested. More than 1,100 buildings were damaged or destroyed and property losses totaled more than $1 billion. The glimpse of anarchy that simultaneously terrified and thrilled the nation was over.

In the summer of 1992, Koon, Powell, Briseno, and Winn were indicted on Federal charges of violating Rodney King's civil rights. Koon and Powell were found guilty and each served 30 months in jail, while Winn and Briseno were acquitted. All four men subsequently left the LAPD, as did Chief Daryl Gates. Willie Williams, hired from Philadelphia as Los Angeles's first African-American Police Chief, replaced Gates. Rodney King was awarded $3.8 million in damages from the city of LA. Much it went to pay his lawyers and King even started a short-lived rap record company. At the time of the beating, King was on probation and in the years since had several minor run-ins with the law. He also earned his high school equivalency degree, but rarely spoke in public. Rodney King's legacy seems to be that of a reluctant icon who happened to get caught up in issues that he was neither inclined nor equipped to deal with. King drowned in his swimming pool at home on June 17, 2012.

As the smoke cleared from what was the deadliest and most expensive civil uprising in modern United States history, there was a sense of vindication on the part of many within the West Coast rap music culture. As Ice-T told *The Los Angeles Times* on May 2, 1992:

> I'm not saying I told you so, but rappers have been reporting from the front for years. Ice Cube, Public Enemy, we were all saying that you have a potentially explosive situation. Black people look at the cops as the Gestapo. People thought it might come to an end [with the Rodney King trial] and they might get some justice. That was a false hope. People saw [that] justice is a myth if you're Black. Of course people will riot.

Some felt that as a result of these events rappers would essentially become community leaders. However, Eazy-E argued:

> Nobody wants to hear us lecture them. What they want is to see something done to those four officers. They want justice. They want to see something done to that grocer who shot that

little girl. They want the government to make an example of those four officers the way they made an example of Mike Tyson. What this boils down to is a matter of respect.

In a separate *Los Angeles Times* story, Ice Cube worked to define the terms of the debate, saying, "First of all, I don't even call it a riot, I call it an uprising." Ice Cube, the musician and the personality, was still a hard sell for the mainstream, and the media could not help itself, implying that rap, and artists like Ice Cube, were as much instigator as recipient of social conditions. The *LA Times*, in the same piece in which Ice Cube was quoted, asked:

Why keep reflecting the anger at a time when the community is aching for healing? Didn't the uprising or riots raise new challenges for rappers? After the hours of sobering television footage, is there really any need to continue expressing rage?

Ice Cube responded:

The media and authorities like to concentrate on

the looting and say it was just a bunch of

criminals or thugs out there, but there were all

kinds of people out there, women and children...

poor people who wouldn't have to loot if they

had money to buy things.

That's why, to me, it was a protest. It was a

protest against the conditions and the injustice.

The looting that was done in South Central was

nothing like the looting done by the savings and

loans [financial scandal during the 1980s].

Another *LA Times* article finally gave props that hip-hop had

been subconsciously craving since its birth, but with a caveat:

For those who have rejected the raw, street spawned

music as exploitative and contrived, it is time to recognize the

genuine artistic impulses of the field's most gifted figures,

including Ice Cube and Chuck D. At the same time, it's no

longer enough for rappers to convey just the anger and rage of

the inner city. Those emotions were amply documented for the

world to see in the sobering, heartbreaking footage of burnings, looting and beatings. To continue to serve as a network of information and change, rappers must explore the challenges and consequences facing the community, both inside and outside the 'hood.

Obviously, one could not argue that these MCs now had unprecedented access to mainstream platforms that were previously unavailable. Having essentially predicted history, West Coast artists like Ice-T, Ice Cube and NWA now had a level of credibility that caused many people, especially youth, to look to rappers for some social direction. If they saw all of this coming, what would they say next?

I Told You it Would Happen and You Heard it Read it But All You Could Call Me Was Anti-Semitic

The energy within and surrounding the West Coast hip-hop music scene following the King uprising produced several works that continued to challenge the status quo with even more fury. One example was Ice Cube's *The Predator*. As he had on *Death Certificate*, Ice Cube used the album's liner notes to set the stage for the music. He took aim at "White America's continued commitment to the silence and oppression of Black men," "the failure of the public school system to teach all of its students about the major contributions made by our African-American scientists, inventors, artists, scholars and leaders," and "America's cops for their systematic and brutal killings of brothers all over the country." Ice Cube's remarks were flavored by Black Nationalist/Pan-African hip-hop culture. Ice Cube concluded:

You say Ice Cube is a problem – well you're
right, he's two people in the same body, one
African, one American. I see myself through the
eyes of Africa and I will continue to speak as an
African. I will become an African-American
when America gives up oppression of my people.
KEEP RAP LEGAL!

Ice Cube' popularity as a celebrity figure was evidenced by
referring to himself in the third person, but he was also reflecting
a widespread hip-hop social consciousness that felt a strong
connection to Africa.

The album opened with a sample from the movie
American Me, depicting the humiliation new prisoners face as
they are booked into jail. The bell sounds, the door slams, and a
guard tells a group of men to "Shut the fuck up!" While dramatic
music plays in the background, the inmates must "raise their nut
sacs" and then turn around, "bend over, grab your ass, spread
your cheeks and give me two good coughs!"

As had become standard among the top artists in
hip-hop, there were radio/video friendly tracks that seemed ready
made to deliver Ice Cube to the mainstream. The track "Wicked"

incorporated a funky, reggae inspired chant, a trend also present in the NWA song "Always Into Somethin." And Ice Cube did kick mainstream friendly lines like:

> *Shake that nigga and pass me the pill*
> *And I'll slam dunk it like Shaquille O'Neal*

But he also continued to put pressure on the power structure:

> *Through with Daryl Gates but is Willie Williams*
> *Down with the Pilgrims? Just a super slave*
> *We'll have to break his ass up like Super Dave*

The removal of Daryl Gates and the hiring of Willie Williams could be viewed as progress. But Ice Cube clearly understood that a change in the skin color of the police chief did not constitute a change in the culture of the police department. Ice Cube continually mixed mass appeal with a social change agenda; there might be party music but Cube knew where he wanted it to lead.

"It Was a Good Day" was an easy going description of the 'perfect' day according to Ice Cube. Set to a sample from the Isley

Brother's classic "Footsteps in the Dark," Ice Cube described an "odd" day that saw him: Wake up to a morning in Los Angeles with no smog, eat a breakfast with no pork, hop in his drop-top on hydraulics, get paged by a female, play basketball, not get harassed by the police, shoot some dice, play dominoes, not have any friends murdered, hook up and have sex with a girl he'd been trying to get at since high school, get a Fat Burger, see the Goodyear Blimp ("and it read Ice Cube's a pimp"), and not have to use his AK-47.

Ice Cube's extensive flirtation with the Nation of Islam and the 5 Percent Nation also continued to influence the content and direction of his music. The Nation had a long history of being active within the prison system, and has turned around the lives of thousands of people. The Nation and Ice Cube worked the same turf, agreeing politically on many issues. Jail was a very real factor in the communities Ice Cube's music represented and the Nation had a long history of resistance against the United States government that was overpopulating jails with young Black males.

However, some accused Ice Cube of being a hypocrite; the Nation of Islam required abstinence from alcohol while Cube had become a well-known spokesman for St. Ides Malt Liquor. The growth in popularity of cheap, highly potent malt liquor was a contentious issue within hip-hop culture. Chuck D, a fellow Nation supporter wrote "1 Million Bottle Bags," which appeared on the album *Apocalypse 91... The Enemy Strikes Black*, to address the abuse of malt liquor.

In addition, the Nation's message of Black unity contrasted with violent Black-on-Black violence skits like the beginning of "Now I Gotta Wet'Cha." With the Lench Mob's "Guerilla's in the Mist" playing in the background, someone said, "Yo Cube, there go that muthafucka right there." Ice Cube responded, "No shit, watch this." As he walked over to this person the following exchange took place:

> *Ice Cube: Ay whasup man?*
> *Guy: Not too much.*
> *Ice Cube: You know you won, G.*
> *Guy: Won what?*
> *Ice Cube: The wet T-shit contest, muthafucka!*
> *[gunshot]*

The popular image of the 'gangsta' rapper and how things were handled in the streets was also reflected in scenes from movies such as *New Jack City, Boyz N The Hood,* and later *Menace to Society.* Depending on which side of the reporting/glamorizing debate you stood, Ice Cube certainly appeared to be sending mixed messages.

The highly charged track "When Will They Shoot," set to a sample from "We Will Rock You" by Queen, did address the nature of Ice Cube's relationship with the Nation of Islam:

> *I met Farrakhan and had dinner*
> *Now you ask am I a 5 percenter well*
> *No but I go where the brothers go*
> *Down with Compton Mosque Number 54*

The song also sampled Michael Jordan saying, "You better eat your Wheaties," and Ice Cube's observation of who has been most responsible for violent death within the Black community:

> *Most got done by a Black man's bullet*
> *Give a trigga to a nigga and watch him pull it*
> *Negro assassin*
> *I'ma dig a ditch bitch and throw yo ass in*
> *When they shoot it won't be a cracker*

They'll use somebody much Blacker

Of all the music that reflected commentary on the King uprising, perhaps no song captured the fury of the time more than "We Had to Tear This _____ Up." An intro sample contained a southern sounding White man saying, "Peace, quiet, and good order will be maintained in our city to the best of our ability. Riots, melees and disturbances of the peace are against the interest of all our people, and therefore cannot be permitted." Any question of what the song was about was answered next as a newscaster announced, "... the jury found that they were all not guilty" [fading echo, "not guilty, not guilty, not guilty, not guilty, not guilty..."]. Another newscaster then described breaking news: "We've been told that all along Crenshaw Boulevard that there's a series of fires, a lot of looting is going on, a disaster area, obviously."

A prickly bass riff with a hard kick drum, produced by DJ Muggs of Cypress Hill gave the track a hectic, chaotic feel that set the tone for the vibe of the song. The collaboration between Ice Cube and Muggs was deeply rooted in the influence of Public Enemy. Ice Cube's prior work with Chuck D and the Bomb Squad is the obvious link. As the architect of Cypress Hill's

442

sound, Muggs had developed a style that was reminiscent of a West Coast Public Enemy feel with beats that were at times busy and contained those high-pitched, shrieking samples (compare "Hand On the Pump" by Cypress Hill and "Don't Believe The Hype" by Public Enemy).

Wasting no time, Ice Cube spit fire on the first verse:

Not guilty the filthy devils tried to kill me
When the news get to the hood the niggaz will be
Hotter than cayenne pepper cuss bust
Kickin up dust is a must
I can't trust a cracker in a blue uniform
Stick a nigga like a unicorn
Born wicked Laurence Powell foul
Cut his fuckin throat and I smile
Go to Simi Valley and surely
Somebody knows the address of the jury
Pay a little visit who is it yo its Ice Cube
Can I talk to the Grand Wizard then boom
Make him eat the barrel modern day feral
Now he's zipped up like Leather Tuscadero
Pretty soon we'll catch Sergeant Koon
Shoot him in the face run up in him with a broom

Stick prick devils ain't shit

Introduce his ass to the AK-40 dick

Two days niggaz laid in the cut

To get some respect

We had to tear this muthafucka up

This verse summarized the fiery yet complex feelings in many

young people as they witnessed what was taking place, and Ice

Cube's stutter-step rhyme method brought emphasis to the

continued mistrust of police, the unanswered question of how

the trial got moved to predominantly White Simi Valley in the

first place, and the natural desire to seek some sort of justice

through vigilante action.

Ice Cube's mainstream power and recognition was

immense, as reflected in an article from *The Washington Post*:

Ice Cube must have gloated when his new

Predator album opened on the *Billboard* charts

at No. 1. After all, in the "Wicked" cut, he disses

the music trade magazine and its editor, Timothy

White, for printing an editorial last year

denouncing him and urging a boycott of the

Death Certificate album for what *Billboard*
called racist and homophobic lyrics. *Predator*
went platinum in four days.

As history reflects on the issues behind the Rodney King
uprising, the event is often used as a reference point in gauging if
and when something similar might happen again in the United
States. As predictor and narrator, no one articulated the dynamic
of these events through music more effectively than Ice Cube.
Throughout "We Had to Tear This _____ Up," Ice Cube
exclaims, "Make it rough!" When it came to the rebellion that
fueled the heart of West Coast hip-hop music during the early
1990s, no one made it rougher.

Hmm Let Me Think About It

In the way that "Same Song" by Digital Underground
introduced the world to Tupac, another song in 1992 would do
the same for the West Coast's next up and coming hip-hop
superstar. The movie *Deep Cover* starred Larry Fishburne as a
disillusioned Los Angeles police officer who got caught up going
too far undercover trying to get to the top of a cocaine
distribution ring. The soundtrack to the movie included the
film's theme song, which was highly significant for two reasons.
It was the debut single for Dr. Dre following his departure from
NWA. Rumor had it that Suge Knight, co-founder of Death
Row Records, had threatened Eazy-E with a baseball bat in an
attempt to secure Dr. Dre's contractual release from Ruthless
Records. Whatever the case, all eyes were on Dr. Dre as he looked
to prove himself as a solo artist with the weight of the theme
song to a major motion picture squarely on his shoulders.

Though Dr. Dre was never considered a master lyricist, the effective use of other group members and his production skills nearly always made up for whatever Dre lacked as an MC. The song "Deep Cover" would be no different. A hard kick drum beat and a funky, rising bassline offered up a musical treat:

> *Kingpin kickin back while his workers slang his rocks*
> *Coming up like a fat rat big money big cars*
> *Big bodyguards on his back*
> *So it's difficult to get him*
> *But I got the hook up*
> *with somebody who knows how to get in contact with him*
> *Hit him like this and like that*
> *Let 'em know that I'm lookin for a big fat dope sack*
> *With ends to spend so let's rush it*
> *If you want to handle it tonight we'll discuss it*
> *On a nigga's time at a nigga's place*
> *Take my strap just in case*
> *One of his boys recognize my face*
> *Cause he's a sheisty motherfucker*
> *But I gives a fuck cause I'm going deep cover*

When Dr. Dre and his production talents left NWA, it meant

the end of the group. As Dre moved into his solo career the

question was: Would there be a lyricist that could properly

compliment what Dre was doing musically? The answer was yes,

and he came to Dr. Dre as a member of a group called 213, named

after the telephone area code for downtown Los Angeles and

Long Beach. One member of this group, Warren Griffin aka

Warren G., was Dr. Dre's younger half-brother. Warren had

constantly been telling Dre about his MC partner in 213, a kid

from Long Beach named Snoop Doggy Dogg. This is what led

Dre to give Snoop his big time debut on "Deep Cover," where

his vocal chops, in concert with Dr. Dre's beats, had immediate

impact:

> *Creep with me as I crawl through the hood*
> *Maniac lunatic call me Snoop Eastwood*
> *Kickin dust as I bust fuck peace*
> *And the motherfuckin punk police*
> *You already know I gives a fuck about a cop*
> *So why in the fuck would you think that it would stop*
> *Plot yeah that's what we about to do*
> *Take yo' ass on a mission with the boys in blue*
> *Whattup Snoop?*

Yo I got the feelin
Tonight's the night like Betty Wright and I'm chillin
Killin feelin no remorse
Yeah so let's go straight to the motherfuckin source
And see what we can find
Crooked-ass cops that be gettin niggaz a gang of time
And now they wanna make a deal with me
Scoop me up and put me on they team and chill with me
And make my pockets bigger
They want to meet with me tonight at seven o'clock so
*   whassup nigga?*
What you wanna do? What you wanna do?
I got the gauge an Uzi and my motherfuckin .22
So if you wanna blast nigga we can buck 'em
If we stick 'em then we struck 'em so fuck 'em

Snoop's voice, delivery, vocal agility and overall bad boy microphone presence was seamless, and it was only a matter of time before the combination of Snoop vocals over Dr. Dre beats would become the hip-hop equivalent of Michael Jordan and Scottie Pippen.

Yes Indeedee I Wrote Graffiti on the Bus

As the stage for West Coast artists grew, Ice-T worked to challenge himself artistically. While his first three albums had distinct thematic elements, *O.G. Original Gangsta* marked a departure of sorts from this tried and tested formula. *Billboard* magazine noted that the album's 23 tracks contained:

> ...philosophy, commentary, attitude, and finely detailed stories of confrontation and conquest on the streets of LA. Unlike his last album, *The Iceberg/Freedom of Speech... Just Watch What You Say*, *O.G.* contains few tirades against censorship, drugs, or violence, and avoids almost completely any graphic sex talk. Instead, says Ice, he returned to the basics, as in "New Jack Hustler (Nino's Theme)" – also featured on the soundtrack to *New Jack City* – which is rising

fast on the Hot R & B Singles chart. "One thing about this album, there is not that guaranteed message there... That got boring to me; if we know there's gonna be a message then it's no fun."

In addition to continuing his recording career, Ice-T branched out into heavy metal. Having already dabbled in rock laced tracks on both *Power* and *The Iceberg*, Ice-T developed his former rock tendencies into a fully loaded, furious sound. The name of Ice-T's new heavy metal band was Bodycount, and its most infamous single was a track called "Cop Killer." Numerous police groups and public figures, including President George H.W. Bush, and Tipper Gore, whose husband Al was the Democratic vice presidential candidate running with Bill Clinton, quickly denounced the song. Several dozen police officers and their supporters even showed up with signs at an Ice-T show in North Hollywood to protest.

A police officer responded to "Cop Killer" by recording his own single, as *The Los Angeles Times* reported:

Outraged by rap artist Ice-T's controversial song

"Cop Killer," Hawthorne Police Officer
Roosevelt Matthews Jr. has recorded a rap of his
own. Matthews, a former gang member whose
conversion to motorcycle officer was dramatized
last year on network television, has just cut a
debut single called "Role Model." He hopes the
slickly produced, four minute tune will serve as
an antidote to Ice-T's song, which he believes is
sending a poisonous message to youths.

"I'm not personally attacking Ice-T," said
Matthews, who in the past has performed before
student audiences as 'Blade,' his musical
moniker. "I'm attacking the product he puts out.
The lyrics in his music are, like, devastating to
society." The Ice-T anthem, released in April –
the same month as the riots – is sung from the
point of view of a frustrated inner-city youth
who resolves to 'dust some cops off.'

Meanwhile, artists from Los Angeles continued to push the
boundaries of hip-hop expression. One example was The

Pharcyde and their debut album *Bizarre Ride II The Pharcyde*. Visually, here again was another artist using illustrated album cover art. Musically, the most widely recognized song on this record was "Passin Me By." With its smooth delivery over a Quincy Jones sample, it told that age-old tale of juvenile infatuation, love, and rejection that was absent in most of the 'gangsterism' dominating the Los Angeles hip-hop scene. However, with other song titles such as "Return Of The B-Boy," The Pharcyde also demonstrated a revived effort to remain connected to the essence of hip-hop culture.

Acts like the Pharcyde, Del Tha Funkee Homosapien and his crew Hieroglyphics, provided an alternative vibe that acted as a counterbalance to the overpowering popularity and heavy subject matter of 'gangsta' rap. The streets were not the experience or preferred subject matter of all rappers from the West Coast, many emphasized the importance of expressing differing points of view. Because of the volume of diversity in content, West Coast hip-hop attracted unprecedented numbers of young people from very different places and backgrounds, shifting the balance of power in the hip-hop world from east to west.

Now I'm Smellin Like Indonesia

If "6 'N The Morning" by Ice-T was the seminal work that
signaled the beginning of the period covered in this text, then Dr.
Dre's *The Chronic* would be the one to mark the end. As he
approached his first solo album, Dre carried the weight of his
reputation as genius producer, by the end of '92 he had earned
his status as one of the hottest producer/artists in all of music,
but it was unknown whether Dre could carry the mail lyrically
on the solo tip for an entire album. The general hip-hop public
expected nothing less than greatness from any new Dre sound. A
huge piece of putting together the album became the vocals. By
combining deep funk arrangements with the tantalizing vocal
debut of Snoop Doggy Dogg, Dre reinvented himself and gave
the hip-hop world a new sound to imitate and sample.

The Chronic's cover was made to look like a pack of
Zig-Zag rolling papers, with Dr. Dre's picture where the old

White man with the beard usually was. As for the album's name, the website www.rapdict.org defines it:

Chronic – (n) See marijuana. Incredibly potent marijuana, it started out as weed laced with coke.

The inset photo featured Dre sitting on a tricked out 1964 Chevrolet Impala. Again, the image of the ball cap wearin, expensive car havin, chronic smoking, chin checkin, bitch killin, gun shootin, Tanqueray drinkin, not givin a fuck Compton G took center stage.

There is always pressure on any artist leading up to the debut of a project that they completely control artistically. However, it is easy to imagine Dr. Dre embracing the opportunity to have full creative control over the music he was going to make. The result was a trademark sound that was stamped across the landscape of hip-hop. The thick, heavy bass lines and the high pitched synthesizer combined with the West Coast vibe to introduce the world to what would become known as the G-Funk era.

"The Chronic [Intro]" could hardly wait to tell Dre's side of the story surrounding the dramatic disintegration of NWA.

Snoop Doggy Dogg, the introductory spokesman, gave an evil laugh and proclaimed, "Niggaz Wit Attitudes? Nah loc, niggaz on a muthafuckin mission." So if it's not NWA, then who is it? Snoop again; "The notorious Compton G, D-R-E, on the solo tip. Fuck them other fools. What up, Ren." While this shout out to MC Ren indicated that Dr. Dre's anger was not towards everything associated with his old group (though Ren did not appear on the album), it got real specific real quick. Snoop once more; "Oh yeah: P.S., fuck Mr. Rourke and Tattoo, aka Jerry and Eazy." The comparison of Jerry Heller and Eazy-E to the characters from the 1980s television show "Fantasy Island" was purposeful and resonated on a couple of levels. First was the racial juxtaposition of the powerful White man (Mr. Rourke) and his little colored sidekick/servant (Tattoo). Second was the implied power dynamic between the two, the idea that Eazy-E simply followed Jerry Heller around, took orders, and exploited those that trusted him. Ice Cube had expressed the same opinion on "No Vaseline."

Dr. Dre left NWA feeling persecuted to the extent that the first song on *The Chronic* was called "Fuck Wit Dre Day [And Everybody's Celebratin']." In the aftermath of the animosity that had spilled out of the departure of Ice Cube and eventual breakup of the group, 'beef' between artists all over hip-hop had become more personal and threatening. "No Vaseline" had made dismantling someone on a record an art form and an open invitation to say pretty much anything you wanted to say about another person. So when Dre said:

> *Used to be my homie used to be my ace*
> *Now I wanna slap the taste out your mouth*
> *Make you bow down to the row*
> *Fuckin me now I'm fuckin you little ho*

It wasn't necessarily that big of a deal for him to come at Eazy-E this way. Tim Dog, a member of the pioneering New York group Ultramagnetic MCs, who in 1991 had released a song entitled "Fuck Compton," was called out, as was Luke Skyywalker of Miami's Two Live Crew. In the process of dissing Luke, Dre and Snoop combined for some ill homoerotic visuals, keeping with the spirit behind the title of Ice Cube's "No Vaseline":

> **Snoop:** *Now understand this my nigga Dre can't be touched*
> **Dre:** *Luke's bendin over*

> **Snoop:** *So Luke's getting fucked*

And then:

> **Dre:** *If it ain't another ho that I gots to fuck wit*
> *Gap teeth in your mouth so my dicks gotsta fit*
> **Snoop:** *Wit my nuts on your tonsils*
> *While you're on stage rappin at your wack ass concerts*

Hip-hop has a rooted connection to incarceration. Since homosexuality is a fact of life in jail, there is an overlap between these two cultures. Hip-hop references such as Dre's and Cube's reflect a conceptual understanding that has always existed on the margins of hip-hop.

The most enduring song from *The Chronic* was "Nuthin But a 'G' Thang." It featured both Dr. Dre and Snoop Doggy Dogg, with Snoop getting the writing credit. Portions of the vocals featured Dre and Snoop simultaneously repeating "It's like that and like this and like that," and Snoop spelling out his name; "It's the capital S, oh yes I'm fresh, N double O-P, D-O double G-Y D-O double G you see." Though it was only the early 1990s, by this time the term "fresh," which www.raptdict.org defined as, "1) (adj) New; 2) (adj) Very Good," was not fresh anymore, given the constant turnover in hip-hop based slang. Snoop's word choice reflected hip-hop music's history and a respect for the earlier styles that had influenced him. Visually this song exhibited warm weather, barbeques, driving around in low-riders, parties with people dancing, and refrigerators filled with ice cold 40 ounce bottles of malt liquor.

In addition, it was "Nuthin But a 'G' Thang" that solidified Snoop's status as a star among the masses. It's safe to say that he pretty much had everybody with, "1, 2, 3 into tha 4, Snoop Doggy Dogg and Dr. Dre is at the do..." Snoop's performance on "Nuthin But a 'G' Thang" set the stage for what would become one of the most anticipated albums in hip-hop's short history to that point, his solo album *Doggystyle*.

Often overlooked on *The Chronic* was the political/protest material that gave the album a social backbone. "The Day The Niggaz Took Over" presented Dr. Dre's view of the Rodney King uprising, the aftermath of which was still hanging over the city like smog. A repeated chorus of "Break em off somethin!" on top of a busy, driving track that brought to mind the chaos and anger that existed at all stages of the King saga. The beginning of the song quotes a man speaking to a group of people in the middle of the action:

> Im'a say this and I'ma end mine
> If you ain't down for the Africans here
> In the United States, period point blank
> If you ain't down for the ones that suffered in South
>   Africa
> From apartheid and shit dammit you need to step your
>   punk ass to the side
> And let us brothers, and us Africans step in
> And start putting some foot in that ass!

Dre's decision to open a song discussing the King uprisings with a quote that invokes the comparison between the Black American experience and apartheid in South Africa was appropriate, after all, apartheid was simply South African speak for Jim Crow. Dre's social awareness underscored its prevalence, even amongst the hardest of the hardcore, within hip-hop music at the time.

Similar to Ice Cube's "We Had to Tear This
_____ Up," audio clips from news broadcasts

were inserted for effect:

> Yes, we have, there have been riots, ahh, rioting
> well I don't wanna say rioting but there's been
> looting downtown! But right now, Bree, what I
> want to show you is they have started fires down
> at the end of the street!

The beauty of that clip was in the tension of the reporter's voice and the understanding that under no circumstances did she want to call what was happening 'rioting.' If "there's been looting downtown" and people "have started fires down at the end of the street," at least 9 out of 10 times that shit is a riot.

Though perhaps not as articulate as Ice Cube, Dr. Dre still got his point across regarding his feelings about the King verdict and what followed:

> *Sittin in my livin room calm and collective*
> *Feelin that gotta get mine perspective*
> *Cause what I just heard broke me in half*
> *And half the niggaz I know plus the niggaz on the Row*
> * is bailin*
> *Laugh now but cry much later*

Ya see when niggaz get together
They get mad cause they can't fade us
Like my niggaz from South Central Los Angeles
They found out they couldn't handle us
Bloods Crips on the same squad
With the Ese's help and nigga it's time to rob and mob
And break the White man off something lovely
I don't love them so them can't love me

The idea of being broken 'in half' by the not guilty verdict, while acknowledging crying and emotional vulnerability, was not normal protocol for the macho driven world of hip-hop, particularly coming from a 'G.' In addition, there was the observance of unity between the Bloods, the Crips, and Latinos in the face of a common enemy, the White male power structure.

The song "Lil Ghetto Boy" played like a knowledge pipeline from OGs (Original Gangstas) to the BGs (Baby Gangstas). The song talked to urban kids growing up without parents, mentors, or jobs, facing a compromised adult world that had not acknowledged their presence in the world, and offered emotional, musical understanding and support. The chorus asked:

Little ghetto boy livin in the ghetto streets
Whatchya gonna do when you grow up
And have to face responsibility?

The song's intent to pay attention to youth is displayed prominently at the beginning. After a set of remarks covering community economic development, another anonymous man speaking in front of a crowd concludes by saying:

> *I'ma tell you right now, if I have to die today for this little African right here to have a future, I'ma dead muthafucka!*

Every child wants and needs someone who they feel will go all out for them in their life. The question that should have come from all this was: Who will advocate for kids growing up in the social conditions of places like South Central Los Angeles?

As he offers his bit of advice, Snoop almost sounds like an instructor ready to teach an important lesson:

> *I spent four years in the county*
> *With nothing but convicts around me*
> *But now I'm back at the Pound and we*
> *Expose ways for the youth to survive*

Some think it's wrong but we tend to think its right

"Lil Ghetto Boy's" grass roots appeal and stories about the differing perspectives of OGs and BGs wasn't preachy and judgmental. Instead it acknowledged that anonymous young man as a "hustlin ass youngsta, clockin your grip." For that unnamed young man to be recognized as such by someone like Snoop might contribute to getting that young man to think about having to "face responsibility."

While there was what some would consider a social element to *The Chronic,* there was also more than enough material to keep hip-hop's critics busy. The most obvious was the drug reference, not only in the name of the album, but also in the fact that a big green 'chronic' leaf on a black background was pictured on the face of the compact disc. Skits in-between songs portrayed Dr. Dre as a ruthless, mega-sexual superhero who watched ill game shows on television. One involved Dre confronting a man who apparently said something wrong. Dre eventually puts a gun in the man's mouth. How do we know? He says, "What's wrong nigga? You can't talk with a gun in your mouth?" It ended with the following exchange:

> **Dre:** *Listen up nigga, you know Lucifer?*
>
> **Guy:** *Nah!*
>
> **Dre:** *Well you about to meet him muthafucka!*
> *[gunshot]*

Later on, while sitting around watching television, Dre stumbles on "The $20 Sack Pyramid," a game show with contestants playing for a "$20 sack of indo and a $35 gift certificate to the Compton Swap Meet." One player gives the clues and the other player must guess what the hell he's talking about, similar to the format of the old school TV game show "$20,000 Pyramid." For instance:

> **Player 1:** *VCRs, uhh, TVs and shit, uhh, them socks and shit, oh that box in your room!*
>
> **Player 2:** *Shit I came up on lootin?*

Another insert, called "The Doctor's Office," features a woman coming to a busy sounding office for an appointment with Dr. Dre. When told by the receptionist that the doctor is busy, the 'patient' becomes agitated and bursts into an office where she finds Dr. Dre having sex, presumably with a woman who had an earlier appointment.

The mainstream was now infatuated with the flavor of established West Coast artists like Dr. Dre, despite the presence of hardcore material, critics arrived bearing high praise. *The Michigan Citizen*, in Highland Park, Michigan gushed:

> Whether dealing with the LA riots ("The Day The Niggaz Took Over") or everyday life in the violent world of the gangsta ("Nigga Witta Gun," "Rat-Tat-Tat-Tat," "Lil' Ghetto Boy"), whether dissing and boasting (the first single "Nuthin But A 'G' Thang," "F--- Wit Dre Day") or having a low riding good time ("Let Me Ride") and partying ("Deez Nuts"), on *The Chronic* Dre displays a range of style and subject unheard of on a rap album. Using R & B funk vocals and melodies as well as samples from the likes of George Clinton, Donny Hathaway, and Isaac Hayes, his songs flow into each other, creating a sense of life as it's lived on the street, the anger, the sex, the warfare, the dope, the rhythm, even the humor.

A final track, "Bitches Ain't Shit," went unlisted on the
CD case. Dr. Dre's verse was dedicated to more Eazy-E bashing
("I used to know a bitch named Eric Wright..."), and he delivered
more insight into his side of the story behind the breakup of
NWA. It also further pushed the misogyny envelope:

> Bitches ain't shit but hos and tricks
> Lick on these nuts and suck the dick
> Get the fuck on after you're done
> Then I hops in my coup to make a quick run

Dre had put it right out there on *The Chronic* with "Nuthin But
A 'G' Thang":

> And I'ma continue to put the rap down
> Put the mack down
> And if you bitches talk shit
> I'll have to put the smack down

Thinking back to "6 'N The Morning," little had changed in
West Coast hip-hop music regarding notions of violence toward
women, further highlighting a societal failure to effectively
address issues of domestic violence. It would not be until the OJ

Simpson case in 1994 that the general public began to really pay attention to such things.

The Chronic represented an example of what critics point to when they decry hip-hop's lack of respect for women. Tricia Rose, author of the book Black Noise, has called the problem the 'power of the funk.' These songs may have messages that are foul and detrimental to women's struggles and equal rights, but what to do when those messages are wrapped in some of the illest drumbeats and bass lines ever heard? If we are on the dance floor with our hands in the air, or even just bobbing our head to this music, are we somehow guilty by association?

Outro

By the early '90s, mainstream culture was firmly under the spell of rap music, especially the West Coast version that had its start in the late '80s. The *Billboard* charts reflected hip-hop's expansive influence in the culture at large. Tone Loc's "Wild Thing" surpassed "We Are the World" to become the highest selling single of all time to that point. NWA's *Efil4zaggin* debuted at #2 on the Billboard 200 and then went to #1 the next week. Soon afterward Ice Cube's album, *Predator*, debuted at #1. In reality the controversial material in some West Coast hip-hop that caused so much mainstream excitement and anxiety was just a reflection of the increase of sex and violence in mainstream media overall.

The Chronic established new conventions for what had come to be known in the mainstream as 'gangsta' rap. With its recognizable, mainstream friendly, funk-laden samples it could have been more accurately described as 'gangsta' pop. Dr. Dre represented the evolution of the hardcore West Coast rap that started in the early 1980s. The cross-pollinating relationship between this style of hip-hop music and mainstream culture was now official, becoming a blueprint for numerous other artists not just from other areas of the United States, but all over the world.

Similarly influential, MC Hammer had developed rap as a flashy mega show. With his infamous 'Hammer pants' and suspenders, his style echoed the early days of hip-hop, a la Grand Master Flash and The Furious Five circa 1982's "The Message." Hammer's formula of easily recognizable samples and multitudes of backup dancers brought crossover rap into a new phase that was refined and recycled by Sean "Puffy" Combs aka Puff Daddy aka P. Diddy during the second half of the 1990s.

The NWA versus Ice Cube conflict showed the rap industry, and the rest of the world, the artistic and promotional value of beef. The flurry of media attention around the exchange of insults and records created a sensation unlike anything in hip-hop or pop to that point. Even though Ice Cube attempted to take the high road on *Amerikka's Most Wanted*, he understood that remaining silent in the face of attack was not an option in hip-hop. The foundation for the infamous East Coast versus West Coast beef of the mid-1990s was generated by the NWA/Ice Cube episode. While numerous people got involved, the stars of this conflict were Tupac and the Notorious B.I.G. The tragedy is that after the sale of millions of records, magazines, newspapers and other beef related items, both of them were dead.

The expansion of any cultural movement is never a smooth process. West Coast hip-hop music faced opposition from both its hardcore and mainstream-friendly camps. The hardcore riled up conservative America enough for President George H.W. Bush and Vice President Dan Quayle to angrily denounce Ice-T and his record "Cop Killer" by name in 1992. Mainstream acceptance even provoked the ire of conservative hip-hop, such as Q-Tip of A Tribe Called Quest on 1991's "Check The Rhime:"

> *Proper - what you say Hammer? Proper*
> *Rap is not pop if you call it that then stop*

In truth, by that time plenty of rap was in fact pop, but that pop was present in both mainstream and hardcore sounds and content.

West Coast rap and hip-hop's cultural emergence served as a bridge between the beginnings of a national and a global movement. As the more people paid attention to it, corporate interests began to exert more and more influence. In addition to this, the music and the culture around it changed as newer generations began expressing their own interpretations of what hip-hop music had come to mean to them. Hip-hop's general inclusiveness and the arrival of the ability to share information over the internet, continue to foster diverse artistic communication between ethnic and cultural groups, all couched in hip-hop dialect.

The prior artificial social barriers that had effectively kept young people culturally separated were reduced, largely due to an increased level of awareness communicated by hip-hop music and culture. In the article "What the White Boy Means When He Says Yo," Charles Aaron talked about hip-hop opening the eyes of White (and I would add, other non-Black) listeners to race and American society, while at the same time, heightening their sensitivity to people unlike themselves.

The first generation of West Coast hip-hop artists brought cultural understanding and large changes that they used to raise and mentor following generations in what was essentially a different world. Bakari Kitwana has labeled this phenomenon the 'New Racial Politics' in his book *Why White Kids Love Hip-Hop*. For example, open cross-racial admiration of an urban Black artist by a rural White teenager, perhaps once considered taboo for the White kid, was now not such a big deal. This new sense of cultural and racial normalcy helped establish a base of opportunity for Barack Obama to be taken seriously as a presidential candidate less than two decades later, and contributed to his ability to win re-election after what even many of his supporters considered somewhat of a lackluster first term. The old adage that someone Black had to do twice as well as someone White in order to receive the same amount of credit appeared to have been put to the ultimate political test, and it was seemingly disproved. In the end, the legacy of this time would appear to be that millions of people in the United States, and the world, came to realize that we have a lot more in common than we thought.

***

Made in the USA
San Bernardino, CA
18 August 2015